Introduction to
Machine and Assembly
Language: Systems/360/370

Introduction to Machine and Assembly Language: Systems/360/370

FRANK D. VICKERS
University of Florida

HOLT, RINEHART AND WINSTON, INC.

New York Chicago San Francisco Atlanta Dallas Montreal Toronto London Sydney

To my parents
Frank C. and Estelle L. Vickers

Preface

This text is designed for a second course in computer science. Primarily it studies the behavior of a computer at the machine-language level, including the various representations of data and instructions, the basic structure of the computer from the programmer's viewpoint, and the behavior of the computer under program control. A study of this kind is better made with an actual machine rather than a generalized one. The System/360 computer was chosen because it is the largest selling machine and because I have access to one.

Included within this study is an incomplete development of the Assembly Language for the 360. This text does not provide a complete presentation of this subject, because many of the Assembler features are used only by very experienced systems programmers. It is more important that the student obtain a strong understanding of the behavior of the computer in all of its aspects. Assembly language is required only as a vehicle toward this end. In the same spirit, the Fortran language is used as an input and output tool until enough background is provided for the study of Assembly Language I/O.

This text covers the majority of the concepts included in the second course of the ACM Curriculum 68 as follows:

1. Machine structure and language, registers, storage, control, and I/O. Instruction types, formats, execution. Arithmetic, program control, I/O operations, and interrupts.

2. Addressing techniques including absolute, indexing, indirect, relative, and base addressing.

3. Representation and conversion of integer, floating-point, decimal, character, and logical data.

4. Assembly systems including symbolic coding of mnemonic codes, labels, and addresses, literals, extended and pseudo operations. System and user macro programming is included.

5. Program segmentation and linkage between like and unlike languages. Storage allocation and reentrant programming. Systems organization including storage hierarchies.

6. New developments as exhibited by IBM System/370.

I hereby acknowledge the generous permission granted by the International Business Machines Corporation to reprint several figures and tables from various System/360 publications. These include Form Numbers A22-6821-7, C20-1646-4, C28-6535-1, C28-6646-0, C28-6647-1, GA22-7000, and X20-1703-6.

I also wish to publicly acknowledge those who directly or indirectly have significantly influenced the concepts and philosophy of presentation within this text. A partial list would include, in chronological order, W. W. Peterson, C. A. Taylor, A. A. Broyles, R. G. Selfridge, C. B. Periman, and R. N. Braswell. Special acknowledgment is given my wife for her patience, encouragement, and help throughout the writing of this text.

June 1971   *F. D. VICKERS*
Gainesville, Florida

Contents

Table of Definitions

Chapter **one**

Computer Software System Space

This text offers the fundamental knowledge one needs in order to understand the organizational structure and behavior of high-speed electronic computers. The level of knowledge presented here is not that of electronic circuitry, but rather of the machine organizations and the machine operations most useful to the computer user and the computer scientist. This could be called a study of the *designed behavior* of the computer—or, stated differently, the behavior of the computer under fundamental programming conditions. Or we might say this is the study of a *basic machine language*. In most academic as well as practical situations this becomes the study of an *assembly language*.

For a thorough understanding of the basic concepts in computer and information science the student must obtain an intimate knowledge of the fundamental workings of a computer. This intimate knowledge can be gained only through extensive experience involving actual programming using the language of the machine itself.

It is assumed that the reader has had some experience with computers and computer programming, particularly with a high-level language such as Fortran or PL/I. These computer languages are always translated by compilers or interpreters into a basic machine language before the actual computations can be performed. Thus the user of Fortran or PL/I has already been indirectly involved with the subject matter of this book. No doubt such experience has already produced an awareness of the existence of other programming languages and systems. The purpose of this first chapter is to place within perspective the wide range of computing systems found in modern large-scale computational environments.

1.1   SYSTEM-SPACE PARAMETERS

This section and the next will develop a concept for describing as precisely as possible the universe of *computing system space*. This space, an abstract one, includes all programming languages and/or systems. Like other system spaces, computing system space has certain dimensions, but unlike other spaces these dimensions are not measured in commonly accepted units.

The three major dimensions of computing system space are sophistication, orientation, and proceduration. Proceduration is a coined word indicating the degree of proceduralness. All units of measurement are qualitative rather than quantitative; thus the various dimensions are described in terms such as low, high, or intermediate.

Sophistication is a measure of the degree of removal of tedious and time-consuming attention to detail from the programmer's work load. For example, Fortran is a language of relatively high sophistication. At the other extreme, a basic machine language is of very low sophistication. When programming in a basic machine language, the programmer must describe the program procedure in much more detail than is obvious when programming in Fortran. A good measure of sophistication is the translation ratio between the sizes of a source program and the corresponding object program. If, during translation or compilation, a program expands from a few instructions to a large number of individual machine commands, the language is said to be highly sophisticated. Therefore, the programmer can state a complicated procedure in a relatively few statements when using a language that is sophisticated.

The second dimension measures the degree of *orientation* between the two extremes of pure machine and pure problem orientations. A machine-oriented language is one that is closely related to the basic functions and operations of the computer. On the other hand, a problem-oriented language is completely divorced from the basic functional behavior of the machine. Usually, a problem-oriented language allows a problem to be stated in the professional terms familiar to a particular user. In most cases a procedure for solving a problem is not even specified by the user; he merely states the problem. The particular system being used contains a predetermined procedure for solving the problem being stated. A few examples of such problem-oriented systems are: a General Purpose Simulation System called GPSS, a structural problem-solving system called STRESS, a continuous system or time-incremented simulation system called DYNAMO, and an electrical-circuit problem-solving system called ECAP. All of these languages allow the user to describe a problem at hand in terms used in his everyday technical jargon and do not require construction of detailed procedures. Another way of describing orientation is the degree of generality of a system. The more general a system becomes, the more flexible it becomes within the capability range of the basic machine. On the other hand, as a system becomes less general and is used for a narrowing field of application, the system quite naturally loses some of the flexibility that is characteristic of the basic machine. Thus whenever a new language or system is designed, the loss of flexibility must be weighed against the gain in simplicity and usefulness to a selected group of users.

The third parameter is, for the lack of a better name, referred to by the author as *proceduration*. This measurement describes the degree of procedural-ness of a language. A language that is totally procedural involves the specification of a sequence of operations to be performed by the computer in a step-by-step fashion. As mentioned above, some languages do not yield proce-dural programs, while others are almost purely procedural, such as a basic machine language. Still others are intermediately procedural, in that within a procedure certain steps may be predetermined by the system itself, such as in the Snobol language.

Creating these dimensions as three distinct entities allows most languages to be contrasted with each other in a meaningful way and eliminates some of the confusion that exists when certain languages are described. Fortran characteristics, for example, remain indistinct until the properties of proceduralness and problem orientation are separated. It seems obvious that Fortran is problem oriented (oriented toward mathematics), yet unlike most problem-oriented languages Fortran is highly procedural. Even though a three-dimensional space is difficult to show on paper, the advantage of less confusion in language characteristics seems to outweigh the disadvantage.

There are many other ways of describing programming languages, such as difficulty of learning and using, or speed of, or accuracy of execution and translation, but the three parameters given above seem to be the major ones. From the academic viewpoint, these descriptors provide relatively clear methods of discussing the major interrelationships and characteristics of the thousands of computer systems and/or languages that exist.

1.2   COMPUTER SYSTEM SPACE

Figure 1.1 shows a perspective view of computing system space using the three dimensional parameters discussed above. The reader will note that the space is formed by a cube placed within a three-dimensional space with one corner at the origin. The computer could be considered to reside at this origin. All the various systems within the space can now be considered as various approaches to the machine that can be made by the human programmer. As a system appears further away from the origin, it becomes more and more divorced from the characteristics of the machine itself.

The left-hand face of the cube represents systems that are totally machine oriented, while the right-hand face represents systems that are totally problem oriented. The top face represents the highest degree of sophistication, the bottom face the lowest. The front face represents the nonprocedural systems, the back face the procedural systems.

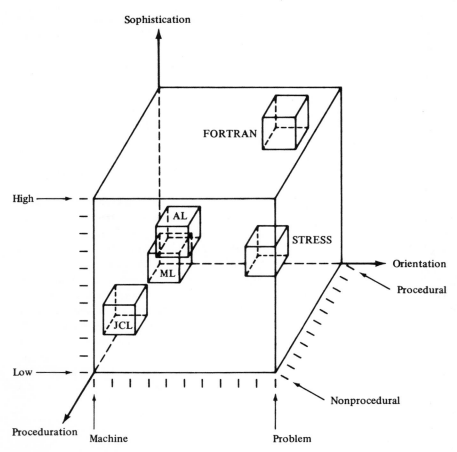

FIGURE 1.1   Computer System Space

To reduce confusion, only a few languages are shown in their respective positions. If all systems were to be inserted, very little empty space would remain. Probably the empty space, if any, would occur near the edge of the cube with nonprocedural machine-oriented characteristics. The only structures that can be found resembling a language with these characteristics are the job command languages. These languages usually are not very procedural, yet they do describe program parameters in terms of physical computer components, particularly input, output, and storage devices.

Shown in the computing system space at the extreme corner of the cube at the origin are the machine languages. A machine language is that language understood by a computer standing alone. This is the major subject matter presented within this text. No other known approach gives the clear and precise knowledge of computer behavior that is required for advance study in computer and information science. Even the technical and specialized approach of electrical engineering involving the design of computers in terms of electrical circuits is not sufficient. The machine designer must also have a full and complete understanding of how a computer should behave from the user's viewpoint before an optimal design can be made. Thus, the only reasonable route to the understanding of the concepts and behavior of a computer is through the extended study of a machine language and its applications.

Slightly above and slightly more problem oriented than machine language is assembly language. In actual practice very few programmers ever program in a machine language. An assembly language is used instead. Machine languages are usually very archaic in nature and are written in forms that are hard to remember. Most machine languages are made up of machine commands and operands coded by either binary numbers, alphabetic characters, or some combination of characters. These coded commands are not designed for human understanding and therefore are hard to deal with. Assembly languages are symbolic forms of machine languages involving mnemonic operation codes and symbolic operand references designed for easier programming. However, the penalty of requiring a translation must be paid. This translation operation is called the assembly phase. For the most part, assembly-language operations are in a one-to-one correspondence with the commands in machine language; thus the translation is a very simple one compared to Fortran compilation. Because assembly language is easier to learn and use than machine language, the presentation in subsequent chapters uses assembly language as a vehicle for teaching the concepts involved in the basic objective of machine language. Further discussion of assembler characteristics and its operating environment appears in Section 1.4.

Fortran would probably appear within the space near the top, near the right face, and very close to the back face. There are more sophisticated languages than Fortran, such as PL/I. Fortran is not totally problem oriented either, since a great many mathematical operations are not provided for in the language. There are hundreds of dialects of Fortran as well as many other similar languages. A few similar languages are Algol, Mad, Jovial, and Basic, while some Fortran dialects are Fortran II, Fortran IV (Fortran III made only a brief appearance), Fortransit, Flatran, and Quicktran. All of these languages have varying degrees of sophistication, problem orientation, and proceduralness, and the exact placement within system space could be a highly subjective decision.

Another example of a language in system space is the language called STRESS. This language is used by construction engineers who are concerned with structural problems. The language is very much problem oriented and is completely nonprocedural. Relatively speaking, STRESS is probably about 70 percent sophisticated, as shown in Figure 1.1. To solve a problem involving a structure, the programmer specifies the coordinates of the joints of the structure, the type of joint, the type of beams making up the structure, and the amount and locations of loads to be placed on the structure. The STRESS system then solves the problem, yielding desired information about the structure, such as the reactions at the joints, tensions or compressions within the beams, and other stress or strain relations expressing the physical behavior of the structure. Thus, the engineer can solve problems using terminology with which he is familiar without specifying the complex computer procedure required for solving such problems. The computer procedures for analyzing the structure were built into the STRESS system by the systems programmers who originally designed and implemented the system. Most systems such as STRESS are originally written in an assembly language; thus most systems programmers must know and use assembly language in their work.

As a final example for discussion of system space and its membership is Job Control Language, called JCL. Most computing systems have some form of control language in which the user can direct his job through the system. Whereas the order of JCL commands is not totally irrelevant, the order is not as critical as the order of statements in a Fortran program or other highly procedural language. At the same time, most JCL commands have a direct relationship with a physical device or function of the machine or system. Thus JCL is a language that has the slightly unusual characteristic of being somewhat machine oriented but not completely procedural. Since this language is needed during the study and use of assembly language, some attention will be given to JCL in later chapters of this book. The JCL for IBM System/360 computers appears in several versions; the one used with large systems has the preceding characteristics.

1.3   A SPECIFIC ASSEMBLY LANGUAGE FOR FURTHER STUDY

The author feels that a specific machine, or type of machine, in actual use should be chosen, along with its machine language and assembly language, for extended study. A full appreciation of the subject can only be developed with extensive practice and experience using a real, live computer. Make-believe computers, even those having simulators that operate on existing machines, and their associated systems never approach the sophistication and complexity exhibited by a real system used everyday for normal computing use. Thus the author has chosen a particular system knowing full well that fewer people will use this book, even though it still may be as useful as those books utilizing fictitious machines. The specific machine chosen is the IBM System/360. Furthermore, the specific version of supervisor system chosen is Operating System/360, usually referred to as OS/360. This particular machine was chosen for two rather obvious reasons: System/360 is the largest-selling machine and the author happens to have access to a System/360, model 65. The choice of OS over the other supervisor systems is simply that most large System/360 machines operate in this environment, as may the model 65. The choice of OS is not a limiting factor to the reader, since OS is the most sophisticated and generalized version of all of the various supervisors available from IBM for use on System/360 computers.

1.4   THE ASSEMBLY-LANGUAGE ENVIRONMENT

Most computing systems allow an assembly language to be used in many contexts. This section describes one typical way that assembly language can be used with System/360. To a large extent, this particular method of application is used in the first nine chapters for programming examples and student exercises. Just as any high-level language such as Fortran or PL/I must first be compiled or translated into an object program before it can be executed, so must assembly language. However, the translation of assembly language is referred to as an *assembly* rather than a compilation. In addition, a second transformation exists between either the compilation or assembly phase and the final objective, the execution phase. In System/360 this *new* operation is called the *Linkedit* phase. Besides this complication, System/360 provides the capability of combining program segments, called subprograms, written in a number of different languages, into one larger program to be executed as a single task. Thus the various phases or job steps that make up a total job can become more numerous.

Figure 1.2 illustrates in a very general fashion how a job is broken into job steps. It further demonstrates how the inputs and outputs of each job step relate to all the others. It also shows the sources available for the various inputs and destinations for outputs. This particular job is made up of a Fortran compilation step followed by an assembler-language assembly step, the Linkedit step, and finally the execution step. Other variations include reversing the first two steps, replacing the Fortran step with a PL/I step, adding a separate PL/I step, or many other possibilities involving one or more languages.

The particular illustration in Figure 1.2 is chosen for the following reasons. This text is concerned primarily with the assembly-language step and the effect of the resulting program on the computer. However, for purposes of simplification, Fortran is also used during the first nine chapters of the text as a means of providing access and data to an assembly-language program. This allows a delay in the discussion of input and output under assembly language until the latter part of the book. The subject of input and output, under normal OS/360 conditions, is quite complicated and requires that a considerable amount of groundwork be laid first.

The first job step shown in Figure 1.2 is a Fortran compilation. Any reasonable number of Fortran subprograms, called Fortran *source modules*, can be presented to the Fortran compiler. A number of these source modules can be obtained from within the system library, provided they have previously been stored there by an earlier job. The output of the compiler is a series of *object*

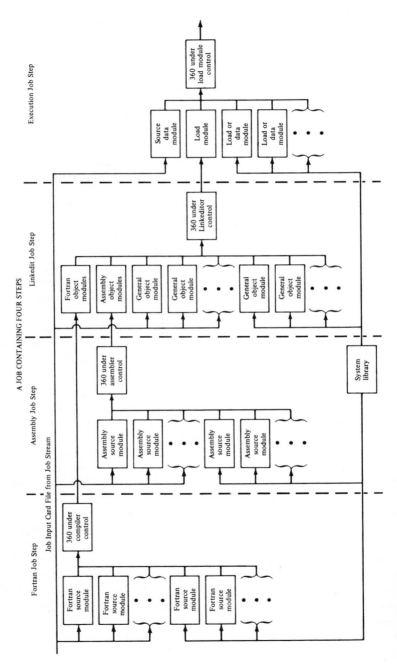

FIGURE 1.2   Job Steps Involving Fortran and Assembly Language

8

modules, one for each source module. These object modules are saved in auxiliary storage for input to the Linkedit phase.

The second job step is an assembly phase. Any reasonable number of assembler-language subprograms, called assembler source modules, can be presented to the assembler. Again, several source modules may be supplied to the job step from the system library. Output from the assembler is a series of object modules, one for each of the source modules. Again, these object modules are saved in auxiliary storage for input to the Linkedit phase.

The third job step, referred to as Linkedit, takes the various object modules produced by the first and second job steps together with any previously compiled or assembled object modules, either supplied in card form by the user during this run or supplied from the system library, and presents the total package to the Linkeditor, a component of the Operating System. The Linkeditor resolves and completes all the various references between the object modules and produces one executable *load* module. This load module is then loaded into the computer's main memory along with any other load modules that are necessary for execution.

The final job step is the actual execution of the combined load modules by the computer. Provided the various subprograms are written correctly, the data supplied during execution are correct, and the computing system is operating correctly, the desired result is produced as output. More details of job steps and job-step control are presented at appropriate points throughout the balance of this text. While the successful execution of a program depends on the job control information supplied by a user, this subject is secondary to the major intent of this text.

1.5   THE ORGANIZATION OF THE TEXT

Chapter 2 discusses various aspects of number systems to the extent required for full understanding of the operation and behavior of the modern computer. This involves the binary and hexadecimal number systems. The architectural structure of the computer is presented in Chapter 3. This is an abstract discussion without regard to electronic or logical circuit considerations. An attempt is made to describe this structure in terms of design advancements made between first-, second-, and third-generation computers. It is felt that a stronger understanding of the newer concepts is obtained if they are contrasted to older concepts. Chapter 4 is an introduction to machine language within the context of the organization of the computer and its relationship to assembly language. A simple example, the solution of $A = B + C$ is developed, and actual computer operation involving integer arithmetic is demonstrated. Chapter 5 presents all of the various machine instructions that involve integer arithmetic as well as the various fundamental concepts of address logic. Chapter 6 deals exclusively with branching operations. This includes conditional branching, looping instructions, and index control. The various operations involving character manipulation and code conversion are presented in Chapter 7. Logical operations and decimal arithmetic are presented in Chapters 8 and 9. The subject of real or floating-point arithmetic is discussed in Chapter 10. The concepts of program interrupts, supervisor services, and system macro operations are the subjects of Chapter 11. The generalized concepts of input and output at the machine-language level are introduced in Chapter 12. An introduction to the Data Management services division of the Operating System is also presented. Chapters 13 and 14 deal with two particular methods of performing input and output operations within the environment of OS/360. Chapter 15 describes the concept of user-defined macros. The final chapter, Chapter 16, presents the major differences between the IBM Systems/360 and 370.

The author takes the position that a few well-designed problems of graded difficulty are much more informative than many simple exercises. Therefore, a single programming problem is provided at the end of each chapter beginning with Chapter 4. However, for those students who wish to test their knowledge based on several simple questions, a number of such exercises are also included at the conclusion of each chapter. It is emphasized, however, that a reasonable understanding of computer behavior can be obtained only through the actual programming and running of a sufficient number of programs on a real machine under a real system. For this reason, some concepts are discussed within the paragraphs that present the programming problems themselves. Thus the student must at least read the problem statements to find this additional information.

EXERCISES

1. Discuss the three dimensional parameters of system space.
2. Discuss the major characteristics of machine and assembly languages in terms presented in Chapter 1.
3. Contrast the five languages shown in Figure 1.1, using the qualitative measurements in computing system space.
4. Contrast one or more languages that you might know with the five shown in Figure 1.1.
5. Draw a block diagram similar to Figure 1.2 for a job containing one Fortran source program, one assembly source program, and one data deck, all in the form of cards. Four steps are required.
6. Redraw the diagram of Exercise 5, leaving out the assembly-language program. How many steps are involved?

7. Redraw the diagram of Exercise 5, leaving out the Fortran-language program. How many steps are involved?

8. Redraw the diagram of Exercise 5, assuming the two source programs had been compiled and assembled on a previous job and object decks had been punched. How many steps are involved in only the current job?

Chapter **two**

Number Systems

Most large high-speed computers do not utilize decimal numbers for their fundamental counting system. For primarily economic reasons, the binary number system is used. It is much easier to build electronic circuits that maintain and operate on binary numbers rather than decimal. The two binary digit values, 0 and 1, correspond conveniently with such natural electrical phenomena as a switch being open or closed or a light being off or on. Therefore, the user of such a machine should be familiar with the binary number system in order to appreciate the operations that are performed.

For reasons of convenience, a second number system must also be studied. This second system has a special relationship with the binary number system and is used to write binary numbers in a shorter form. This second system has a base of 16 and is called the hexadecimal system.

This chapter will familiarize the reader with the fundamentals common to all number systems through comparison of these two *new* systems with the decimal system. Also methods of transformation from one system to another are discussed along with the basic mathematical operations of addition and subtraction within each particular system. It should become obvious that one number system is as good as another as far as results are concerned. For example, it is possible that the most common number system in use today would have been the duodecimal system had human beings originally been created with 12 fingers.

To avoid possible misunderstanding, notice that no distinction is being made here between number systems and numeration systems, as a precise treatment of number theory might require. Throughout this chapter the symbolic representation of a number, which is a numeral, is used interchangeably with its abstract value. Strictly speaking, there is only one natural number system; therefore what is being discussed in this chapter is actually numeration systems.

2.1   REVIEW OF THE DECIMAL NUMBER SYSTEM

Fundamental to each and every number system is a value called the *radix* or base of the system. The radix of the decimal system is 10. The value of the radix enters into a number in the following way. The decimal number

$$375$$

is actually a shorthand notation for the expression

$$3 \times 10^2 + 7 \times 10^1 + 5 \times 10^0$$

At the same time it is understood that each individual digit in the notation will be less than the radix. Thus in the decimal system each digit must lie between 0 and 9 inclusively, or the value of each digit must be less than 10.

Decimal fractions are also notations for expressions similar to the above involving negative powers of 10. Thus the decimal number

$$3.842$$

is a notation that represents the expression

$$3 \times 10^0 + 8 \times 10^{-1} + 4 \times 10^{-2} + 2 \times 10^{-3}$$

All of the specific information above can be presented in a general fashion. Consider a decimal number containing digits, each of which is represented by the subscripted variable X as follows:

$$X_m \dots X_2 X_1 X_0 . X_{-1} X_{-2} \dots X_{-n}$$

This, then, is the notation for the following expression:

$$X_m \times 10^m + \cdots + X_2 \times 10^2 + X_1 \times 10^1 + X_0 \times 10^0 + X_{-1} \times 10^{-1}$$
$$+ X_{-2} \times 10^{-2} + \cdots + X_{-n} \times 10^{-n}$$

with the added restriction that $0 \leqslant X_i < 10$.

A definition (2.1 on p. 14) can now be stated that is true for any number system with radix R.

The decimal point (.) used to separate the integer from the fraction in decimal numbers actually should be called a radix point in the general definition 2.1.

2.1 Number System with Radix R

The notation for a number with radix R is

$$X_m \ldots X_2 X_1 X_0 \,.\, X_{-1} X_{-2} \ldots X_{-n}$$

which represents the expression

$$X_m \times R^m + \cdots + X_2 \times R^2 + X_1 \times R^1 + X_0 \times R^0 + X_{-1} \times R^{-1}$$
$$+ X_{-2} \times R^{-2} + \cdots + X_{-n} \times R^{-n}$$

and where $0 \leqslant X_i < R$.

2.2   THE BINARY NUMBER SYSTEM

A binary number is a notation representing an expression involving a radix of 2. Thus by Definition 2.1 each digit in a binary number, conventionally called a *bit*, must be either 0 or 1 (equal to or greater than zero and less than 2) and each place in the notation represents a power of 2.

Therefore the following binary number

$$1011001 \tag{1}$$

is a notation for the expression

$$1 \times 2^6 + 0 \times 2^5 + 1 \times 2^4 + 1 \times 2^3 + 0 \times 2^2 + 0 \times 2^1 + 1 \times 2^0 \tag{2}$$

For those who have never seen binary numbers in use before, Table 2.1 contains the first seventeen values along with an interesting method suggested by Bowers and Bowers[1] for naming binary numbers. It should be apparent to the reader that the basis of these names is the same as it is in the decimal system applied in the context of the new radix. The reader will find it helpful if the first sixteen binary number configurations are committed to memory.

The appearance of expression (2) should immediately suggest a method for converting the binary number (1) to its equivalent decimal number. By simply executing the indicated mathematical operations we obtain the following sequence:

$$1 \times 64 + 0 \times 32 + 1 \times 16 + 1 \times 8 + 0 \times 4 + 0 \times 2 + 1 \times 1 =$$
$$64 + \quad 0 + \quad 16 + \quad 8 + \quad 0 + \quad 0 + \quad 1 = 89$$

---

[1] Henry Bowers and Joan E. Bowers, *Arithmetical Excursions: An Enrichment of Elementary Mathematics* (New York: Dover Publications, Inc., 1961). Reprinted through permission of the publisher.

TABLE 2.1   Binary Numbers

Decimal	Binary	Names
0	0	Zero
1	1	One
2	10	Twin
3	11	Twin one
4	100	Twindred
5	101	Twindred one
6	110	Twindred twin
7	111	Twindred twin one
8	1000	Twosand
9	1001	Twosand one
10	1010	Twosand twin
11	1011	Twosand twin one
12	1100	Twosand twindred
13	1101	Twosand twindred one
14	1110	Twosand twindred twin
15	1111	Twosand twindred twin one
16	10000	Twin twosand

Therefore it can be stated that 1011001 to the base 2 is equal to 89 to the base 10. The following notation is used to avoid confusion in indicating the base of a given number.

$$1011001_2 = 89_{10}$$

Mixed binary numbers are expanded and converted in a similar fashion. Thus the following sequence of operations is possible:

$$
\begin{aligned}
10.1011_2 &= 1 \times 2^1 + 0 \times 2^0 + 1 \times 2^{-1} + 0 \times 2^{-2} + 1 \times 2^{-3} + 1 \times 2^{-4} \\
&= 1 \times 2 + 0 \times 1 + 1 \times 0.5 + 0 \times 0.25 + 1 \times 0.125 + 1 \times 0.0625 \\
&= 2 + 0 + 0.5 + 0 + 0.125 + 0.0625 \\
10.1011_2 &= 2.6875_{10}
\end{aligned}
$$

Conversion of a decimal integer number into an equivalent binary number

2.2 Conversion of Base N Numbers to Base 10

In general, to transform a number of base other than 10 to a number of base 10, one simply expands the notation according to Definition 2.1 and performs the indicated operations using base 10 arithmetic.

is accomplished through successive divisions of the decimal number by 2. The remainders, all 0 or 1, taken in reverse order from that used in obtaining them, form the equivalent binary number. Using 89 to the base 10 as an example, the following sequence of divide operations is performed:

$$89 / 2 = 44 \qquad \text{and 1 remainder}$$
$$44 / 2 = 22 \qquad \text{and 0 remainder}$$
$$22 / 2 = 11 \qquad \text{and 0 remainder}$$
$$11 / 2 = 5 \qquad \text{and 1 remainder}$$
$$5 / 2 = 2 \qquad \text{and 1 remainder}$$
$$2 / 2 = 1 \qquad \text{and 0 remainder}$$
$$1 / 2 = 0 \qquad \text{and 1 remainder}$$

As the zero quotient signals the completion of the sequence, the final result is obtained by reading the remainders in the reverse order from that in which they were obtained. This yields 1011001 as the equivalent binary number.

A decimal fraction is converted to binary by a series of multiplications involving the factor 2. The integer portions of the products are used for digits in the resulting binary number. Only the fraction portion of each product is used in the next multiplication operation. The resulting binary digits are written in the same order in which they are obtained. To illustrate this procedure, the decimal number 0.6875 is now converted to binary:

$$0.6875 \times 2 = 1.3750, \qquad \text{integer part} = 1$$
$$0.3750 \times 2 = 0.7500, \qquad \text{integer part} = 0$$
$$0.7500 \times 2 = 1.5000, \qquad \text{integer part} = 1$$
$$0.5000 \times 2 = 1.0000, \qquad \text{integer part} = 1$$

Since the fraction part has reached zero, no further multiplications are useful. Thus the final binary result is 0.1011. In the case when the original decimal number is not divisible by a power of two, the fraction never reaches zero. Therefore a decision must be made as to when sufficient accuracy has been obtained in the result for the conversion to be terminated. For example, the decimal number 0.45 has no finite binary equivalent. The following sequence illustrates this point.

$$0.45 \times 2 = 0.90, \qquad \text{integer part} = 0$$
$$0.90 \times 2 = 1.80, \qquad \text{integer part} = 1$$
$$0.80 \times 2 = 1.60, \qquad \text{integer part} = 1$$
$$0.60 \times 2 = 1.20, \qquad \text{integer part} = 1$$
$$0.20 \times 2 = 0.40, \qquad \text{integer part} = 0$$
$$0.40 \times 2 = 0.80, \qquad \text{integer part} = 0$$
$$0.80 \times 2 = 1.60, \qquad \text{integer part} = 1$$

Notice that the results of the multiplications repeat. This yields a binary result of infinite length containing a repeating sequence of zeros and ones as follows:

$$0.45_{10} = 0.0111001100110011001100..._2$$

A second, quicker method of converting from binary to decimal is given for more practical use. Since the method depends on mentally doubling values, the method is not very applicable to large numbers. One begins by inspecting the bit on the left or high-order end of the number to be converted. Then, for each remaining bit, moving from left to right, one doubles the number so far computed and adds the current bit. Using the previous example again, the following sequence of operations demonstrates this technique.

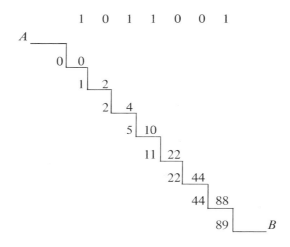

The reader will note, while following line $A-B$ through the sequence, addition occurs while the line is horizontal and the doubling operation occurs while the line is vertical. The process is speeded up slightly if the first three or four bits are converted to decimal directly from memory before proceeding with the doubling and adding for each additional bit.

2.3 ADDITION AND SUBTRACTION OF BINARY NUMBERS

Addition and subtraction of binary numbers are basically the same as in other systems, except that the addition table is much simpler than in any other system. Table 2.2 contains all possible combinations of two bit values with and without the presence of a carry.

TABLE 2.2   Binary Addition Table for $X + Y$

		Without Carry		With Carry	
	$X =$ 0		1	0	1
$Y =$	0	0	1	1	10
	1	1	10	10	11

Three examples of binary addition are shown below, illustrating simple carry conditions.

1.	1010	2.	1001	3.	1011
	+1001		+101		+101
	10011		1110		10000

The more complex problems shown next involve carries beyond one column.

4.	101	5.	111	6.	101
	1101		100		11
	10		101		111
	+111		+1101		110
	11011		11101		1011
					+1111
					101111

In subtraction, it should be remembered that borrowing is in terms of twos, not tens. Three examples of subtraction follow.

1.	1010	2.	1010	3.	10000
	−110		−101		−101
	100		101		1011

A more thorough discussion of binary subtraction is presented in Section 2.7 in connection with two's-complement arithmetic operations.

Multiplication and division, which are quite easy to perform, will not be presented here. The reader is encouraged to attempt one or two multiplication problems on his own. The technique is no different than for the decimal operation.

2.4   THE HEXADECIMAL NUMBER SYSTEM

The reader will have realized by now that a large value expressed as a binary number will contain many bits. As a simple matter of convenience, the hexadecimal number system (referred to henceforth as hex) is introduced and used as a compact means for representing binary numbers. This is possible because of a straightforward relationship between the binary and hex number systems. This relationship is expressed by the fact that the radix of the hex system, 16, is a power of two. Since 16 is equal to 2^4, one column of hex numbers repeat exactly at the same time as four columns of binary numbers. Table 2.3 shows this relationship along with the symbols used for the six hex digits above 9. A system of names suggested by Magnuson,[2] which could be used in reading hex numbers aloud, is also shown.

TABLE 2.3   Hexadecimal Numbers

Decimal	Binary	Hexadecimal	Names
0	0	0	Zero
1	1	1	One
2	10	2	Two
3	11	3	Three
4	100	4	Four
5	101	5	Five
6	110	6	Six
7	111	7	Seven
8	1000	8	Eight
9	1001	9	Nine
10	1010	A	Ann
11	1011	B	Bet
12	1100	C	Chris
13	1101	D	Dot
14	1110	E	Ernest
15	1111	F	Frost
16	10000	10	Ten
.	.	.	.
26	11010	1A	Annteen
27	11011	1B	Betteen
.	.	.	.
160	10100000	A0	Annty
176	10110000	B0	Betty
192	11000000	C0	Christy
.	.	.	.

[2]Robert A. Magnuson, *A Hexadecimal Pronunciation Guide.* Reprinted with permission of Datamation ®copyright 1968, F. D. Thompson Publications, Inc., 35 Mason Street, Greenwich, Conn. 06830.

The simple relationship between binary and hex numbers allows the user to convert from one system to the other by inspection, provided he has memorized the first 16 lines of Table 2.3. As an aid in this memory chore, the following rule is given. Notice that if the four binary numbers for 4, 5, 6, and 7 are doubled (as in a previous rule) and a zero added, the even numbers 8, A, C, and E are obtained. If a one is added, the odd numbers 9, B, D, and F are obtained. In summary:

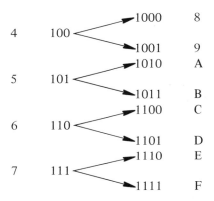

Thus, actually only four three-bit configurations need be memorized along with the even and odd modifier.

As for all number systems, the hex number system also is based on Definition 2.1, with R equal to 16. Thus, the following hex number

$$3A74E$$

is a notation representing the expression

$$3 \times 16^4 + A \times 16^3 + 7 \times 16^2 + 4 \times 16^1 + E \times 16^0$$

To convert this number to decimal, replace all hex digits in the expression by their decimal equivalents. Thus the expression becomes

$$3 \times 16^4 + 10 \times 16^3 + 7 \times 16^2 + 4 \times 16^1 + 14 \times 16^0$$

Performing the indicated operations, we obtain the following sequence:

$$3 \times 65536 + 10 \times 4096 + 7 \times 256 + 4 \times 16 + 14 \times 1 =$$
$$196608 + \quad 40960 + \quad 1792 + \quad 64 + \quad 14 = 239438$$

Therefore

$$3A74E_{16} = 239438_{10}$$

The reader's attention is called to the hex and decimal conversion chart shown in Table 2.4. For convenience, this chart is reproduced in Appendix 6.

This conversion chart can be used to convert six-digit hex numbers to

TABLE 2.4   Hexadecimal and Decimal Conversion Chart

Hex Digits											
1		2		3		4		5		6	
Hex	Dec	Hex	Dec	Hex	Dec	Hex	Dec	Hex	Dec	Hex	Dec
0	0	0	0	0	0	0	0	0	0	0	0
1	1048576	1	65536	1	4096	1	256	1	16	1	1
2	2097152	2	131072	2	8192	2	512	2	32	2	2
3	3145728	3	196608	3	12288	3	768	3	48	3	3
4	4194304	4	262144	4	16384	4	1024	4	64	4	4
5	5242880	5	327680	5	20480	5	1280	5	80	5	5
6	6291456	6	393216	6	24576	6	1536	6	96	6	6
7	7340032	7	458752	7	28672	7	1792	7	112	7	7
8	8388608	8	524288	8	32768	8	2048	8	128	8	8
9	9437184	9	589824	9	36864	9	2304	9	144	9	9
A	10485760	A	655360	A	40960	A	2560	A	160	A	10
B	11534336	B	720896	B	45056	B	2816	B	176	B	11
C	12582912	C	786432	C	49152	C	3072	C	192	C	12
D	13631488	D	851968	D	53248	D	3328	D	208	D	13
E	14680064	E	917504	E	57344	E	3584	E	224	E	14
F	15728640	F	983040	F	61440	F	3840	F	240	F	15

decimal or decimal numbers less than 16777216 to hex. Note the table is made up of six columns. These six columns correspond to the powers of 16 in a hex number. The rightmost column corresponds to the units digit or the 16^0 digit. The leftmost column then corresponds to the 16^5 digit, with each intervening column corresponding to each intervening digit.

To convert from hex to decimal, one looks up each hex digit in its appropriate column and adds up the indicated decimal values. Thus for the hex number 3BE8, one adds up 12288, 2816, 224, and 8 to obtain 15336 as the equivalent decimal number.

To convert from decimal to hex, one reverses the process. For example, assume the decimal number to be converted is 357614. The largest decimal value is found in the table that will still be less than or equal to the initial decimal value. This value is 327680, which is equivalent to hex 50000. Subtracting 327680 from 357614, one obtains 29934, which is then used as the next value for conversion. The largest value now is 28672, equivalent to 7000 in hex. Subtracting again, one obtains the value of 1262. The table yields 1024 as the closest value with an equivalent value of 400 in hex. The difference of 1262 and 1024 is 238. The table yields 224 as the next value with equivalent value of E0 in hex. The final difference of 238 minus 224 is 14, whose hex equivalent is E. Adding all five hex equivalents together, in hex, one obtains the final result of 574EE.

2.5   ADDITION AND SUBTRACTION IN HEXADECIMAL

To efficiently carry out addition and subtraction in hex, the user would need to memorize a different addition table from the usual one for decimal addition. However, for relatively infrequent use of hex arithmetic, a less drastic method is probably sufficient. Since most debugging aids for assembly-language programming yield information in terms of hex values, a certain amount of addition and subtraction in hex will need to be performed. Therefore the degree of dexterity in hex arithmetic that one needs will depend more or less on one's proficiency as a programmer. The fewer program errors made, the less one needs to be concerned with hex arithmetic. Thus the author recommends a hybrid approach to hex arithmetic, using partial conversion with the addition being performed in decimal and a reconversion to hex for each column of hex numbers. It is very seldom that a programmer is called upon to add more than two digits at a time plus a possible carry. Usually small values are involved, up to 30 in decimal; therefore, conversion from decimal to hex and hex to decimal is relatively simple.

For example, to add 3C75 and 3E7, the following arithmetic,

$$
\begin{array}{r}
3C75 \\
+3E7 \\
\hline
405C
\end{array}
$$

involves certain mental operations. Let us see what they are. Partial hex-to-decimal conversion is needed only if a digit of A, B, C, D, E, or F appears in a column being currently added. Therefore, in adding 5 and 7 no preconversion is necessary. Adding 5 and 7 in decimal, a result of 12 is obtained. This is then converted to hex, as the digit C, and is written beneath the column. Notice there is no carry. The second column contains 7 and E. The E on conversion to decimal yields 14, plus the 7 yields 21, and reconversion yields a 5 with a carry of 1. Thus a 5 is written beneath the second column. The third column contains a C and a 3 plus the carry. Thus in decimal, 12 plus 3 plus 1 yields 16, which in hex is a 0 with a carry of 1. Thus a 0 is written beneath the third column. The fourth column is simply 3 plus the carry to yield a 4. Thus the final sum is 405C in hex.

Subtraction is done in essentially the same way; the actual subtraction is done mentally in decimal while all digits written are always in hex. It also must be remembered that a borrow involves a value of 16, not 10. Reversing the example above, the following arithmetic,

$$
\begin{array}{r}
405C \\
-3E7 \\
\hline
3C75
\end{array}
$$

can be described as follows. Converting the C to 12 and subtracting 7, one obtains 5. Since E, or 14, is larger than 5, a borrow must be performed for the second column. In so doing, the 4 becomes 3 and the 0 becomes F (if actual changes are to be made) and the 5 becomes 21, in decimal. Subtracting 14 from 21, a difference of 7 is obtained. Converting the F to 15, subtracting 3 to yield 12, and reconverting yields C for the third column. Finally the 3 is left in column four, making the final result 3C75.

For those who would like to do their hex arithmetic in pure hex, Table 2.5 gives the addition table that must be memorized.

TABLE 2.5   Hexadecimal Addition Table

+	0	1	2	3	4	5	6	7	8	9	A	B	C	D	E	F
0	0	1	2	3	4	5	6	7	8	9	A	B	C	D	E	F
1	1	2	3	4	5	6	7	8	9	A	B	C	D	E	F	10
2	2	3	4	5	6	7	8	9	A	B	C	D	E	F	10	11
3	3	4	5	6	7	8	9	A	B	C	D	E	F	10	11	12
4	4	5	6	7	8	9	A	B	C	D	E	F	10	11	12	13
5	5	6	7	8	9	A	B	C	D	E	F	10	11	12	13	14
6	6	7	8	9	A	B	C	D	E	F	10	11	12	13	14	15
7	7	8	9	A	B	C	D	E	F	10	11	12	13	14	15	16
8	8	9	A	B	C	D	E	F	10	11	12	13	14	15	16	17
9	9	A	B	C	D	E	F	10	11	12	13	14	15	16	17	18
A	A	B	C	D	E	F	10	11	12	13	14	15	16	17	18	19
B	B	C	D	E	F	10	11	12	13	14	15	16	17	18	19	1A
C	C	D	E	F	10	11	12	13	14	15	16	17	18	19	1A	1B
D	D	E	F	10	11	12	13	14	15	16	17	18	19	1A	1B	1C
E	E	F	10	11	12	13	14	15	16	17	18	19	1A	1B	1C	1D
F	F	10	11	12	13	14	15	16	17	18	19	1A	1B	1C	1D	1E

2.6   BINARY AND HEXADECIMAL CONVERSIONS

As mentioned above, hex numbers are used primarily as a convenience in representing long strings of binary bits. This can best be described by example. The binary number

$$1010111000100110111110001$$

is equivalent to the hex number AE26F1, a number one-fourth the length. Furthermore, one should be able to convert from one base to the other by simple inspection. Taking the example again, mark off groups of four bits starting at the right or low-order end. Each four-bit number is then replaced by its hex equivalent, as follows.

$$1010 \mid 1110 \mid 0010 \mid 0110 \mid 1111 \mid 0001$$
$$\text{A} \quad \text{E} \quad 2 \quad 6 \quad \text{F} \quad 1$$

Any odd group of bits left over at the high-order end can be mentally padded with zeros to form a four-bit group if desired.

An alternate method of converting decimal numbers to binary, which may be quicker in most cases, is to first convert from decimal to hex, then convert the hex value to its binary equivalent.

2.7   ARITHMETIC USING COMPLEMENT NOTATION

The operation of subtraction can be performed by complementing the subtrahend and adding. This is illustrated by the following example. All numbers are in decimal. The conventional statement

$$631729 - 375418 = 256311$$

can be replaced by the statement

$$631729 + (1000000 - 375418) - 1000000 = 256311$$

where the quantity in parentheses is called the *ten's complement*. The value of the ten's complement,

$$1000000 - 375418 = 624582$$

added to 631729 yields

$$631729 + 624582 = 1256311$$

a value which is 1000000 larger than the original result. Thus, if the high-order carry is ignored, the same result is obtained. Therefore, for arithmetic involving numbers of a particular length, subtraction can be produced by complementation followed by addition.

The formal definition for complementation, in decimal, is given by

$$10^n - N$$

where N is the number to be complemented and n is the number of digits in N. The reader will note that 10 raised to the n power is one larger than the maximum number containing n digits. This fact leads to the rule that the ten's complement of a number can be obtained by first subtracting each individual digit in the number from nine, yielding the *nine's* complement, and then adding a one to the low-order digit. Thus complementation can usually be performed by inspection.

In general, the *radix complement* for a number of radix R is given by

$$R^n - N$$

where N is a base R number to be complemented and n is the number of digits in N. If the original number N is added back to its radix complement, the following result is obtained:

$$R^n - N + N = R^n = 100000 \ldots$$

The reader will again note that this result represents a number that is one larger than the maximum number containing n digits. In a fixed-length arithmetic system of n digits, ignoring the high-order carry into the $n + 1$ place produces a result of zero in the operation above. Thus the following general statement can be made as an alternate definition for the radix complement. The radix complement of any number in a *fixed-length arithmetic system* is that number which, when added to the original number, produces all zeros. Note that the term fixed-length arithmetic system implies the high-order carry is to be ignored.

Now turning to the binary number system, the ten's and nine's complement in decimal is seen to correspond to the two's and one's complement in binary. Using the previous general definition for radix complement, the *two's complement* is given by

$$2^n - N$$

where n and N are the same as before. For example, the two's complement of the binary number 00100110 in a fixed-length system containing eight digits is computed in binary, as

$$100000000 - 00100110 = 11011010$$

Complementing in binary turns out to be a very simple operation, done readily by inspection. Each bit in the number is *inverted*; that is, all ones become zeros and all zeros become ones, yielding the *one's complement*. Adding a one to the low-order digit then yields the two's complement. Thus the example shown above would appear as

original number	00100110	
inverting	11011001	= one's complement
adding one	1	
yields	11011010	= two's complement

Now suppose the original number, 00100110, is to be subtracted from a second binary number, 00110011. As in the decimal system, the two's complement of the subtrahend can be added as

Complement arithmetic		*Conventional arithmetic*	
original minuend 00110011		00110011	original minuend
complemented subtrahend +11011010		−00100110	original subtrahend
yields 100001101		00001101	yields

Therefore, just as in the decimal system, if the high-order carry is ignored in the complement arithmetic, the same answer is obtained as in conventional arithmetic. To investigate the behavior of negative numbers within complement arithmetic, the same problem is repeated with a minuend that is smaller than the subtrahend.

	Complement arithmetic	*Conventional arithmetic*	
minuend	00010101	00010101	minuend
complemented subtrahend	+11011010	−00100110	original subtrahend
yields	11101111	−00010001	yields

It is interesting to note that a high-order carry has not occurred in the complement arithmetic. At the same time, note that the answer obtained is actually the complement of the result obtained in the conventional arithmetic, only with the opposite sign. The answer should be recomplemented to obtain the correct result as a negative value.

If one chooses, negative numbers may be represented and maintained in the two's-complement form, thus eliminating the need for the recomplementation operation. At the same time, precomplementation operations are avoided in the addition of negative numbers. Thus the only actual complementing necessary occurs before subtract operations.

As true in most binary computing systems, the high-order or leftmost bit of a number indicates the sign of the number. A high-order zero represents a positive number, while a high-order one represents a negative number. This remains true even though the number is in two's-complement form. The operations of addition and subtraction remain valid, the only requirement being that the high-order carry is to be ignored as part of the result. The only remaining concern is the possible occurrence of an overflow, or that condition where the maximum capacity of an n-digit number is exceeded. However, this condition can be detected quite easily by observing the carries into and out of the high-order position of the number. If these carries agree, the answer is acceptable. If the carries do not agree, the answer is not correct and overflow has occurred. A proof of these statements follows.

Assumptions:

1. Number length $n = 8$

2. Using two's-complement notation:

    (a) Positive number in true form has at least one leading zero.

    (b) Negative number in complement form has at least one leading one.

3. Owing to assumptions 1 and 2:

    (a) Largest-magnitude positive number is 127.

    (b) Largest-magnitude negative number is −128.

4.   Two cases yield overflow:

   (a)   Two positive numbers whose sum is > 127.

   (b)   Two negative numbers whose sum is < -128.

Proof that overflow is indicated by unlike carries for

1.   Case I—two positive numbers.

   carries $\rightarrow$ 0C

$$0XXXXXXX \leqslant 127$$
$$0XXXXXXX \leqslant 127$$
$$0XXXXXXX \leqslant 127$$

   $\uparrow$ must be zero for positive result

Therefore C must be zero to be consistent.

2.   Case II—two negative numbers.

   carries $\rightarrow$ 1C

$$1XXXXXXX \geqslant -128$$
$$1XXXXXXX \geqslant -128$$
$$1XXXXXXX \geqslant -128$$

   $\uparrow$ must be one for negative result

Therefore C must be one to be consistent.

Looking at Case I, one can state that all zeros shown must be zero in the absence of overflow. The carry out of the eighth place must be zero, since at least two zeros appear in the eighth column. To obtain a positive result, the digit in the eighth place of the sum must be zero, otherwise contradiction of assumption 2(a) results. Thus, C must also be zero to produce the sum of zero. Therefore, the two carries must be both zero for a valid result.

Looking at Case II, one can state that all ones shown must be one in the absence of overflow. The carry out of the eighth place must be one, since at least two ones appear in the eighth column. To obtain a negative result, the digit in the eighth place of the sum must be one, otherwise a contradiction of assumption 2(b) results. Thus, C must be one to produce the sum of one. Therefore, the two carries must be both one for a valid result.

The behavior of two's-complement arithmetic and the possible overflow condition are fully illustrated by the six problems that follow. All possible combinations of operands are accounted for in these examples. Each example is shown using both two's complement and conventional arithmetic. Please note that for simplicity the arithmetic is based on a number length of eight bits. Thus the largest positive number allowed is 01111111 or 127 in decimal. The largest negative number is 10000000 or -128 in decimal.

1. | two's complement | conventional | decimal |
    | --- | --- | --- |
    | 00111110 | +00111110 | +62 |
    | +00011011 | +00011011 | +27 |
    | 01011001 | 01011001 | +89 |

    (No high-order carries = no overflow)
    (Answer is positive and in true form)

2. | two's complement | conventional | decimal |
    | --- | --- | --- |
    | 00111110 | +00111110 | +62 |
    | +11100101 | −00011011 | −27 |
    | 00100011 | +00100011 | +35 |

    (Both high-order carries = no overflow)
    (Answer is positive and in true form)

3. | two's complement | conventional | decimal |
    | --- | --- | --- |
    | 00011011 | +00011011 | +27 |
    | +11000010 | −00111110 | −62 |
    | 11011101 | −00100011 | −35 |

    (No high-order carries = no overflow)
    (Answer is negative and in complement form)

4. | two's complement | conventional | decimal |
    | --- | --- | --- |
    | 11000010 | −00111110 | −62 |
    | +11100101 | −00011011 | −27 |
    | 10100111 | −01011001 | −89 |

    (Both high-order carries = no overflow)
    (Answer is negative and in complement form)

5. | two's complement | conventional | decimal |
    | --- | --- | --- |
    | 00111110 | +00111110 | +62 |
    | +01011001 | +01011001 | +89 |
    | 10010111 | 10010111 | +151 |

    (Only one high-order carry = overflow)
    (Answer is unacceptable)

6. | two's complement | conventional | decimal |
    | --- | --- | --- |
    | 11000010 | −00111110 | −62 |
    | +10100111 | −01011001 | −89 |
    | 01101001 | −10010111 | −151 |

    (Only one high-order carry = overflow)
    (Answer is unacceptable)

It should be obvious in the last two examples that overflow did occur, since the sums are both larger than the eight-bit number can hold and still allow one bit to represent the sign of the number.

A great deal more can be said about binary and hex numbers, and particularly about number systems in general; however, the material within this chapter provides sufficient background for a full understanding of the remaining chapters within this text.

EXERCISES

1. Consider a number system with 5 as a radix. Expand the base 5 number 312.34 into its equivalent mathematical expression. What is the decimal equivalent for this number?
2. Convert the decimal numbers 43.0 and 16/49 to base 7 numbers.
3. Convert the decimal numbers 17, 26, 31, 53, and 76 to their binary equivalents.
4. Expand each of the binary numbers obtained in Exercise 3 by Definition 2.1.
5. Convert each of the binary numbers obtained in Exercise 3 to decimal, using the memory method discussed in Section 2.2.
6. Add the binary numbers obtained in Exercise 3 in binary to obtain a single sum. Convert the sum to decimal and check against a sum obtained from the original decimal equivalents.
7. Subtract in binary each binary number found in Exercise 3 from the binary sum obtained in Exercise 6.
8. Convert the decimal numbers 3791, 255, 5097, and 30177 to hexadecimal.
9. Add the four hex numbers obtained in Exercise 8 to form one hex sum. Convert this sum to decimal and compare with the sum of the original four decimal values.
10. Convert the five binary numbers of Exercise 3 to hex.
11. Convert the hex numbers obtained in Exercise 8 to binary.
12. Subtract 5DA from 736C in hex. Likewise, subtract F28 from E78A.
13. Write the decimal numbers −17, −26, −31, −53, and −76 in two's-complement binary form using a number length of eight bits.
14. Add the binary number 00011111 to each of the five two's-complement values obtained in Exercise 13. Make a comment about the acceptance, sign, and form of each result.

Chapter **three**

System/360
Architecture

Integral to any automatic digital computer is a memory, the contents of which can be modified by the machine itself. Without access to such a storage device, computers could not exist in their present state. The concept of an automatically modifiable memory is central to the fundamental law referred to as the *stored-program principle,* first postulated during the 1940s by John von Newmann, a noted mathematician. This law also contains an essential point, the placing of a calculating machine under its own control to obtain reliable, high-speed computation. The self-control is provided by a *program* stored within the memory. Another requirement is the ability to change the control sequence, within one problem as well as between entirely independent problems. Thus the concept of a modifiable program is generated from within this need for flexible self-control, or control sequences that can be altered either manually or automatically.

One of the earliest applications of flexible, automatic control was in the Jacquard loom in France in 1747. Here a sequence of cards with coded holes would mechanically pass through a mechanism to control the loom in weaving a particular design into cloth. To change the design, a new set of cards could be coded and placed in the control mechanism. Thus, without rebuilding of the machine, the same general-purpose loom could be used for weaving a number of different designs. The cards in the Jacquard loom were the forerunners of the modern computer punched cards.

3.1   COMPUTER STORAGE IN GENERAL

To obtain the desired flexibility in computation along with reliability and high speed, some suitable device had to be devised to hold the program or control sequence within easy access of the calculator portion of the computer. Many different types of devices have been used over the years for storing computer programs and their associated data within the computer. Quite naturally, the early devices were very slow in terms of access time and could remember only a few pieces of information at a time. Access time, the time required to store or retrieve one item of information, was measured in seconds or, at best, in tenths of a second. Memory size was limited to perhaps twenty or thirty ten-digit numbers. Needless to say, these computers were somewhat limited in their ability to solve problems. However, it was obvious to the designers of these machines that they had great promise, and the major key to success was only higher speed and larger capacity. These problems were solved fairly rapidly, and by the early 1950s storage access time had dropped to milliseconds and capacity had grown to several thousand ten-digit numbers. Some of the typical devices used for storage were electromechanical relays, flying-spot storage tubes, sonic delay lines, and electromagnetic drums.

The major breakthrough came with the design of memories made up of magnetic cores. A magnetic core is a simple device that can remember one of two possible states; thus it was very amenable to representing a binary digit or bit. During the 1960s memory access time dropped to the microsecond and, in the most expensive equipment, even to fractions of microseconds. At the same time memory capacities grew to hundreds of thousands and, in some cases, millions of basic memory units called *bytes*. (A byte in System/360 computers is composed of eight binary bits.) Owing to the widespread use of core memories, the most common way of referring to storage became *core storage* or simply *core* (as in phrases such as "the program is then loaded into core to be executed"). Newer memories using thin-film magnetic devices promise to extend the speed and capacity boundaries even further. Whether the reference name *core* will change remains to be seen.

Regardless of the size or operating characteristics, size or radix of numbers being stored, or physical makeup, the basic purpose of computer memories has always been essentially the same. The basic purpose of storage is to provide a medium in which information concerning the problem at hand can be held in suspension, retrieved, updated, or otherwise modified and used. An essential part of this storage concept must be an organization that will yield efficient storage and retrieval of each item of information to be stored. Of even more importance is the placing of information in a particular location within the memory device so that it can again be found and identified. This particular problem is solved through a technique called *addressing*. Each storage location is given a name or address that is unique from all other locations within the memory. Thus, once information is stored, it can again be retrieved, provided the address of the location is remembered and used during the retrieval operation.

More discussion of addressing techniques is presented in later sections. Before leaving the general discussion of storages, however, we should consider the subject of storage hierarchy. Complexity of computer systems has grown to the point where storage has become stratified into various levels of use. These levels can be characterized in several ways, such as purpose, access speed, capacity, and cost. Some typical hierarchy levels are now presented along with their respective characteristics.

At the top level is found main storages, usually made up of high-speed magnetic core memories. Since almost every calculation or operation performed by the computer depends on accessing information in memory, then the speed of a computer depends, for the most part, on how fast this memory access can be performed. Thus main memories must be as fast as possible within the cost restraints placed on the machine. Owing to the relatively large cost involved in high-speed memories, the corresponding capacity is relatively limited. Typical parameters are an access time of one microsecond with a capacity of 250,000 bytes for a computer costing in the neighborhood of $1 million (based on total computer cost in 1970).

A second level of storage hierarchy not usually included in most systems is a slower-speed but larger-capacity bulk core memory. Here speed is sacrificed for more capacity at a comparable cost of main memories. Access speed might be about 8 or 10 microseconds with a capacity between 1 and 8 million bytes.

A third level is typified by high-speed magnetic drum memories involving a cylindrical drum coated with a magnetic material on which data can be recorded. The drum is then rotated while the read-write heads are fixed at close proximity for storage and retrieval. Access speeds range between 5 to 20 milliseconds, with capacities around 4 million bytes. Data transfer rates are in the neighborhood of 1 million bytes per second. The relative cost is lower than main or bulk core memories.

A fourth level is typified by a direct-access device called a disk drive. This memory unit is made up of a stack of disks, about 14 inches in diameter, which are coated with magnetic material. Read-write heads move between the disks to reach the various recording tracks in which data is stored. Access speed is measured in milliseconds, with capacities for a single disk drive around 10 million bytes. Usually several disk drives are accessible by the same computing system, increasing the available storage accordingly.

A fifth level, also direct access, includes data cells composed of many thin plastic strips coated with magnetic material. These strips are kept in bins or cells, which can be moved to a reading station. When information is transferred into or out of the data cell, a strip is selected from a bin, data is read or written, and the strip is then returned to its bin. Access speed ranges from a few milliseconds up to a half second or more, depending on where the desired bin and strip is located relative to the read station. Capacity can be as high as 400 million bytes.

A sixth level is typified by magnetic tape and tape drives. Here access time can be quite long, since access is of a sequential nature. However, capacity can be considered limited only by the number of tapes available to a user. Cost is relatively low compared with the other devices in the higher levels.

A final level, made up of ordinary punched cards, must also be considered as a valid memory or storage device, for certainly cards can store information. Access time is usually very slow, sometimes even hours for large files of information, but capacity can be very large at very low cost. The costs of providing cabinets for card storage and rooms for cabinets are much higher than the cost of the cards themselves.

3.2   SYSTEM/360 MAIN MEMORY

We now focus exclusively on the organization and concepts involved in main memories of System/360 computers. Other levels of memory are considered in later chapters.

Main memories are composed of magnetic cores, arranged in groups of nine. One core in each group is used for a parity check—a means of increasing the reliability of the memory system. Thus eight cores are left in each group for the purpose of storing information. Each group of cores is called a *byte* and has a capacity of eight binary bits. Therefore, a byte contains numbers equivalent to decimal 0 through 255, corresponding to the binary values of 0 and 11111111 or hex numbers of 0 and FF.

Each byte of storage represents one memory location or cell and has associated with it a unique address. These addresses are simply binary numbers ranging from zero up to a number that represents the maximum capacity, in bytes, of the particular model of System/360. Memory capacities are usually manufactured in groups equal to powers of 2, such as 32768, 65536, 131072, 262144, and so on. For sake of convenience, these memory sizes are usually referred to as 32K, 64K, 128K, 256K, and so forth. To avoid the obvious inconsistency, it has been suggested to let the value of K, within this context, be equal to 1024. At any rate, for a particular model of machine, the highest memory address would be a power of 2 minus 1, since the first address begins with zero. Thus a typical machine might have addresses running from 0 through 131071 corresponding to a memory size of 131072 bytes.

In order to allow several bytes of storage to be considered as a single unit of information, storage bytes can be considered as being side by side, as in Figure 3.1. Binary bits are represented by the variable X. When two or more consecutive bytes are considered as a single group containing an integral piece of

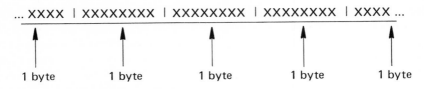

FIGURE 3.1   One-Byte Storage Locations

information, the group is referred to as a *field*. Certain fields of two, four, and eight bytes have special names and are respectively called half words, words, and double words. To qualify as being such, however, the addresses of half words, words, and double words must be multiples of 2, 4 and 8, respectively. This concept is illustrated in Figure 3.2. The binary numbers shown represent the low-order four bits of the address of each byte.

Binary Address (Low-order four bits)

0000	0001	0010	0011	0100	0101	0110	0111	1000	1001	1010 ...
Byte	Byte	Byte	Byte	Byte	Byte	Byte	Byte	Byte	Byte	Byte ...
Half word		Half word		Half word		Half word		Half word		...
Word				Word				Word		...
Double word								Double word		...

FIGURE 3.2   Storage Boundaries

The reader will note that a binary number ends in zero if it is an even number or is divisible by 2. One that is divisible by 4 ends in two zeros. Therefore, word boundary addresses end in two zeros. Since a number divisible by 8 ends in three zeros, double-word boundaries have addresses that end in three zeros.

A storage field containing more than one byte is always addressed or is referred to by the address of the leftmost byte in the field. Thus, if a field is made up of three bytes with addresses 511, 512, and 513, the address of the field as a unit is 511.

3.3   INDEPENDENCE OF ADDRESS AND CONTENT

Students often find it difficult to understand the independence of the address of a memory location and the storage contents of that location. An address is merely the *name* of the location; it has no other relation to the contents of the location. The same concept is involved in algebra or programming languages, where variable names are used to refer to quantities. As pointed out in Chapter 2, numerals are names that represent abstract values. To illustrate the universality of this concept, let us depart somewhat from the subject and discuss an interesting excerpt from literature. The following discussion between the White Knight and Alice is taken from Lewis Caroll's *Through The Looking Glass.*

> "You are sad," the Knight said in an anxious tone. "Let me sing a song to comfort you."
>
> "Is it very long?" Alice asked, for she had heard a good deal of poetry that day.
>
> "It's long," said the Knight, "but it's very, *very* beautiful. Everybody that hears me sing it—either it brings the *tears* into their eyes, or else—"
>
> "Or else what?" said Alice, for the Knight had made a sudden pause.
>
> "Or else it doesn't, you know. The name of the song is called *'Haddocks' Eyes.'* "
>
> "Oh, that's the name of the song, is it?" Alice said, trying to feel interested.
>
> "No, you don't understand," the Knight said, looking a little vexed. "That's what the name is *called*. The name really is *'The Aged, Aged Man.'* "
>
> "Then I ought to have said, 'That's what the *song* is called?' " Alice corrected herself.
>
> "No, you oughtn't; that's quite another thing! The *song* is called *'Ways and Means'*; but that's only what it's *called*, you know!"
>
> "Well, what *is* the song, then?" said Alice, who was by this time completely bewildered.
>
> "I was coming to that," the Knight said. "The song *is* '*A-sitting on a Gate*'; and the tune's my own invention."

The author wishes to be impertinent and attempt to draw the following conclusions from this rather amazing conversation. It is amazing in that it was written many years before computers ever existed. The four *names* found in the presentation can be correlated in one-to-one correspondence with similar concepts in computer storage and addressing. This correspondence is now given in the following outline.

Proper Name	Common Name	Corresponding Concept
A-sitting on a Gate	song	storage content value
Ways and Means	song is called	storage content numerals
The Aged, Aged Man	name of song	address value
Haddocks' Eyes	name of song is called	address numerals

The reader will notice that the relationship between abstract value and symbolic representation is also involved in the excerpt. This is probably what Lewis Carroll was primarily concerned with, but it still is interesting to note that there is a definite demarcation between the song and its name. This break occurs with the statement: "That's quite another thing!" This distinction and its correlation with the corresponding distinction between storage contents and storage addresses is the impressive point. One hardly expects it of the nineteenth century, even though Carroll was a noted mathematician and logician.

3.4   DATA AND ARITHMETIC CONCEPTS

Manipulation of data in System/360 computers can occur in several different modes, depending on the interpretation of data involved in the operation. All data stored within the machine are basically stored in only one form and are made up of the eight-binary-bit bytes discussed earlier. The calculator or control component of the machine has the capability, however, of interpreting these binary numbers in several different specific formats. There are essentially five ways of interpreting data: Integer or fixed-point, real or floating-point, packed decimal, zoned decimal, and finally the plain unsigned binary number called logical data. Each of these modes of data is used for different purposes and is operated upon by the computer in different ways. Each mode of operation will be developed in detail in one or more chapters of this book. We shall undertake here a preliminary discussion in connection with the architecture of the system.

Integer or fixed-point numbers, identical to the Fortran numbers of the same name, are manipulated by the machine in a particular section of the computer called the integer arithmetic module. Within this module are found sixteen registers, which can be compared to the dials of an ordinary desk calculator. These units also can be thought of as small memory devices, although they have the additional capability of performing arithmetic. Each register holds a binary number of 32 bits, the same as a word or four bytes of main storage. Since these registers have purposes other than use in integer arithmetic, they are called the sixteen General-Purpose Registers (GPR). Figure 3.3 shows an abstract view of these sixteen registers. In order to distinguish between the registers, each has an address associated with it. These addresses, just as in main memory, begin with zero and run through 15 in decimal, 1111 in binary, and F in hex.

Real or floating-point arithmetic, identical to the Fortran arithmetic of the same name, is carried out by a different part of the computer, which contains a set of floating-point registers. Unlike the GPR, floating-point registers (FPR) can not be used for any purpose other than floating-point arithmetic, except perhaps for temporary storage of information. There are four of these FPR, each is 64

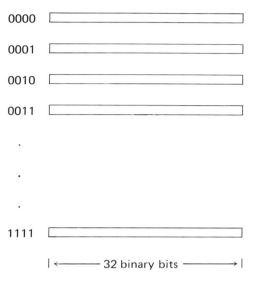

FIGURE 3.3 General-Purpose Registers

bits long. However, the first half of each can be used independently. Figure 3.4 shows the abstract view of the floating-point registers. Notice that their addresses go in steps of two.

No special registers are provided for the other data types, as arithmetic involving zoned and packed decimal values is performed within main storage. This is also true for the logical data.

Any further hardware devices or features, such as those that input and output operations might require, are discussed along with their respective detailed presentations.

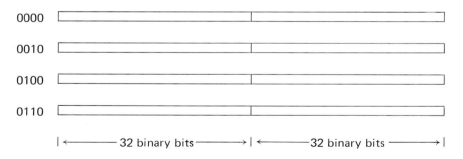

FIGURE 3.4 Floating-Point Registers

3.5   CONTROL CONCEPTS

Fundamental to any automatic computer is a set of basic operations that can be performed by the machine. Each basic operation involves an elementary and specific manipulation of data. Within System/360, each basic operation is also identified at the basic machine-language level by a unique binary number between 0 and 11111111. To simplify programming, the assembly language provides a unique, alphabetic and mnemonic representation for this binary number. These operations are invoked by *instructions*, and the binary number associated with each is called either an operation code or an instruction code. A *program* is an ordered set or collection of instruction codes that specify a particular sequence of operations to be performed by the computer.

Besides the instruction code, a valid instruction to the computer must also involve information concerning the data to be operated upon. Data referred to are called *operands* of the indicated instruction. Thus each instruction found within a program appears with an instruction code along with certain operand specifications.

Within System/360 computers there are five types of instruction formats. They are called Register to Register (RR), Register with Indexing (RX), Register to Storage (RS), Storage Immediate (SI), and Storage to Storage (SS). The precise appearance of each of these five formats is shown in Figure 3.5. Shown within each format are certain components or constituents presented by symbols. These symbols are defined briefly in Table 3.1 and are discussed in detail in the paragraphs that follow.

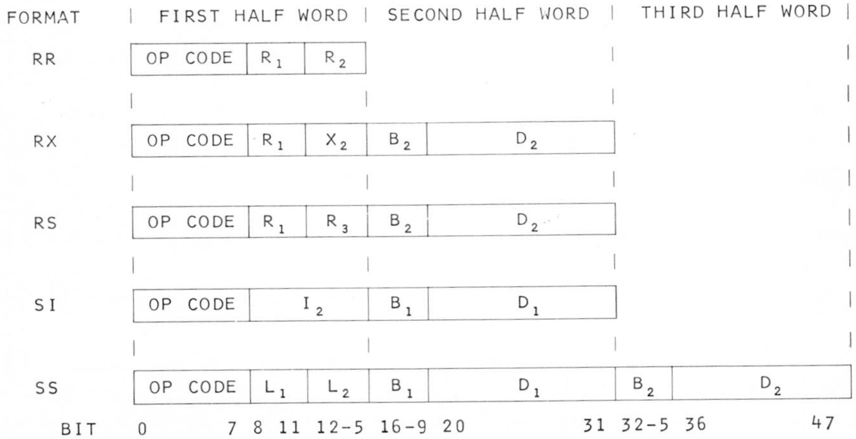

FIGURE 3.5   Instruction Formats

TABLE 3.1   Symbol Representation in Figure 3.5

Symbol	Representation Refers to a Number
B_i	of a GPR used as a Base Register
R_i	of a GPR or FPR used as an Operand Register
X_i	of a GPR used as an Index Register
D_i	used as a Displacement
I_i	used as an Immediate Operand
L_i	used as an Operand Length

Implied by the data within Figure 3.5 and Table 3.1 is a wealth of information, which is difficult both to understand as well as describe. Even after a detailed presentation, many of the concepts will escape the reader until he has gained some experience with actual application.

The major concept being described here is that of placing within the same computer memory both instructions and data during the same period of time. This not only allows the interpretation of data information as data and instruction information as instructions but also the very useful ability to interpret instruction information as data and even data information as instructions. Even though this is a very powerful concept, it is also very simple. The third type of interpretation allows program instructions to be modified by the machine under program control. The fourth type of interpretation, although a common source of error, allows a program to create from data additional and new instructions for further execution. This concept is the basis for all automatic computation and is the culmination of the stored-program principle.

The computer actually has no way of distinguishing between data and instructions from the stored information itself. The determination is made within the sequence control module of the computer by constantly alternating between two modes of operation. One mode, called *instruction fetch*, is the time when the next sequential instruction is retrieved from storage. The other mode, called *instruction execute*, is the time when the fetched instruction is executed. Any information retrieved during this second mode is interpreted as data. Thus as long as the correct information appears in storage at the right time and at the right place, effective results are obtained. This then becomes the *simple* duty of the programmer.

The simplest operations within System/360 are those falling within the RR type of instructions. These instructions cause the machine to perform an arithmetic or logical operation on data contained within one or two general-purpose or floating-point registers. A typical operation might be the addition of the contents of one GPR to the contents of a second GPR. Other operations include subtraction, multiplication, division, logical arithmetic, or duplication of the contents of one register into a second. No reference is made to main storage for operand data. The only main storage reference is to obtain the instruction itself. All other types of instructions cause the computer to make reference to main storage for one or more operands during the execution of an instruction.

RX type instructions make reference to both a register and main storage for operands. In addition, an index register, also a GPR, may be specified for the purpose of *indexing* the main storage operand reference, a technique similar in effect to subscripted variables in Fortran or PL/I. Indexing provides an easy method of stepping through a table of values by incrementing the contents of the index register. RX instructions are the only ones that may be indexed. Main storage operands referred to by RX instructions are always a fixed length of either a byte, half word, word, or double word. The specific length is determined by the instruction code itself.

RS type instructions, except for shift and certain branch instructions, refer to one or more register operands as well as the main storage operand. The length of the storage operand is a multiple of four bytes and must be on a word address boundary. Shift instructions refer to only one register operand, and the storage operand address is actually a shift count, not a data reference. Certain branch instructions also refer to one or more register operands, but the storage operand address is actually a branch address, not a data reference. These peculiarities are discussed in detail in Chapters 4 and 5.

SI type instructions, besides referencing main storage for one operand, also contain one-byte operands within the instructions themselves, called immediate operands. All main storage operands are also one byte in length.

SS type instructions refer to main storage for two operands. In some cases, each operand may be of a different length, thus two length codes are included within the instruction format to specify each length. Lengths can be from 1 to 16 bytes for these cases. In other cases, both operands must be of the same length; thus only one length code is indicated in the instruction. This length can be from 1 to 256 bytes.

3.6   THE CONCEPT OF BASE REGISTER ADDRESSING

Computers in use before the advent of System/360 had instruction formats that contained a complete operand address. In other words, enough room was provided in the instruction to refer to the operand by its actual and complete address. Thus, if a machine had a total capacity of 32768 memory locations—a typical size—then addresses would go as high as fifteen binary bits in length. Therefore, fifteen binary places were alloted for the address within each instruction. As storage capacities grew toward the million mark, address size could have approached 20 bits and more if the entire address continued to be included within the instruction.

System/360 designers, realizing that a typical program would be much smaller than total memory size, developed the base register and displacement approach to operand referencing. The advantage of this approach is the reduction of the length of the operand reference in an instruction, thus conserving storage. A displacement length of twelve bits (refer to Figure 3.5.) plus the base register number of four bits equals sixteen, which is less than the 24 bits needed to address a memory size of 16777216, the maximum size of all System/360 memories. Thus memory requirements for operand references are reduced by one-third.

Using the base register and displacement method has other advantages as well. The concept is very useful in dynamic storage allocation and in reentrant and recursive programming, subjects discussed in Chapter 11. The method may help to simplify the initial loading of a program, but no advantage exists in the problem of dynamic relocation once execution has been initiated.

The concept of base register addressing is based on the following technique. At the beginning of a program a general-purpose register, called the base register, is loaded with a *base address*. This base address is usually at or near the first location used by the program. Then throughout the program, all operand referencing is made relative to the base address by using a *displacement* value equal to the difference between the base address and the actual operand address. This technique is shown in Figure 3.6. The actual programming of this method is made somewhat easier by the assembler, the system-supplied program that translates the assembly-language program into a machine-language program. The assembler, knowing which register is to be the base register and also what the base address is to be, computes the displacement and creates the correct instruction image containing the proper base register number and the correct displacement value so that the operand address reference is correct. Therefore, during the execution of a program, each reference to a main storage operand causes the machine to add the contents of the specified base register and the specified displacement value to obtain the real address of the operand.

In addition, RX type instructions provide an indexing capability. The contents of a specified index register, a general-purpose register, is also added to the address represented by the sum of the base address and displacement. Thus, by varying the contents of the index register, the storage reference can be altered in some desired fashion without disturbing the base register or the displacement. An important point is that a base or index register number of zero indicates that particular component of the address is not to be included in the address computation.

3.7   CONDITION-CODE CONCEPT

Any automatic computer must have a method of altering the path of control within a program based on conditions within the machine at the time the

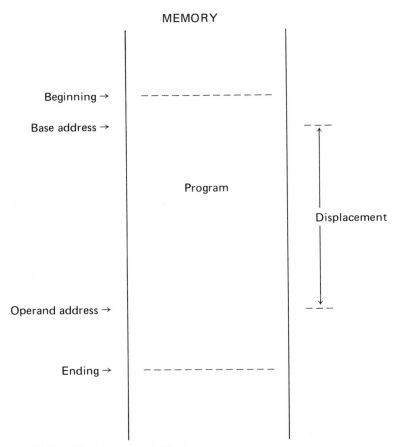

FIGURE 3.6   Base Address and Displacement

program is being executed. Older machines used the technique of providing a separate and independent instruction to test for each condition that might be useful to know about. If the condition existed, the machine would perhaps branch to a given location within the program; otherwise it would continue executing the program in sequence. System/360 uses a different and more powerful approach. Within the control module of the machine a *condition-code* indicator is maintained, which constantly reflects pertinent information about conditions with which the programmer might be concerned. One branching instruction is then provided that causes a branch depending on the status of the condition-code indicator. For example, following the execution of an addition operation, the condition code is set to one of the four possible settings of the code. If the result of the addition is zero, the code is set to zero. If the result is negative, or less than zero, the code is set to one. If the result is positive, or greater than zero, the code is set to two. If the sum results in a number too large for the machine to handle, the code is set to three, indicating an overflow condition. Not only can the programmer test for the occurrence of a particular condition-code setting, such as one; he also has the very powerful ability to test for an occurrence of a condition-code value from among several settings, such as zero or two. Because there are four possible values, there are sixteen possible combinations in which a test can be made. For example, if a programmer wished to check for a sum that is either zero or less than zero, he would test the condition code for either a setting of zero or one. The flexibility allows for a more sophisticated level of decision making by programmers than that provided for in older machines.

3.8   PROGRAM-INTERRUPTION CONCEPT

Most machines of pre-System/360 vintage had no procedure for avoiding the possibility of being told by the programmer to do something impossible. For example, if an instruction was found in a program that contained an invalid operation code, most machines would simply stop in frustration and give up. Or if someone attempted to divide by zero, a similar behavior might be exhibited. Also, most older machines actually had a stop instruction. Of all things a computer could do, this was needed the least.

System/360, and other modern computers, have built into them the ability to recognize certain conditions to be either invalid, impossible, or unwise to allow to continue beyond a certain point. System/360 contains an *interrupt system* that handles these special problems. Five levels of interrupt are possible; only the *program* level is discussed in this section. This level contains most of the possible situations that can arise during the execution of the user's program. The names of the other levels are input/output, supervisor-call, external, and machine-check interrupts. Within the program-interrupt level fifteen different problems can exist; these are coded with numbers from 1 to 15, as shown in Table 3.2.

Some of the program interruptions are easy to understand; others are more difficult to explain at this point. However, a short statement is given here about each. The *operation* interrupt occurs when the machine attempts to execute an invalid operation code. The *privileged operation* interrupt occurs when the user's program attempts to use an instruction that is restricted to use by the Operating System. Input and output instructions are examples of privileged operations. All input and output in System/360 is performed by the Operating System at the request of the user's program. The *execute* interrupt occurs when the subject instruction of an execute instruction is a second execute. The *protection* interrupt occurs when a program attempts to store into a region of main storage that is reserved for another user's program. Up to fifteen separate areas of main storage can be protected from each other. This allows undebugged programs to

TABLE 3.2   Program Interrupts

Interruption Code	Interruption Cause
1	Operation
2	Privileged operation
3	Execute
4	Protection
5	Addressing
6	Specification
7	Data
8	Fixed-point overflow
9	Fixed-point divide
10	Decimal overflow
11	Decimal divide
12	Exponent overflow
13	Exponent underflow
14	Significance
15	Floating-point divide

run at the same time as other programs that are in operation, without the danger of the former destroying the latter. The *addressing* interrupt occurs if a program makes a main storage reference beyond the maximum address allowed for a particular model of System/360. The *specification* interrupt occurs when a main storage reference is not on the proper boundary or when certain register references are not correct. The *data* interrupt occurs in decimal arithmetic when a datum being used is not a valid decimal number. *Fixed-point overflow* occurs when an integer number is generated that is too large for register capacity. This interrupt can be ignored if the programmer so desires by a procedure called "masking off the interrupt." *Fixed-point divide* occurs when an attempt is made to divide by zero in integer arithmetic. *Decimal overflow* is similar to fixed-point overflow except that it occurs in decimal arithmetic. This interrupt can also be masked off. *Decimal divide* is similar to fixed-point divide except it occurs in decimal arithmetic. *Exponent overflow* occurs in floating-point arithmetic when the exponent of a result is larger than approximately 10^{75}. *Exponent underflow* occurs when the exponent becomes smaller than approximately 10^{-78}. This interrupt can also be masked off. *Significance* occurs when accuracy is lost in some particular operations. This interrupt can also be masked off. The final interrupt of *floating-point divide* occurs when an attempt to divide by zero occurs during floating-point arithmetic. These fifteen conditions represent all of the possible errors that can be made by programmers that might cause damage to another program, including the Operating System program.

EXERCISES

1. Cite the essential points contained within the stored-program principle.
2. State the major breakthrough that led to modern computer memories.
3. Discuss the concept of memory addressing.
4. Name and discuss the seven levels of computer storage.
5. What is the smallest unit of addressable storage in a System/360 main memory called? What is the capacity of the storage unit?
6. What is a field? What are the special two-byte, four-byte, and eight-byte fields called and what restriction is placed on their addresses?
7. What are the connections between the contents of a memory location and its address?
8. Name five ways data can be interpreted as data.
9. What are general-purpose and floating-point registers? What are they used for?
10. What are the four fundamental ways information can be interpreted by the computer?
11. Name and describe five ways instructions are interpreted by the control module of the computer.
12. What is the concept of base register addressing?
13. What is the condition code? How many conditions are possible? How many combinations of conditions are possible?
14. What is a program interrupt? How many kinds of program interrupts are possible?

Chapter four

An Introduction to Machine Operations and Programming

The point has now been reached where topical boundaries must become vague for proper understanding and presentation. The essentially independent concept of machine behavior becomes easier to discuss if it is introduced almost simultaneously with the elementary procedures and conventions of assembly language. Thus, two different but interacting concepts are discussed within this chapter. The primary concept is concerned with the integer arithmetic operations found within System/360; however, it is difficult to discuss these operations to any extent on an independent basis. Therefore, both concepts are presented in parallel, although an attempt is made to distinguish between the two.

Before beginning the discussion of the primary topics, we consider the advantages of two's-complement arithmetic. Binary integer arithmetic in System/360 computers is not performed in the conventional manner. Negative numbers are maintained in two's-complement form, providing several improvements over conventional binary arithmetic.

All System/360 binary integer operations have instructions that fall within the RR, RX, and RS formats. However, these operations by no means exhaust all of the possible instructions within these three categories. Floating-point, logical, and branching operations also make use of these formats.

This chapter describes the fundamental behavior of the machine with respect to a limited set of uses for the general-purpose registers, main storage, and the combination of registers and storage. Several notational devices are introduced to help clarify and emphasize pertinent factors in the behavior of the machine.

At the same time as behavioral characteristics are being described, some elementary techniques in assembly-language programming are also introduced to provide an easier method of describing further machine behavior. Major programming techniques, including all variations, are given for RR, RX, and RS instructions beginning in Chapter 5. The reader will be encouraged to know that programming conventions are the same for all instructions within a given format type. Thus, once a particular type has been studied and mastered, the same conventions and techniques can be applied to other instructions of the same type with relative ease.

4.1   ADVANTAGES OF THE TWO'S-COMPLEMENT NOTATION

Two's-complement notation provides at least three advantages over the conventional method of representing data, usually referred to as the sign-and-magnitude method. In this latter approach, each number has its magnitude represented in true form regardless of sign.

One advantage of two's-complement form is related to the arithmetic capability described in Chapter 2. It is easier to implement two's-complement arithmetic in computer hardware than conventional arithmetic. This is primarily true because algebraic sign control is essentially automatic in complement arithmetic, and the need for hardware for performing subtraction is eliminated.

A second advantage is the elimination of a negative zero under two's-complement notation. In older machines using conventional arithmetic, both positive and negative zeros were possible. This condition had to be taken into consideration by programmers and was a source of error. The following example of conventional arithmetic illustrates this behavior. Note that the high-order bits are sign bits, with 0 representing the plus and 1 the minus.

$$
\begin{array}{ll}
10011011 & \longleftarrow \text{ register operand} \\
+00011011 & \longleftarrow \text{ storage operand} \\
\hline
10000000 & \longleftarrow \text{ register result}
\end{array}
$$

In conventional arithmetic, addition of numbers with unlike signs is done by finding the difference and taking the sign of the larger magnitude for the sign of the result. When magnitudes were equal in older machines, the sign of the register operand was taken for the result. Thus when a negative number in the register was added to a number of equal magnitude, the result was a negative zero. Using the same example in two's-complement notation, we obtain the following results:

$$-00011011 \longleftarrow \text{original register operand}$$
$$11100100 \longleftarrow \text{inverting to one's complement}$$
$$11100101 \longleftarrow \text{adding one for two's complement}$$
$$\underline{+00011011} \longleftarrow \text{adding original storage operand}$$
$$00000000 \longleftarrow \text{result ignoring high-order carry}$$

Since there is a carry both into and out of the high-order bit position, the result is valid and is a positive zero. Furthermore, since no concern is given to the determination of the larger number for sign control, no other result is possible. In general, two's-complement notation and its associated arithmetic provides very simple and automatic sign control.

A third advantage is the ability to easily extend or retract the precision, or length, of a number represented in two's-complement form. Perhaps the reader has noted that all bits to the left of the most significant bit in a two's-complement-notation number are the same as the sign bit. This is true for both negative and positive values. For example, the values of 13 and −13 represented as eight-bit two's-complement-notation numbers appear as

$$+13 = 00001101$$
$$-13 = 11110011$$

The precision, or length, of such a number can be extended quite easily by propagating the sign bit to the left the desired number of binary places, filling each bit position with a bit equal to the sign. Thus, +13 and −13 can be extended to sixteen-bit numbers as

$$+13 = 0000000000001101$$
$$-13 = 1111111111110011$$

The cutting back of the length of a two's-complement-notation number is accomplished in the opposite manner, provided the magnitude of the number is less than the maximum allowed for the length of the final result.

System/360 makes provision for two sizes of integer numbers, both represented by two's-complement notation. These are the half-word and full-word lengths of sixteen and 32 bits, respectively. Instructions within the machine's repertoire of operations convert one size to the other using the expanding and contracting technique discussed above.

4.2   A LIMITED SET OF MACHINE OPERATIONS

This section discusses three specific machine operations. A problem example is solved. The method of writing an assembly-language program for the problem using these three operations is shown in Section 4.3. After this informal introduction to machine instructions and programming conventions, Section 4.4 discusses additional assembly-language techniques required to write a complete program. Section 4.5 presents a complete program and the results obtained upon execution. Chapter 5 returns to a more formal presentation of the integer arithmetic operations.

We consider first the load instruction. Its operation code in hex is 58. The corresponding assembly-language mnemonic code is the letter L. This instruction is of RX type; thus its format in hex appears as

$$58RXYZZZ$$

where 58 is the operation code, R represents a four-bit number of a general-purpose register used for the first operand, X represents a four-bit number of a general-purpose register used for an index register, Y represents a four-bit number of a general-purpose register used as a base register, and ZZZ represents a 12-bit number used as a displacement value. Taken together, the contents of register X plus the contents of register Y plus the value of ZZZ specify the location in main storage of the second operand, a full word, used by the instruction. To simplify discussion in the future, this last statement can be represented by the following notation. The letter C preceding a pair of parentheses means *contents of* the indicated register or storage location.

$$\text{Operand 2 address} = C(X) + C(Y) + ZZZ$$

The purpose, and thereby the definition or meaning, of the instruction L is to cause the machine to load the general register specified by the number R with the full word located in main storage at the address specified by the second operand address, or $C(X) + C(Y) + ZZZ$. The original contents of register R are lost in the process. The original contents of location $C(X) + C(Y) + ZZZ$ remain unchanged. This behavior is always true for all instructions having a similar effect on the machine. The total concept of this operation can be represented by the following notation, a simple extension of the notation just introduced:

$$C(C(X) + C(Y) + ZZZ) \longrightarrow C(R)$$

In English, this statement reads: the contents of the full word at the memory location specified by $C(X) + C(Y) + ZZZ$ replace the contents of register R.

The second instruction of interest is the *add*. Its operation code in hex is 5A and has the mnemonic code A. Since the format of this instruction is also RX, the same comments can be made about the various components of the instruction. The notational representation for the A instruction is

$$C(R) + C(C(X) + C(Y) + ZZZ) \longrightarrow C(R)$$

or in English it states that the original contents of register R plus the contents of the full word at the memory location $C(X) + C(Y) + ZZZ$ replace the contents of register R. The contents of main storage remain unchanged.

The third and final instruction for this preliminary discussion is *store*. Its hex coed is 50 with a mnemonic code of ST. Its type is also RX. Notationally, this instruction is written as

$$C(R) \longrightarrow C(C(X) + C(Y) + ZZZ)$$

meaning that the contents of register R replace the original contents of the full word at memory location $C(X) + C(Y) + ZZZ$. The original contents of register R remain unchanged.

Figure 4.1 shows a segment of main storage represented in hex and containing an application of the three instructions just introduced. The problem being solved is the equation $C = A + B$. The first instruction loads the value of A into register 5. The second instruction adds the value of B to register 5. The third instruction stores the contents of register 5 as the value of C back into storage. The first digit of each instruction and data word is shown by a marker. The only pertinent address value, that of A, is also shown. Storage contents appear as they would at the conclusion of execution of all three instructions. The contents of register 12 can be assumed to contain 00010000 in hex. Storage contents that have no meaning in the example are shown by decimal points.

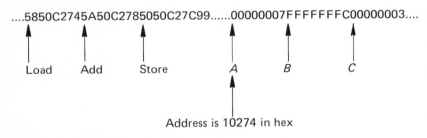

FIGURE 4.1   Example of Program for $C = A + B$ in Core

Several comments can be made about the information shown in Figure 4.1. First, the line of hex numbers resembles a core dump obtained from a debugging run. (Core-dump listings are discussed in detail in Section 4.5.) Second, notice how one instruction immediately follows another in storage. The same is true for data. To aid in interpretation, the value of A is 7, B is −4, and the result C is 3. Notice that the value of B is stored in two's-complement form. We shall postpone until Section 4.3 any discussion as to how the values of A and B came to be stored in this manner.

The first instruction can be seen as 5850C274. The 58 is the operation code for the load operation. Register 5 is being loaded. No index register is being used. The base register is C or 12 in decimal. The displacement is 274 in hex. Therefore, the storage operand address is the contents of register 12, given as 00010000 in hex, plus 274 in hex or 10274. Notice that location 10274 is the beginning of the full word containing the value of A, or 7. At the completion of the operation, register 5 contains the value 7 and the contents of location A remain unchanged.

The second instruction can be seen as 5A50C278. The 5A is the operation code for the add operation. Register 5 is being used to create the sum. No index register is being used. The base register is still register 12. The displacement is now 278. Thus the storage operand address is now 10278, or the location of B, which contains the −4. The contents of register 5 after the instruction is completed are the value 3. The contents of location B remain unchanged.

The third instruction can be seen as 5050C27C. The first 50 is the operation code for the store operation. Register 5 is being stored. No index register is being used. The base register is still register 12. The displacement is now 27C. The storage address is 1027C, the location of the full word that is to contain the value of C, or 3. After the operation is completed, the original value of register 5 remains unchanged. In other words, it still contains the value 3. The original contents of location 1027C are lost and are replaced by the value of 3.

As a bonus, this example in Figure 4.1 also illustrates how a program interrupt can occur. The number 99, following the third instruction, is not a valid operation code. Therefore, the machine interrupts the execution of the program, and under normal conditions terminates the job and flushes it from the system.

4.3   SOME ASSEMBLY-LANGUAGE FUNDAMENTALS

As in most computer languages, assembly-language programs are made up of statements. Each statement normally appears on one or more lines or cards. Comments cards are usually indicated by an asterisk in column one. Continued cards usually contain a nonblank character, not part of the statement, in column 72, and continuation cards usually begin in column 16.

Each statement can be made up of four entries or fields. They are, from left to right, the *name* entry, the *operation* entry, the *operand* entry, and the *comments* entry (see Figure 4.2). These four entries must be separated by one or more blanks and must be written in the order given. Normally these fields begin in columns 1, 10, and 16, with the comments following the operand separated by one or more blanks. However, these columns do not have to be adhered to if the programmer so desires. The coding can be in free form except for five rules:

1. The entries must not go beyond column 71 of a line.

2. The entries must be in the order of name, operation, operand, and comments.

3. The entries must be separated by one or more blanks.

4. If a name is to be used in a statement, it must begin in column 1; otherwise column 1 should be left blank.

5. The name and operation fields must be completed on the first line of the statement, including at least one blank following the operation field.

Each of the four entries is discussed in more detail in the paragraphs that follow. Complete descriptions of all possible options are not given here—only what is necessary and reasonable at this point. The assembly language has a great many features that are used only by very experienced programmers. For example, the statement begin, end, and continuation columns indicated above as 1, 71, and 16 can be altered at the discretion of the programmer through the use of a special instruction to the assembler. See IBM Reference C28-6514 for these special operations.

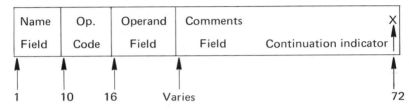

FIGURE 4.2   Assembly-Language Coding Layout

The *name* field contains a symbol, one to eight letters or digits the first of which is a letter, created by the programmer and is used to identify the statement. Sometimes the name symbol is referred to as a statement label, much as in Fortran or PL/I. More accurately, the statement name or label represents a main storage location or address where the instruction or datum represented by the statement is stored during execution. Thus, this field is sometimes also called the location field—a reference preferred by the present author. The name entry is optional. If omitted, column 1 must be blank. A blank, as well as a nonblank, location field entry implies the current statement will follow the previous statement in the final program as stored in main storage during execution.

The *operation* entry is a mnemonic operation or instruction code that specifies the operation to be performed. This operation code may be a machine instruction, an assembler instruction, or a macro operation. A machine instruction is replaced by its hex code and placed within the instruction being assembled for use during the execution of the program. An assembler instruction, however, is a command to the assembler itself to be used to control the process of assembly in some way; thus this type of instruction does not find its way into the final object program. A macro instruction is a special assembler feature that allows the programmer to represent a sequence of machine or assembler instructions by a single operation code. This feature is discussed in

Chapter 15. An operation entry is mandatory and must appear in the first line of a statement with at least one blank before and after.

The *operand* field contains entries that identify either register operands, storage operands, masks, storage field lengths, or various types of data, all of which are to be involved in the operation specified in the operation field. All machine instructions require one or more operands, although some assembler instructions require none. Each operand is separated from the others by commas with no intervening blanks. The first blank encountered in the operand field is interpreted by the assembler as the end of the operand field and the beginning of the comments field. An exception to this occurs in some operands where blanks may appear between apostrophes.

The *comments* field may contain any of the 256 possible characters (see Appendix 2) including blanks. At least one blank must precede the comments field following the operand field. The purpose of the comments field is to allow the programmer to enter descriptive comments about the program. Prospective programmers will find it useful to use comments. It is very difficult to read a program written either by someone else or by oneself after a passage of time unless appropriate comments are included.

The assembly-language program for the problem of Section 4.2 is now shown in Figure 4.3. We can make several statements about this program. To

```
LOCATION OP. OPERAND ...   COMMENTS          ...
        .       .    .      STATEMENTS  REQUIRED
        .       .    .      TO BEGIN A PROGRAM
        L     5,A          LOAD REG 5 WITH A
        A     5,B          ADD B TO REG 5
        ST    5,C          STORE REG 5 INTO C
        .       .    .      OTHER PROGRAM
        .       .    .      STATEMENTS
A       DC    F'7'         A FULL WORD CONSTANT 7
B       DC    F'-4'        A FULL WORD CONSTANT -4
C       DS    F            RESERVE A FULL WORD
        .       .    .      BALANCE OF
        .       .    .      PROGRAM
```

FIGURE 4.3   Assembly-Language Program Example

avoid confusion, program statements required at the beginning and ending of a program are not shown explicitly; these are presented in the next section.

The first program statement of interest is the load instruction. Since this statement follows the preceding instruction in a natural sequence, no location entry is necessary. Location field entries are needed only when a reference is to be made to this particular location from some other instruction. The mnemonic code L is written in the operation-code field. This is replaced by the hex 58 during assembly. Two operands are shown written in the operand field. The first operand, 5, represents general-purpose register 5. The second operand is the main storage operand and is referred to by its symbolic name. To work correctly, this symbolic name, the A, must appear somewhere in the program in the location field. The name A is found later on in the program on the line that defines a constant within a full word equal to the value 7. During the assembly phase, the assembler resolves the symbolic reference to A and inserts into the instruction for the load operation the proper base register designation and the correct displacement value. Thus, the proper instruction is created to load the contents of the full word at symbolic location A into register 5.

A similar set of comments can be made about the next instruction, except that it adds the contents of symbolic location B to the contents of register 5. The only additional point that might be made is that since the value within the base register has not changed, the displacement for location B is four greater than the displacement for location A.

The third instruction stores the contents of register 5 into main storage at the symbolic location C, a displacement of four more than for B.

Other instructions would probably appear between the store instruction and the data found in symbolic locations A, B, and C.

The program statements for locations A, B, and C involve instructions that are commands to the assembler, not to the machine. At this point, a standard and formal technique for defining new instruction codes and operations is introduced. Throughout the rest of the text this same formal presentation is used to introduce each new instruction or set of instructions. For assembler instructions, the format is presented in Definition 4.1.

4.1 Sample Definition for Assembler Instructions

The first partition contains the term being defined, stated in English. This second partition contains the prototype, or standard form for writing the instruction into an assembly-language program. Additional information is given to completely define the syntax involved.

This third partition contains the semantic description of the instruction in terms of the effect of the instruction on the operation of the assembler.

Definitions are now presented for the two assembler instructions having mnemonic operation codes of DC and DS. Portions of these definitions refer to additional subdefinitions and are presented before discussion continues.

4.2 Assembler Instruction *Define Constant*

NAME   DC   *X,Y,Z,...*

where *NAME* is an optional symbol and *X,Y,Z,...* represent one or more operands specifying various constants. See Definition 4.4 for methods of specifying constants.

Specifies that the indicated constants are to be translated, if necessary, into a hex number according to the specified data format and prepared for loading into main storage with the object program at the location represented by *NAME.*

4.3 Assembler Instruction *Define Storage*

NAME   DS   *X,Y,Z,...*

where *NAME* is an optional symbol and *X,Y,Z,...* represent one or more operands specifying various constants. See Definition 4.4 for methods of specifying constants. The constant subfield used in the DC operation is optional for the DS operation.

Specifies that the proper amount of storage is to be reserved for each type of constant specified. No constant is assembled, thus no information is loaded into the corresponding locations at execution time. Original contents of storage before program loading remain unchanged. No storage clearing is performed.

4.4 Assembly-Language *Constant Specifications*

ntmc

where *n* is an optional duplication factor, *t* is a constant type code (see Definition 4.5), *m* is an optional modifier (to be discussed later), and *c* is one or more constants containing digits and characters enclosed in apostrophes or parentheses to conform with the type *t*. Only one *c* can be specified for types C, H, or B (see Definition 4.5).

Specifies that the indicated constants *c* of type *t* modified by *m* are to be converted to the proper form, and duplicated *n* times.

4.5   Assembly-Language Constant *Type Codes*

The letters C, X, B, F, H, E, D, P, Z, A, Y, S, V, and Q.

Code	Type of Constant	Implied Length and Format
C	Character	Eight-bit code for each character
X	Hexadecimal	Four-bit code for each hex digit
B	Binary	Binary format
F	Fixed-point	Full-word two's-complement integer
H	Fixed-point	Half-word two's-complement integer
E	Floating-point	Full-word floating-point format
D	Floating-point	Double-word floating-point format
P	Decimal	Packed decimal format
Z	Decimal	Zoned decimal format
A	Address	Full-word address value
Y	Address	Half-word address value
S	Address	Half-word base register and displacement
V	Address	Full word reserved for address
Q	Address	Space for dummy section offset

Most of the type codes defined in Definition 4.5 are not needed until later in the text; all are given here for completeness. The only one of interest at this time is the F type code used in the program example of Figure 4.3. In the line with the name A, a constant is being defined of type F. No duplication factor or modifier is being used. The constant, shown between apostrophes, is the decimal 7. The assembler, upon seeing the DC instruction, creates a full-word constant of 00000007 in hex for subsequent loading at the time the object program is loaded into main storage for execution. Thus, the translation from decimal 7 to a hex 7 occurs during assembly. Loading into main storage occurs at object-program load time. Loading into register 5 occurs during execution of the object program.

The program line containing the name B produces a full word containing the value FFFFFFFC in hex and is loaded into the full word following the previous full word containing 00000007.

The program line containing the name C does not produce a constant during assembly. It does reserve a full word of storage, however, according to the type code F. This full word follows the word containing FFFFFFFC. Nothing is loaded into this reserved word at object-program load time; thus the original contents of this word, left over from the previous user, remain unchanged until the store operation is executed, placing the value of 00000003 in hex into the reserved area.

4.4   ADDITIONAL ASSEMBLER INSTRUCTIONS

In order to complete the program shown in Figure 4.3 sufficiently for it to run, three more assembler instructions plus one machine instruction must be introduced and discussed. Enough Job Control Language (JCL) is also provided to allow the program to be submitted to a real system. By purposely placing an error in the program to cause an interrupt, a core dump can be obtained for output. Section 4.5 interprets this core-dump listing as well as the printed output obtained from the assembly phase of the job.

The three new assembler instructions are called START, USING, and END. START and END have fairly obvious uses. The USING operation is needed to specify to the assembler the numbers and contents of the base registers to be used during execution of the program. The assembler must be made aware of this information in order to resolve symbolic storage references into actual base address and displacement components.

Precise definitions of START, END and USING are as follows.

4.6 Assembler Instruction START

NAME   START   *n*
where *NAME* is an optional symbol and *n* is an optional decimal number used as the initial relative location by the assembler for allocation of storage for instructions or data.

If a symbol is supplied in the location field, it is considered the name of the subsequent program steps and is the symbolic reference to the first-used location in the program. Normally, the value of *n* is either zero or blank. This causes program locations to begin with zero in the program listing printed by the assembler. In some special cases, a programmer may wish to specify a nonzero starting address. In any event, the program is normally relocated at load time into an unpredictable location in storage.

4.7 Assembler Instruction END

END   *NAME*
where *NAME* is an optional symbol.

Terminates the assembly phase of a job. The symbol in the operand field, if used, specifies the location at which execution is to begin after loading the object program. If no name is given, the first location of the program is assumed to be the starting point.

4.8   Assembler Instruction USING

USING   *v,r1,r2,r3,...*

where *v* is usually a symbol or an asterisk and *r1, r2, r3, ...* are general-purpose register numbers.

Specifies the general-purpose registers that are to be used as base registers and addresses that are to be in each register. Normally, for small programs, only one register is specified. The assembler assumes *r1* will contain the address represented by *v* at execution time. If more than one is specified, the assembler further assumes that *r2* contains an address 4096 bytes higher than *r1, r3* 4096 higher than *r2,* and so forth. An asterisk for the first operand indicates an address equal to the current address being assigned by the assembler. This is the address of the next instruction, since no object code is produced by the USING.

It is important to realize that the USING instruction only provides information to the assembler. The USING does not actually load or place anything into the base register. Thus, a second operation is required for this purpose. Also, since the operation of loading the base register must be accomplished during execution of the object program, a machine instruction is needed. Normally, one of the branching instructions is used even though a branch is never made in this particular application. The instruction is called *branch and link register.* The hex code is 05 and has a mnemonic code of BALR. The type is RR. In general, the instruction appears in hex as

05RS

where 05 is the operation code, R specifies a GPR for operand one, and S specifies a GPR for operand two. The instruction causes the machine to first load the operand-one register with the actual address of the next instruction in sequence. This address is also the address of the BALR instruction itself plus two. If operand two specifies a nonzero register number, the machine will branch to the address contained within the indicated register; otherwise a register number of zero means no branch is to be taken and the next sequential instruction should be executed. This latter behavior is used in the application under discussion.

```
LOCATION  OP.    OPERAND  ...   COMMENTS           ...
BEGIN     START  0             SET LOCATION CNT TO 0
          BALR   12,0          LOAD BASE REGISTER 12
          USING  *,12          INFORM ASSEMBLER
          L      5,A           LOAD REG 5 WITH A
          A      5,B           ADD B TO REG 5
          ST     5,C           STORE REG 5 INTO C
          DC     X'99'         INSERT INVALID OP CODE
A         DC     F'7'          A FULL WORD CONSTANT 7
B         DC     F'-4'         A FULL WORD CONSTANT -4
C         DS     F             RESERVE A FULL WORD
          END    BEGIN         END OF PROGRAM
```

FIGURE 4.4   Complete Assembly-Language Program

Therefore, to completely specify and set up a base register for proper use, both the USING and BALR are required under most circumstances. The program in Figure 4.3 is now shown in Figure 4.4 in a form that will assemble and execute until the machine reaches the invalid operation code 99.

The first instruction in the program of Figure 4.4 tells the assembler that a new program is beginning and to start allocation of storage for the program at relative location zero. The first location in the program also has symbolic name BEGIN.

The second instruction is a machine operation that causes the machine during execution to load register 12 with the location of the next instruction in the program. This next address is the location of the load instruction, since the USING instruction does not produce any object-program information. Because the second operand of the BALR is register zero, no branch is taken. Thus the next instruction to be executed is the load.

The third instruction, the USING, informs the assembler that register 12 is being specified as the only base register. The asterisk in the first operand field specifies the current location being maintained by the assembler is to be used as the base address. This address is the location of the load instruction. An asterisk can usually be used in this fashion in all instructions to indicate the current contents of the location counter being maintained by the assembler. This location counter is increased by the length of each instruction as each instruction is assembled.

The next three instructions—the L, A, and ST—are as before. The next entry in the program inserts the invalid operation code 99 following the ST instruction. This provides not only a core dump but also the experience of seeing what happens when an interrupt occurs.

The balance of the program is the same as before, with the exception of the END instruction at the physical end of the program. This informs the assembler that there is no more program to be assembled and that the program is to be executed, beginning with symbolic location BEGIN after the object program is produced and loaded.

```
CARD COLUMN GUIDE
00000000011111111112222222222333333333344444444445555555555666666666677777
1234567890123456789012345678901234567890123456789012345678901234567890123456789012
//FIRSTJOB JOB (NNNNN,NN,010,01,000),'PROGRAMMER NAME'
//:PASSWORD NNN,PASSWORD,NEWPSWD
// EXEC ASMFCLG
//ASM.SYSIN DD :
BEGIN    START 0              SET LOCATION CNT TO 0
         BALR  12,0           LOAD BASE REGISTER 12
         USING :,12           INFORM ASSEMBLER
         L     5,A            LOAD REG 5 WITH A
         A     5,B            ADD B TO REG 5
         ST    5,C            STORE REG 5 INTO C
         DC    X'99'          INSERT INVALID OP CODE
A        DC    F'7'           A FULL WORD CONSTANT 7
B        DC    F'-4'          A FULL WORD CONSTANT -4
C        DS    F              RESERVE A FULL WORD
         END   BEGIN          END OF PROGRAM
/:
//GO.SYSUDUMP DD SYSOUT=A
```

FIGURE 4.5 Complete Program with JCL Ready for Submission

4.5   RUNNING A PROGRAM

Before the program in Figure 4.4 is submitted to the machine to be run, several JCL cards must be added at the front and back of the deck. Since JCL is usually somewhat dependent on how local computing systems are operated, some of the following discussion may be untrue and may need modifying. It is suggested that before submitting a job the reader check with an authority to verify that the information is correct. A complete listing of the job, including all JCL, is shown in Figure 4.5.

The first two JCL cards, the Job and Password cards, are more likely to vary from one system to another than any other cards. This is particularly true with regard to the format of punching the various quantities and names. In the cards shown, the following relation exists between card columns and contents.

Job Card Columns	Contents
1-2	//
3-10	Job name, user supplied
12-14	JOB (must appear as shown)
17-20	First four digits of a user job number
22-23	Next two digits of the user job number
25-27	Cutoff time in tenths of a minute
29-30	Limit on printed lines in thousands
32-34	Limit on punched cards
38-52	Programmer's name (limit of 22 columns)

Password Card Columns	Contents
1-10	/*PASSWORD
16-18	User sequence number within job number
20-27	Current password
29-35	New password if desired

The third card, called the execute card, causes the Operating System to retrieve from a catalog of procedures the particular procedure referred to by ASMFCLG and to use it to control the sequence of events during the processing of this job. It is also very likely that this procedure name will vary from one system to another. This particular procedure name stands for the system processing procedure that can assemble (Compile), Linkedit, and execute (Go) an ASseMbly language program using the F level assembler. Other procedure names are available, such as ASMFC which eliminates the execution phase, ASMFC,PARM.ASM=DECK which produces a deck of cards for the object program, ASMFCLG,PARM.ASM=(DECK,LOAD) which produces the object deck as well as executes the program.

The fourth card simply states that the SYSIN (input) data set for the assembly phase follows the card.

The next eleven cards contain the program as before and form the input to the assembler for translation into an object program.

The /* card is the indicator to the Operating System that the end of the SYSIN data set has been reached.

The next card is a special card required to obtain the desired core dump. No core dump is printed, even if there is an interrupt, unless the user indicates where the core-dump data set, referred to through the name SYSUDUMP, is to be located. The word GO associates the data set with the execution phase or the GO job step. The specification, SYSOUT=A, indicates that the destination of the data set is the output data set of general class A. In most systems, output class A is eventually printed on a line printer.

Many of the comments made here about the respective JCL cards have not been made with the expectation that the reader will fully appreciate them, but rather for the sake of completeness. Also it is useful if the user has a few of these JCL characteristics in mind as he begins to explore a computing system. More will be presented on JCL, particularly for data set control, when we reach the subject of input and output.

Figures 4.6, 4.7, 4.8, and 4.9 contain various parts of the output obtained from the program discussed above. Figure 4.6 shows the program listing containing the original source assembly-language and the object machine-language versions of the program. The side-by-side presentation is the normal mode of output from the assembler. Figure 4.7 contains an additional output from the assembler, which provides an analysis of the symbolic references within the program called the cross-reference table. Figures 4.8 and 4.9 show parts of the core dump that are produced by the interrupt. The paragraphs that follow give a detailed analysis of portions of these documents. Upon running the program, the reader finds additional information beyond that shown; however, the information discussed here should allow adequate understanding based on the material so far covered.

Looking at Figure 4.6, we can see the original source program on the right side of the page. Near the middle of the page is a column of decimal numbers under the heading of STMT. These numbers can be called statement numbers and are supplied by the assembler for the purpose of identification if errors are found. The column of hex numbers at the extreme left side of the page, headed by LOC, contains the relative storage addresses assigned to the various instructions and data. Notice that this column begins with zero, as was requested by the START instruction. The various hex digits appearing under the heading OBJECT CODE represent the actual machine-language coding corresponding to each instruction and data item. Numbers that usually appear under the headings ADDR1 and ADDR2 are hex addresses of the first and second main storage operands for those instructions that make reference to storage. Since only three

```
LOC     OBJECT CODE  ADDR1 ADDR2  STMT  SOURCE STATEMENT

000000                             1 BEGIN  START 0        SET LOCATION CNT TO 0
000000  05C0                       2        BALR  12,0     LOAD BASE REGISTER 12
000002                             3        USING *,12     INFORM ASSEMBLER
000002  5850 C00E    00010         4        L     5,A      LOAD REG 5 WITH A
000006  5A50 C012    00014         5        A     5,B      ADD B TO REG 5
00000A  5050 C016    00018         6        ST    5,C      STORE REG 5 INTO C
00000E  99                         7        DC    X'99'    INSERT INVALID OP CODE
00000F  00
000010  00000007                   8 A      DC    F'7'     A FULL WORD CONSTANT 7
000014  FFFFFFFC                   9 B      DC    F'-4'    A FULL WORD CONSTANT -4
000018                            10 C      DS    F        RESERVE A FULL WORD
000000                            11        END   BEGIN    END OF PROGRAM
```

FIGURE 4.6   Program Listing Produced by Assembler

CROSS-REFERENCE

```
SYMBOL   LEN     VALUE   DEFN    REFERENCES

A        00004   000010  0008    0004
B        00004   000014  0009    0005
BEGIN    00001   000000  0001    0011
C        00004   000018  0010    0006
```

NO STATEMENTS FLAGGED IN THIS ASSEMBLY
       26 PRINTED LINES

FIGURE 4.7   Cross Reference Produced by Assembler

63

RX instructions make such references, only three addresses appear, and they are all under the operand two column. Only SI and SS instructions also have entries under the operand-one column.

We shall now analyze each line in the program. As stated before, the START instruction produces no object code. Its only effect is on the location counter, setting it to zero. The BALR instruction is translated to the hex code 05C0. The operation code is 05, register 12 is loaded with the base address, and no branch is taken. Again, the USING instruction produces no object code. However, the assembler does make note that the current location is 000002 and the indicated base register is 12. The L instruction is translated to hex 5850C00E. 58 is the operation code and register 5 is the first operand. No indexing is specified. The base register is 12 and the displacement is E. Note here that the displacement, E, plus the relative contents of the base register, 000002, yield a relative address of 000010 in hex, the same relative address as that allocated to the data word A of statement 8. Therefore, this instruction loads register 5 with the value 7.

The A instruction is translated to 5A50C012 in hex. 5A is the operation code, register 5 is the first operand. No indexing is specified. Here, the contents of the base register plus the displacement, 12, yields the address 000014, the address corresponding to data word B. The ST instruction is similarly translated to 5050C016. The operation code is 50, operand-one register is 5, and no indexing is specified. This time the base address plus the displacement of 16 yields 000018, the address of the data word C. Notice that the $X'99'$ of statement 7 is simply duplicated in the object-code column. Since the constant in line 8 must be on a full-word boundary, specified by the code letter F, the assembler automatically increases the location counter by two bytes to produce the proper alignment. Lines 8 and 9 show the result of specifying full-word constants. The decimal 7 is converted to the hex 00000007 and the minus 4 is converted to the hex FFFFFFFC, the two's-complement equivalent. No object code is produced by the DS or the END.

The cross-reference table shown in Figure 4.7 is also produced by the assembler during the assembly phase. This table lists alphabetically all symbols used within a program. A length attribute is also shown for each symbol. Note that the lengths for A, B, and C are all 4, corresponding to the full word size of each. Under the VALUE heading is found the relative address, or location counter value, assigned by the assembler to each symbol. The statement number of the statement that contains the symbol in the location column in the source program is shown under DEFN. Every statement in which a reference is made to a symbol is shown by its statement number under REFERENCES. This table of cross references is very handy during debugging operations, particularly with a very large program or for a program containing a great many symbols.

Let us now consider the most important parts of the core dump produced by the system upon detecting the invalid operation code 99. Since the appearance of a core dump varies for different versions of the Operating System, two sets of figures are presented. Figures 4.8a and 4.9a contain portions of the dump produced by the MFT (Multiprogramming with a Fixed number of Tasks) version of the Operating System, while Figures 4.8b and 4.9b contain portions of the dump produced by the MVT (Multiprogramming with a Variable number of Tasks) version.

Both dumps, Figures 4.8a and 4.8b, first list the job name, FIRSTJOB; the job step, GO; the time, 141736 or 2:17:36 PM; and the date, April 2, 1970. Both versions then provide a completion code, which can be found within an error-code manual provided by IBM. However, this particular type of code is one that occurs quite often. A system completion code 0CX, where X is any hex digit, is the code for one of the 15 possible program interrupts that can occur. Here, the 0C1 refers to the invalid operation interrupt. (See Table 3.2.)

In the case of the MFT version, in Figure 4.8a, the core dump specifically states the problem on the next line as a program interrupt of type *operation*. Furthermore, the actual storage address of the invalid operation code is given as 06002E. The only other piece of information of interest in Figure 4.8a is the problem program storage boundaries, shown as 00060000 to 00080000. These are the starting and ending addresses of the storage area that was allocated to this job while it was in operation. Normally, under MFT, the beginning of a program is loaded 32 bytes (hex 20) above the starting boundry address. This yields a *load point* of 60020 for the program.

The MVT version, in Figure 4.8b, indicates that the program interrupt occurred at location 24FF2, an address that is four bytes above the offending operation code. This address is found in the APSW entry of the line beginning with PRB and is underlined in Figure 4.8b. The load point for a program running under MVT is usually given by the EPA entry of the first line below CDE. This address is also underlined in Figure 4.8b and is shown as 24FE0.

Figures 4.9a and 4.9b contain more of the same core dumps shown in Figures 4.8a and 4.8b. The only things of interest here are the register contents and storage contents at the time the interrupt occurred. General-purpose registers 0 through 7 and 8 through 15 are identified in both dumps by REGS 0–7 and REGS 8–15. Note that register 5 contains 00000003, the value of 7 plus −4, and the value stored back into memory for the value of C. Register 12 contains 50060022 for the MFT version and 40024FE2 for MVT. Since only the low-order 24 bits of a register are used for address computation, the base address is 060022 for MFT and 024FE2 for MVT. Notice that both base addresses are two bytes greater than the corresponding load points discussed above. Remember, from the assembler listing, the relative base address is 2. Thus, for MFT, if the load point is 60020 corresponding to a relative address of zero, then the actual base address of 60022 corresponds to a relative base of 2. The MVT values have the same relationship.

Finally, identified by P/P -END OF in Figure 4.9a and LOAD MODULE M in Figure 4.9b, the actual contents of storage at the time of the interrupt are found. Each line of the storage dump contains 32 bytes printed in groups of

```
* * *  A B D U M P   R E Q U E S T E D  * * *

JOB FIRSTJOB       STEP GO          TIME 141736    DATE 70092

COMPLETION CODE    SYSTEM = 0C1

PROGRAM INTERRUPTION (OPERATION) AT LOCATION 06002E

INTERRUPT AT 060032

PSW AT ENTRY TO ABEND  800C1000 00000000

TCB 005B60   RB 0007FD80   PIE 00000000      DEB 0007FD0C   TIOT 0007FF28   CMP 800C1000   TRN 00000000
             MSS 00005BE8  PK/FLG 70910408   FLG 000001F5   LLS 00000000    JLB 00000000   JSE 00000000
             FSA 2807FFB0  TCB 00005C90      TME 00005BFC

ACTIVE RBS

PRB 060000   NM M          SZ/STAB 000800C0   USE/EP 00060020   PSW FF75000D A0060032   Q 000000   WT/LNK 00005B60

SVRB 07FDE0  NM SVC-401C   SZ/STAB 0012D072   USE/EP 00006FB8   PSW FF040033 4000717C   Q E003E0   WT/LNK 00060000
             RG 0-7   0000004C  0007FFF8   00080000  0007FF6C   00000003  00005B60   0007FC30
             RG 8-15  0007FF78  00000000   0007FFB0  50060022   0007FFB0  00009018   50060020

SVRB 07FD80  NM SVC-105A   SZ/STAB 000CD072   USE/EP 00006FB8   PSW FF040133 8000722A   Q E003E0   WT/LNK 0007FDE0
             RG 0-7   00060040  00001130   40006FBA  00000000   00000000  00060040   8000716A
             RG 8-15  00005BE8  0006010E   00080000  00005B60   000600A8  50007200   2006002E
```

```
P/P STORAGE BOUNDARIES  00060000 TO 00080000

FREE AREAS        SIZE

     060340      0001F9A8
     07FD50      00000030
     07FEE8      00000008

SAVE AREA TRACE

SA   07FFB0  WD1 00000000   HSA 00000000   LSA 00000000   RET 0007FFC4   EPA 0007FF78   R0  D4404040
             R1  40404040   R2  00000000   R3  00000000   R4  00000000   R5  00000000   R6  00000000
             R7  00000000   R8  00000000   R9  00000000   R10 00000000   R11 00000000   R12 00000000

PROCEEDING BACK VIA REG 13

SA   07FFB0  WD1 00000000   HSA 00000000   LSA 00000000   RET 0007FFC4   EPA 0007FF78   R0  D4404040
             R1  40404040   R2  00000000   R3  00000000   R4  00000000   R5  00000000   R6  00000000
             R7  00000000   R8  00000000   R9  00000000   R10 00000000   R11 00000000   R12 00000000
```

FIGURE 4.8a   First Part of Core Dump (MFT Version)

67

JOB FIRSTJOB   STEP GO   TIME 141736   DATE 70092

COMPLETION CODE   SYSTEM = 0C1

PSW AT ENTRY TO ABEND FFA5000D 40006122

```
TCB 010D20   RBP   000112C0   PIE     00000000   DEB  0001107C   TIO 00011610   CMP   80C1000   TRN 00000000
             MSS   02016DF8   PK-FLG  A0850409   FLG  00008B8B   LLS 000152B8   JLB   00000000   JPQ 000134D8
             FSA   01043FB0   TCB     00010DF8   TME  00000000   JST 00010D20   NTC   00000000   OTC 00010E8
             LTC   00000000   IQE     00000000   ECB  00011680   STA 00000000   D-PQE 00017778   SQS 00010AA8
             NSTAE 00000000   TCT     00011418   USER 00000000
```

ACTIVE RBS

```
PRB 013928   RESV   00000000   APSW   A0024FF2   WC-SZ-STAB 00040082   FL-CDE 00013630   PSW FFA5000D 40006122
             Q/TTR  00000000   WT-LNK 00010D20

SVRB 010C68  TAB-LN 001803D0   APSW   F2F0F1C3   WC-SZ-STAB 0012D002   TQN 00000000   PSW 00040033 50005B76
             Q/TTR  00007D01   WT-LNK 00013928
             RG 0-7  FFFFFF97   00043FF8   00011678   5011668C   00000003   00011608   000161A8
             RG 8-15 00011660   00000000   0000004C   00000000   00043FB0   0008BA66   01024FE0
             EXTSA   000021BE   000447A0   2000FFFF   000445F8   00010CE4   00010CEC   E2E8E2C9
                     C5C1F0F1   C9C5C120   C1C2C5D5   C4000000

SVRB 0112C0  TAB-LN 00080360   APSW   F1F0F5C1   WC-SZ-STAB 0012D002   TQN 00000000   PSW FF040000 500FDFD0
             Q/TTR  00004208   WT-LNK 00010C68
             RG 0-7  00000000   00010CC8   80005868   0006604C   00010C68   00013630   00000000
             RG 8-15 00010D20   40005FDA   00010D20   000447A0   00010CEC   40005AB4   00000000
             EXTSA   E2E8E2C9   C5C6C1D9   01006001   45F0F014   00000000   C9C5C6E2   C4F0F6F5
                     0A079827   901ED00C   05801841   58300010   00000000
```

```
NE 000157C8   RSP-CDE 02013408    NE 000157E0   RSP-CDE 0101B1A0    NE 00016B88   RSP-CDE 0101B160
NE 00016C90   RSP-CDE 0101B290    NE 00000000   RSP-CDE 0101B260

CDE

013630    ATR1 0B    NCDE 000000    ROC-RB 00013928    NM M          USE 01    EPA 024FE0    ATR2 20    XL/MJ 014120
013408    ATR1 31    NCDE 013630    ROC-RB 00000000    NM IGC0A05A   USE 02    EPA 043180    ATR2 28    XL/MJ 013DC8
01B1A0    ATR1 B8    NCDE 01B1D0    ROC-RB 00000000    NM IGG019CF   USE 06    EPA 0FDF00    ATR2 20    XL/MJ 01B190
01B160    ATR1 B8    NCDE 01B1A0    ROC-RB 00000000    NM IGG019CL   USE 08    EPA 0FF808    ATR2 20    XL/MJ 01B150
01B290    ATR1 B8    NCDE 01B2C0    ROC-RB 00000000    NM IGG019BA   USE 0A    EPA 0FE290    ATR2 20    XL/MJ 01B280
01B260    ATR1 B8    NCDE 01B290    ROC-RB 00000000    NM IGG019BB   USE 0A    EPA 0FF008    ATR2 20    XL/MJ 01B250

                                     LN                       ADR           LN        ADR           LN

XL

014120    SZ 00000010    NO 00000001    80000020    00024FE0
013DC8    SZ 00000010    NO 00000001    80000680    00043180
01B190    SZ 00000010    NO 00000001    80000100    000FDF00
```

FIGURE 4.8b First Part of Core Dump (MVT Version)

DATA SETS

```
SYSUDUMP    UCB    003740    DEB 07FDOC    DCB 060040
PGM=*.DD    UCB    002AAC    DEB 07FE94    DCB 07FF78
```

REGS AT ENTRY TO ABEND

```
FL.PT.REGS 0-6    41.100000 00000000   41.100000 00000000   B7.870960 00000000   41.100000 00000000

REGS 0-7    0000004C   0007FFF8   00080000   0007FF6C   00000003   00005B60
REGS 8-15   0007FF78   00000000   0007FFB0   50060022   0007FFB0   50060020
```

P/P -END OF

```
060000  D4404040 40404040 000800C0 00060020  FF75000D A0060032 00000000 00005B60  *M...............................*
060020  05C05850 C00E5A50 C0125050 C0169900  00000007 FFFFFFFC 00000003 00000001  *................................*
060040  00000001 54000000 002C0020 0007FDOC  00480000 00000001 00004000 00000001  *................................*
060060  28022828 4107FEF0 01012158 0001FC40  920124B8 00012650 070601DA 00000372  *.............0..................*
060080  00005B60 00000000 000600F0 00005B60  0000007D 00000001 000020BE 00060040  *................................*
0600A0  00012650 0000730C 000600F0 00005B60  40404040 40404040 50060015E 00000080  *..............0.................*
0600C0  A0072CE 00060219 40404040 40404040   0000739A 006000C0 800071EC 00000080  *................................*
0600E0  0007FEF8 001B0002 98E0D15C 12EE4780  7F000000 40204040 00060040 00060210  *.8.....J....K.O.J...............*
060100  411F007D 191047C0 D0B61BFE 40FD0168  D096D27C F000D16C 41FF007D 50FD0160  *.......K..J.....................*
060120  0048922D 100558F1 000858F0 F03005EF  D203E000 D16841FE 000450FD 0160411D  *....1..00..J....................*
060140  0001480D 005C9560 D1704740 0DCE4720  DOCC1A01 1A011A01 9240D170 D277D171  *.J.K.J..........................*
060160  D1704110 00381901 47ADD0EA 400D005C  07F5481D 005E4111 0014401D 005E92F1  *J.K.J....3.JSJ..0JVK..J..0.....1*
060180  D170D203 D1DDD12C 4E1D0150 F333D1E2  D154960F D1E5D201 D05CD130 47F0D060  *J.....0..PAGE...................*
0601A0  98E0D15C 12EE0785 411E0004 191F0785  0000000A 00060098 000601E0 6C000000  *.....0000.......................*
0601C0  0000000A 00060098 000601E0 00000340  47F0D082 D7C1C7C5 FFFF07FE 00000000  *................................*
0601E0  8000704A 00000000 0007FD80 0000730C  00810000 007D4040 40F0F6F0 F2F0F040  *................................*
060220  40404040 F4F0F4F0 F4F040C6 F4C6F0C6  F4C6F040 C6F4C6F0 C6F4C0C3F6 40C6F4C3  *................................*
        LINES 060240-060260   SAME AS ABOVE
060280  40C74B4B F1F9F0D5 4B4BD24B 4B4BD24B  5CC70000 F1F9F0D5 4180D171 907AD244  *.G..190N.J...K.*
0602A0  18788A0  F14088A0 000589A0 0005D21F  7057A000 41970001F 41800001 925C7056  *....J....K....K.*
0602C0  925C7077 91C07057 4710D230 95407057  47800234 920F7057 943F7057 8778D21C  *.K...K.7....K...*
060300  DC1F7037 D254987A D24407F7 A0007ZCE  00060219 00060340 00000003 4BC1C2C3  *.....ABC*
060300  C4C5C6C7 C8C94B4B 4B4B4B4B 4BD1D2D3  D4D5D6D7 D8D94B4B 4B4B4B4B 4B4BE2E3  *DEFGHI......JKLMNOPQR...ST*
060320  E4E5E6E7 E8E94B4B 4B4B4B4B 4B4B4B4B  F4F5F6F7 F8F94B4B 4B4B4B4B 40001000  *UVWXYZ......0123456789....*
```

FIGURE 4.9a Second Part of Core Dump (MFT Version)

70

REGS AT ENTRY TO ABEND

```
FLTR 0-6      0000000000010DF8      0000000000010C90      00000000000160E8      000000000000000

REGS 0-7   FFFFFF97  00043FF8  00011678  5001168C        00015F60  00000003  00011608  000161A8
REGS 8-15  00011660  00000000  0000004C  00000000        40024FE2  00043FB0  0000BA66  01024FE0
```

LOAD MODULE   M

```
024FE0   05C05850 C00E5A50 C0125050 C0169900    00000007 FFFFFFFC 00000003 00000000
```

LOAD MODULE   IGC0A05A

```
043180   4180D099 1B114313 41330001 95FF3000 47806068 1BEE1BFF 1B001B11   *...........*
0431A0   43E30000 43030001 88F0001C 8C000004 8810001C 1A204AE0 60701A1E   *.T........0.*
0431C0   41818001 44F06076 F384D069 D069DC07 41FFF001 44F0607C 418F8004   *......F...0.*
0431E0   413E3003 47F06010 41330001 D2008000 3002D200 D0692000 D2008000   *.....0..0.SK*
043200   D0695050 D08C5000 D12094FC D1235B00 5800D120 41110003 5010D064   *.....0....J.*
043220   94FCD067 D703D06C D06C1810 54006290 60BC1B10 4010D06C 5810D064   *..........J.*
043240   4A10D06C 1B005D00 66404000 D06A1211 47F0664C 12114770 60E85850   *...P.......J*
043260   D08C5860 D12407F5 4120D121 45B06236 413062C4 48A0D06C 4BA0D06C   *.....J....J.*
043280   88A00002 4580623E 46A06104 9640D112 94BFD112 47F060DE 18A15810   *..J.5..J...D*
0432A0   D1204B10 D06C5010 D0704120 D07145B0 62364810 00011A31 5820D120   *.....J..J.0.*
0432C0   45B0623E 5020D120 9640D112 455062DA 94BFD112 6198 5810 4810D06E   *.J...J....J.*
0432E0   00105810 10A41921 47B061A6 6640D51F 10002000 47706 1A6 4810D06E   *J...J..N..0.*
043300   41110001 4010D06E 41220020 5020D120 47F061B0 1B114010 D06C46A0   *....J.....0.*
043320   611E47F0 60044810 D06E1211 47806019 4800D06E 89000005 1B105010   *.0.M.....J..*
043340   D0704120 D0714810 D06D0610 12114770 D00F629D 41306294 45B0623E   *K...J.....K.*
043360   D20DD0AA 62A2D840 D112 4550 62DA94BF 410306294 12AA4780 60D447F0   *K...J..J.P..*
043380   619ED204 D09F629D 41306297 45B0623E 5810D120 5B106640 5010D070   *...J.P...M.0*
0433A0   41200071 4130629A 45B0623E D20DD0B2 61E64130 62B047F0 65744180   *K...J...0.W.*
0433C0   D0999FF 30004780 627C1B00 43030000 00011A80 44106284 F384D070   *....K...0..3*
0433E0   D070DC07 30062C6 41111001 44106628A 41330002 47F0623E 41330001   *.......J....*
043400   07FB1832 D200D070 2000D200 8000D070 FFFFFFE0 0B02FF0C 02FF1302   *F.........3.*
043420   C5E240E2 C1D4C540 C1E240C1 C2D6E5C5 0002FF09 0312031B 03240330   *ES SAME AS ABOVE....LIN*
043440   034B03FF 0903FF12 03FF1B03 FF2403FF 3003FF39 03FF4203 0339034Z   *ES SAME AS ABOVE*
043460   47806310 D27CF000 D09441FF 007D50F0 00701910 47D06330 D08012EE   *.K...0....0.*
043480   D090D203 E000D090 41FE0004 50F0D084 92201005 58F10008 D08012EE   *.K...0....0.*
0434A0   05EFF110 00858E0 100858F0 E034054F 41000001 4800D05C 95600098   *......1..00.*
0434C0   47206546 1A011A01 1A019240 D098D277 41000038 190147B0 636C4000   *...0..K.....*
0434E0   D05C9140 D1120715 47F060E2 4810D05E 41110001 4010D05E 92F10098   *J...0..S...1.K.J.*
```

FIGURE 4.9b   Second Part of Core Dump (MVT Version)

four. A major space is shown between the fourth and fifth words. The address of the first byte in each line is shown at the left margin; therefore the addresses increase by 32 or 20 in hex. In Figure 4.9a the second line of storage, beginning with address 060020, and the line in Figure 4.9b beginning with address 024FE0, contains the entire program plus a word more. These program and data words are underlined in the figures. The reader should easily find each instruction and each data word to be exactly as in the object program listed in Figure 4.6, except that the data word called C now contains 00000003, the correct results. The balance of both storage dumps represents system program and data modules that are loaded in support of the user's program. For example, a program module is loaded to produce the core dump itself. One final point: the invalid operation code is actually at location 06002E in Figure 4.9a, and location 024FEE in Figure 4.9b, and can be found at these points in the dumps.

PROGRAMMING EXERCISE

Prepare and run the program exactly as shown in Figure 4.5. Locate and identify the various parts of the output that are discussed in Section 4.5.

STUDY EXERCISES

1. State the advantages of two's-complement arithmetic.
2. Modify and rewrite the contents of Figure 4.1 to compute $D = A + B + C$. Assume D is a full word following the full word called C. Further assume C contains 00000003 as shown. Show the contents of storage after the computation is finished.
3. Write the assembly-language program segment corresponding to the answer to Exercise 2.
4. Write DC statements defining full words called ONE, TWO, ..., FIVE containing integer 1, 2, ..., 5. Do the same for −1, −2, ..., −5 called MONE, MTWO, ..., MFIVE.
5. Show the object-code equivalents of the DC statements of Exercise 4.
6. State the purposes for START and END.
7. State the purposes for the USING instruction. Write a USING statement that specifies register 10 as the base register and the base address to be the next address assigned by the assembler.
8. Name the machine instruction used to actually load the base register, and state why such an instruction must be used.

Chapter **five**

Register Address Logic and Integer Arithmetic

The first major section of this chapter presents the various techniques available for referencing an address within a program for System/360. Several different methods of specifying addresses can be used in assembly-language programming other than the simple symbolic reference shown in Chapter 4. The additional procedures are made possible by taking advantage of the register logic capability that is built into the address computation features of the machine. The purpose here is to demonstrate how this machine behavior and certain provisions within the assembler interact to provide an extremely flexible system from the programmer's viewpoint. All of these addressing variations are discussed in detail in Section 5.1. The relationship of each variation to one of the five instruction formats is demonstrated. Thus, as each new instruction in the machine's repertoire is introduced and a format specified, the various addressing techniques that are applicable become immediately apparent. In order to discuss register logic to its fullest, a new machine instruction is also introduced. This instruction, the Load Address operation, is the key to register manipulation of addresses, since it provides a means of determining the value of an address at execution time.

Section 5.2 enters into a formal presentation of all integer arithmetic and related machine instructions. Since a great many instructions are available in System/360, an efficient method of presentation is essential. This is the major reason for discussing many of the machine's architectural features and the purposes of the assembler from a general viewpoint in Chapters 3 and 4.

This chapter concludes with another example of an actual problem and its associated program. A similar problem is provided as an exercise for the reader. Fortran IV is used as a means of obtaining input and output capability by making the assembler-language program play the role of a subroutine to a Fortran IV main program. The linkage conventions between assembler and Fortran must therefore be described. However, these conventions turn out to be extremely simple in light of register address logic.

5.1   REGISTER ADDRESS LOGIC

It has been shown in previous chapters that the main storage address reference in the RX type of instruction causes three possible address components to be added to form an effective address at execution time. This basic address computation can be used in different ways to obtain many different effects. This same capability is extended to a limited extent to the RS, SI, and SS type instructions as well. Main storage references for these instructions also involve a base address and displacement. Thus, only the third component of indexing is missing.

The assembler allows a programmer to write a storage reference in two major forms, each of which has several minor variations. The two major references can be called the *composite* and the *component* methods. The symbolic reference used in Chapter 4 to refer to the values of *A, B,* and *C* is of the composite mode. The reference did not involve a separate base register or displacement specification; those values were determined by the assembler. If an index register is to be used with an instruction, its number is written enclosed by parentheses following the symbol in the operand field. A second level of variation is achieved by what is called address *adjustment*. This adjustment is specified by adding or subtracting a constant to or from the symbolic reference. If both adjustment and indexing are to be indicated, the index specification follows the adjustment value. Thus the composite reference has four variations, as shown in the sample instructions in Table 5.1.

TABLE 5.1   Composite References

L	5,XYZ	Simple symbolic reference
L	5,XYZ(7)	Symbolic reference with indexing
L	5,XYZ+4	Symbolic reference with adjustment
L	5,XYZ+8(6)	Symbolic reference with both

The first example is the same type of reference shown in Chapter 4, causing the assembler to compute the proper displacement value. The second example shows the addition of a general register specification, register 7, which is to be used as an index register. This causes the contents of register 7 to be added to the base address and displacement before the storage reference is made at execution time. The third example illustrates an address adjustment indicated by adding 4 to the reference. This causes the assembler to increase the displacement value, as normally determined, by 4. The fourth example shows an adjustment of plus 8 and indexing using register 6.

The component method of specifying a storage reference allows the programmer to specify the two or three components of an address separately. In general, such a reference is specified as in the following example.

$$L \qquad 5,D(X,B)$$

The letter D stands for a displacement value; the letters X and B refer to general-purpose registers to be used, respectively, as the index and base components of the address computation to take place during execution. A value of zero for any one of the three components means that the indicated component does not enter into the sum. If only a displacement is needed, the (X,B) part of the specification may be eliminated. The assembler assumes zeros are meant for X and B. Likewise, if X is to be zero, the specification may be written as D(,B). If the B is to be zero, D(X) may be specified. If D is to be zero, a zero must be written explicitly preceding the left parenthesis. The examples in Table 5.2 illustrate all of the various ways of writing a component reference.

TABLE 5.2 Component References

L	5,16(7,12)	All three components present
L	5,0(7,12)	Base and index components only
L	5,24(7)	Displacement and index components only
L	5,0(7)	Index component only
L	5,8(,12)	Displacement and base components only
L	5,0(,12)	Base component only
L	5,128	Displacement component only
L	5,0	No components, address is zero

Notice that only four of these variations are possible for the RS, SI, and SS type of storage reference, since indexing is not permitted. In SS instructions, however, where operand length values are specified, a length value is written in the component reference where the index register number appears above. This is also true for the composite method; the length value replaces the index register number between parentheses following a symbolic reference.

To illustrate address adjustment, the program shown in Figures 4.4, 4.5, and 4.6 is modified slightly and presented in Figure 5.1. The only changes

LOCATION	OP.	OPERAND	... COMMENTS ...
BEGIN	START	0	SET LOCATION CNT TO 0
	BALR	12,0	LOAD BASE REGISTER 12
	USING	∷,12	INFORM ASSEMBLER
	L	5,A	LOAD REG 5 WITH A
	A	5,A+4	ADD A+4 TO REG 5
	ST	5,A+8	STORE REG 5 INTO A+8
	DC	X'99'	INSERT INVALID OP CODE
A	DC	F'7'	A FULL WORD CONSTANT 7
	DC	F'-4'	A FULL WORD CONSTANT -4
	DS	F	RESERVE A FULL WORD
	END	BEGIN	END OF PROGRAM

FIGURE 5.1   Program of Figure 4.4 with Address Adjustment

appear in the references to the locations that were called B and C in the earlier version. Realizing that A and B are full words, the programmer is able to reference B and C by adding the proper adjustment constant to the symbolic reference to A. Under these conditions, the symbolic references A+4 and A+8 are equivalent to B and C, respectively.

In order to further illustrate methods of addressing, the Load Address instruction is now introduced. This operation is of the RX type, has a hex code of 41, and a mnemonic code of LA. Like any other RX instruction, the basic format of LA can be represented as

$$41RXYZZZ$$

where R is the first operand register, X is the index register, Y is the base register, and ZZZ is the displacement. However, unlike most other instructions of similar appearance, no actual reference to main storage is made for the second operand. The address itself is loaded into register R instead. Thus the total effect of the operation can be described by the following notation.

$$C(X) + C(Y) + ZZZ \rightarrow C(R)$$

Notice the difference between this description and the corresponding notation for the Load instruction used in the program in Figure 5.1, which appears as

$$C(C(X) + C(Y) + ZZZ) \rightarrow C(R)$$

Thus in the LA instruction the three address components are added in the normal fashion, but the result is loaded into register R, and not used to reference main storage for an operand. The Load Address instruction therefore provides a means of determining the address of a particular location during program execution.

The program of Figure 5.1 is modified again in Figure 5.2 to illustrate the use of the LA instruction. The figure also illustrates how component referencing can be specified. For this particular program this method is slightly less efficient, owing to the extra time required to execute the Load Address. Here the LA

LOCATION	OP.	OPERAND	... COMMENTS ...
BEGIN	START	0	SET LOCATION CNT TO 0
	BALR	12,0	LOAD BASE REGISTER 12
	USING	::,12	INFORM ASSEMBLER
	LA	8,A	LOAD ADDRESS OF A IN REG 8
	L	5,0(,8)	LOAD REG 5 WITH A
	A	5,4(,8)	ADD B TO REG 5
	ST	5,8(,8)	STORE REG 5 INTO C
	DC	X'99'	INSERT INVALID OP CODE
A	DC	F'5'	A FULL WORD CONSTANT 5
	DC	F'-4'	A FULL WORD CONSTANT -4
	DS	F	RESERVE A FULL WORD
	END	BEGIN	END OF PROGRAM

FIGURE 5.2 Program Showing LA and Component Addressing

causes the machine to compute the address of location A and to load its value into register 8. The Load, Add, and STore instructions are coded using the component method of writing an operand reference. Since the exact address of location A is already computed and contained in register 8, the operand reference specified by 0(,8) indicates the same address. By designating the displacement as 4 in the Add instruction, the operand reference is A+4, corresponding to an address adjustment of 4 bytes. Likewise, in the STore instruction, a displacement of 8 causes a reference to location A+8.

Even though it is not very efficient to do so in this example, several interesting and useful techniques can be illustrated by the following variations on Figure 5.2. To save space, only the program segment that changes is shown.

LOCATION	OP.	OPERAND	... COMMENTS ...
.	.	.	
	LA	8,A	LOAD ADDRESS OF A IN REG 8
	L	5,0(,8)	LOAD REG 5 WITH A
	LA	8,4(8)	BUMP REG 8 BY 4
	A	5,0(,8)	ADD B TO REG 5
	LA	8,4(8)	BUMP REG 8 BY 4
	ST	5,0(,8)	STORE REG 5 INTO C
.	.	.	

FIGURE 5.3 Program Showing a Use of the LA

Figure 5.3 illustrates a very powerful application of the Load Address instruction. By making the first operand register in the instruction the same as one of the second operand components, the contents of the register can be increased by the amount of the displacement. The amount contained in the same or a second register can also be added simultaneously. For example, to double the contents of a register and add 14, the following instruction is very useful.

LA   6,14(6,6)   DOUBLE C(6) AND ADD 14

To illustrate how index registers enter into the address specification,

```
LOCATION OP.    OPERAND           ...  COMMENTS           ...
    .        .
             L     5,A                  LOAD REG 5 WITH A
             LA    6,4                   LOAD REG 6 WITH VALUE 4
             A     5,A(6)               ADD B TO REG 5
             LA    6,4(6)               BUMP REG 6 BY 4
             ST    5,A(6)               STORE REG 5 INTO C
    .        .
```

FIGURE 5.4   Illustration of Indexing with Composite Reference

Figures 5.4 and 5.5 are presented. Figure 5.4 contains the program segment using composite referencing with register 6 as the index register. Again, this application of the technique is not efficient and is offered only as an illustration.

Figure 5.5 shows the same application using component referencing. Note that an additional Load Address is needed.

```
LOCATION OP.    OPERAND           ...  COMMENTS           ...
    .        .
             LA    8,A                  LOAD ADDRESS OF A INTO REG 8
             L     5,0(,8)              LOAD REG 5 WITH A
             LA    6,4                   LOAD REG 6 WITH VALUE 4
             A     5,0(6,8)             ADD B TO REG 5
             LA    6,4(6)               BUMP REG 6 BY 4
             ST    5,0(6,8)             STORE REG 5 INTO C
    .        .
```

FIGURE 5.5   Illustration of Indexing with Component Reference

Another feature provided by the assembler is the ability to equate a given symbolic name with a particular value. To do so, the programmer must use the equate (EQU) assembler instruction.

5.1 Assembler Instruction *Equate*

NAME   EQU   *VALUE*
where *NAME* is any symbol and *VALUE* is usually a decimal number or other value using a special type code. See Definitions 4.4 and 4.5.

Specifies that during the assembly phase, any appearance of the symbol *NAME* is to be replaced by its equivalent value.

The program of Figure 5.1, using the modification shown in Figure 5.5, is shown in Figure 5.6, using the EQU instruction to replace register reference numbers by symbolic names. Register 12 is called BASE to mnemonically represent the base register. Register 5 is represented by WORK, since this register is being used to form the sum of A and B data values. Register 8 is called DATA,

```
LOCATION  OP.    OPERAND          ...  COMMENTS          ...
BEGIN     START  0                     SET LOCATION CNT TO 0
BASE      EQU    12                    SET BASE EQUAL TO 12
WORK      EQU    5                     SET WORK EQUAL TO 5
DATA      EQU    8                     SET DATA EQUAL TO 8
INDEX     EQU    6                     SET INDEX EQUAL TO 6
          BALR   BASE,0                LOAD BASE REGISTER
          USING  ::,BASE               INFORM ASSEMBLER
          LA     DATA,A                LOAD ADDRESS OF A INTO DATA
          L      WORK,0(,DATA)         LOAD WORK WITH A
          LA     INDEX,4               LOAD INDEX WITH VALUE 4
          A      WORK,0(INDEX,DATA)    ADD B TO WORK
          LA     INDEX,4(INDEX)        BUMP INDEX BY 4
          ST     WORK,0(INDEX,DATA)    STORE WORK INTO C
   .       .      .
```

FIGURE 5.6   Application of EQU to Register Numbers

since it points to the location of data word A. Finally, register 6 is called INDEX, since it is serving as an index register.

If the programmer wishes to reassign register numbers to the various register names, only the EQU entries need changing. Thus, in a very large program it would be much easier and much more accurate to change register assignments if symbolic register names are used. Therefore, in each variation of addressing technique shown in Tables 5.1 and 5.2, every register reference can be replaced individually by symbolic names at the discretion of the programmer. Even displacements can be specified by symbolic names in the same manner.

For the remainder of this text the following conventions are adopted. As each new instruction is introduced, its appearance in assembly-language coding is presented in the component method of operand referencing. The reader can thereby determine all possible forms of referencing, both composite and component. Table 5.3 summarizes all instruction types and their respective formats.

TABLE 5.3   Summary of Operand Formats by Instruction Type

Instruction Type	Operand Appearance	Remarks
RR	R_1,R_2	
RX	$R_1,D_2(X_2,B_2)$	
RS	$R_1,R_3,D_2(B_2)$	Variation 1
	$R_1,D_2(B_2)$	Variation 2
SI	$D_1(B_1),I_2$	Variation 1
	$D_1(B_1)$	Variation 2
SS	$D_1(L,B_1),D_2(B_2)$	Variation 1
	$D_1(L_1,B_1),D_2(L_2,B_2)$	Variation 2

An even simpler summary of the various operand reference techniques can be produced if one recognizes that only three fundamental main storage reference specifications are possible. Even two of these three appear the same. Table 5.4 shows the appearance of these three reference methods in both composite and component forms.

TABLE 5.4   Fundamental Operand Reference Forms

Component Form	Composite Form
D(B)	NAME±C
D(X,B)	NAME±C(X)
D(L,B)	NAME±C(L)

We note one final point before leaving address logic. If an address of a particular operand is contained within a register, register 6 for example, there is no difference in the following two instructions as far as results are concerned.

$$\text{L} \qquad 5,0(6)$$
$$\text{L} \qquad 5,0(,6)$$

In the first example, register 6 is acting as an index register. In the second case, register 6 is serving as a base register. However, the contents of the full word at the location specified by the contents of register 6 are loaded into register 5 in either case. This should be obvious from the definition of the address computation. Therefore, in most applications, the index and base registers can play interchangeable roles.

5.2   INTEGER ARITHMETIC AND RELATED OPERATIONS

Before any additional instructions are formally introduced, let us examine the format to be used in doing so. If several instructions fall within a general category of behavior, all are presented by the same definition. Any variations are then described. An attempt is made to present all pertinent information about an instruction in a concise yet readable form. The reader is referred to Appendix 1, which contains a summary of all machine instructions and their important characteristics.

Definition 5.2 illustrates a sample definition.

The information found under the heading of SYNTAX provides the standard assembler format for writing the given instruction. The operands are always shown in component reference form. Under the heading TYPE is found one of the five type designations RR, RX, RS, SI, or SS. The corresponding hex operation code is shown under the CODE heading. Under the SEMANTICS heading appears the shorthand notation used in Chapter 4 to describe the behavior of the machine under the control of the indicated instruction. The

---

5.2   Sample Definition of Machine Instructions
Generalized Category Name Appears Here

Within this partition are found four columns of information under the following headings:

NAME   SYNTAX   TYPE   CODE

Within this partition are found three columns of information under the following headings:

SEMANTICS   CC   INTRPTS

---

column headed CC refers the reader to an entry in Table 5.5, which summarizes condition-code settings for integer operations. The column headed by INTRPTS refers to an entry in Table 5.6, which summarizes interrupts for integer operations.

The first set of integer operations, a major one called loading operations, includes nine different instructions. All nine are defined in one group in Definition 5.3. To simplify editorial presentation, subscripts on address and register components are written on the same line with the symbol. Thus R_1 is written as R1.

TABLE 5.5   Condition-Code Settings for Integer Operations

Reference	Code Settings			
Number	0	1	2	3
0	Unchanged			
1	R = 0	R < 0	R > 0	—
2	R = 0	R < 0	R > 0	overflow
3	R = 0	—	R > 0	overflow
4	R = 0	R < 0	—	—
5	R=0 NC	R≠0 NC	R=0 C	R≠0 C
6	—	R≠0 NC	R=0 C	R≠0 C
7	O1=O2	O1 < O2	O1 > O2	—

Notes: R = result, NC = no carry, C = carry, O = operand.

The notation CH in Definition 5.3 means the contents of the half word at the location indicated by C(X2)+C(B2)+D2. During the loading operation, the half word is extended to a full word. Likewise, CnF means the contents of a number of consecutive full words beginning at the location specified by C(X2)+C(B2)+D2. Enough words are loaded to fill registers R1 through R3. In

5.3 Machine Instructions LOAD -

NAME	SYNTAX		TYPE	CODE
LOAD REGISTER	LR	R1,R2	RR	18
LOAD	L	R1,D2(X2,B2)	RX	58
LOAD HALFWORD	LH	R1,D2(X2,B2)	RX	48
LOAD AND TEST	LTR	R1,R2	RR	12
LOAD COMPLEMENT	LCR	R1,R2	RR	13
LOAD POSITIVE	LPR	R1,R2	RR	10
LOAD NEGATIVE	LNR	R1,R2	RR	11
LOAD MULTIPLE	LM	R1,R3,D2(B2)	RS	98
LOAD ADDRESS	LA	R1,D2(X2,B2)	RX	41

SEMANTICS		CC	INTRPTS
LR:	$C(R2) \longrightarrow C(R1)$	0	0
L:	$C(C(X2)+C(B2)+D2) \longrightarrow C(R1)$	0	456
LH:	$CH(C(X2)+C(B2)+D2) \longrightarrow C(R1)$	0	456
LTR:	$C(R2) \longrightarrow C(R1)$	1	0
LCR:	$-C(R2) \longrightarrow C(R1)$	2	8
LPR:	$|C(R2)| \longrightarrow C(R1)$	3	8
LNR:	$-|C(R2)| \longrightarrow C(R1)$	4	0
LM:	$CnF(C(B2)+D2) \longrightarrow C(R1 \text{ thru } R3)$	0	456
LA:	$C(X2)+C(B2)+D2 \longrightarrow C(R1)$	0	0

TABLE 5.6   Interrupts for Integer Operations

Reference Number	Possible Interrupts
0	None
4	Protection[a]
5	Addressing
6	Specification
7	Data
8	Fixed-point overflow
9	Fixed-point divide

[a]Action depends on instruction and installation of protection features.

case R3 is less than R1, register zero follows register 15. The vertical bars around C(R2) indicate the usual absolute magnitude.

Next to be defined are the add instructions. Included with the regular adds are the logical add operations. Logical addition adds all 32 bits of the number in a general-purpose register as though the operands were unsigned. The presence of a high-order carry is recorded in the condition code. Also recorded in the condition code is an indication of a zero or nonzero result. Logical addition is primarily used for higher-precision work than 32 bits. In the definitions that follow, all logical operations are designated by the letter L following the ordinary arithmetic symbol. Thus, logical addition is indicated as +L (read as Add Logical).

5.4   Machine Instructions ADD -

NAME	SYNTAX		TYPE	CODE
ADD REGISTER	AR	R1,R2	RR	1A
ADD	A	R1,D2(X2,B2)	RX	5A
ADD HALFWORD	AH	R1,D2(X2,B2)	RX	4A
ADD LOGICAL REG	ALR	R1,R2	RR	1E
ADD LOGICAL	AL	R1,D2(X2,B2)	RX	5E

SEMANTICS		CC	INTRPTS
AR:	$C(R1) + C(R2) \longrightarrow C(R1)$	2	8
A:	$C(R1) + C(C(X2)+C(B2)+D2) \longrightarrow C(R1)$	2	4568
AH:	$C(R1) + CH(C(X2)+C(B2)+D2) \longrightarrow C(R1)$	2	4568
ALR:	$C(R1) +L\ C(R2) \longrightarrow C(R1)$	5	0
AL:	$C(R1) +L\ C(C(X2)+C(B2)+D2) \longrightarrow C(R1)$	5	456

The set of subtract operations, including the logical subtracts, is given in Definition 5.5. The same comments apply to logical subtract operations as for logical addition.

Next to be defined are multiply operations. Notice that there is a special restriction on register designations in the M and MR instructions. In these two cases, register R1 is an even number and refers to what is called an even/odd pair of registers. In the cases of M and MR, the product appears in both registers of the even/odd pair as a 64-bit number. Signs are determined by ordinary rules of algebra. Notice that no restriction is placed on R1 for the MH instruction, and the result is retained in one register. Overflow can occur and go undetected in this latter case.

5.5 Machine Instructions SUBTRACT -

NAME	SYNTAX		TYPE	CODE
SUB REGISTER	SR	R1,R2	RR	1B
SUBTRACT	S	R1,D2(X2,B2)	RX	5B
SUB HALFWORD	SH	R1,D2(X2,B2)	RX	4B
SUB LOGICAL REG	SLR	R1,R2	RR	1F
SUB LOGICAL	SL	R1,D2(X2,B2)	RX	5F

SEMANTICS	CC	INTRPTS
SR: $C(R1) - C(R2) \longrightarrow C(R1)$	2	8
S: $C(R1) - C(C(X2)+C(B2)+D2) \longrightarrow C(R1)$	2	4568
SH: $C(R1) - CH(C(X2)+C(B2)+D2) \longrightarrow C(R1)$	2	4568
SLR: $C(R1) -L\ C(R2) \longrightarrow C(R1)$	6	0
SL: $C(R1) -L\ C(C(X2)+C(B2)+D2) \longrightarrow C(R1)$	6	456

5.6 Machine Instructions MULTIPLY -

NAME	SYNTAX		TYPE	CODE
MULT REGISTER	MR	R1,R2	RR	1C
MULTIPLY	M	R1,D2(X2,B2)	RX	5C
MULT HALFWORD	MH	R1,D2(X2,B2)	RX	4C

Note: In MR and M, R1 must be an even number.

SEMANTICS	CC	INTRPTS
MR: $C(R1+1) \times C(R2) \longrightarrow C(R1\ \&\ R1+1)$	0	6
M: $C(R1+1) \times C(C(X2)+C(B2)+D2)$ $\longrightarrow C(R1\ \&\ R1+1)$	0	456
MH: $C(R1) \times CH(C(X2)+C(B2)+D2) \longrightarrow C(R1)$	0	456

Next, the divide instructions. Again, the first operand register number is an even value and points to an even/odd pair that initially contains the dividend of the divide operation. Therefore, the dividend is a 64-bit number. After the operation is completed, the even register contains the remainder and the odd register contains the quotient. The sign of the quotient is determined by ordinary rules of algebra. The sign of the remainder is made the same as the sign of the original dividend. The divisor is a 32-bit number located either in register R2 or in main storage. If the relative magnitudes of the dividend and divisor are such that the quotient cannot be expressed as a 32-bit signed number, a fixed-point divide interrupt occurs.

5.7 Machine Instructions DIVIDE -

NAME		SYNTAX	TYPE	CODE
DIVIDE REGISTER	DR	R1,R2	RR	1D
DIVIDE	D	R1,D2(X2,B2)	RX	5D

Note: R1 must be an even number.

SEMANTICS	CC	INTRPTS
DR: C(R1&R1+1)/C(R2) $\longrightarrow$ C(R1+1), R $\longrightarrow$ C(R1)	0	69
D: C(R1&R1+1)/C(Y2) $\longrightarrow$ C(R1+1), R $\longrightarrow$ C(R1)	0	4569
Where R = remainder, Y2 = C(X2)+C(B2)+D2		

Given next are the integer compare operations. These three instructions cause no computation to occur, only the setting of the condition code. The code can then be used for the purpose of making branching decisions. The half word obtained by the CH operation is extended to a 32-bit number before the compare is performed.

5.8 Machine Instructions COMPARE -

NAME		SYNTAX	TYPE	CODE
COMPARE REGISTER	CR	R1,R2	RR	19
COMPARE	C	R1,D2(X2,B2)	RX	59
COMPARE HALFWORD	CH	R1,D2(X2,B2)	RX	49

SEMANTICS	CC	INTRPTS
CR: C(R1) : C(R2)	7	0
C: C(R1) : C(C(X2)+C(B2)+D2)	7	456
CH: C(R1) : CH(C(X2)+C(B2)+D2)	7	456

Note: : = compare.

The operation of returning results to storage is accomplished with one of the store operations. Three such operations are now defined. In the case of the STH instruction, the low-order sixteen bits of a register are stored in a half word in main storage. No consideration is given to the high-order sixteen bits. Thus, if the magnitude of the number in the register is greater than the maximum allowed for a half word, no indication is given.

5.9 Machine Instructions STORE -

NAME	SYNTAX		TYPE	CODE
STORE	ST	R1,D2(X2,B2)	RX	50
STORE HALFWORD	STH	R1,D2(X2,B2)	RX	40
STORE MULTIPLE	STM	R1,R3,D2(B2)	RS	90

SEMANTICS		CC	INTRPTS
ST:	$C(R1) \longrightarrow C(C(X2)+C(B2)+D2)$	0	456
STH:	$CRH(R1) \longrightarrow CH(C(X2)+C(B2)+D2)$	0	456
STM:	$C(R1 \text{ thru } R3) \longrightarrow CnF(C(B2)+D2)$	0	456
Note:	RH = right half.		

Quite often a need exists to shift information either to the left or to the right within a register or a pair of registers. Four instructions are provided for this purpose. One point to remember about shifting is that a shift of one place

---

5.10 Machine Instructions SHIFT -

NAME	SYNTAX		TYPE	CODE
- LEFT SINGLE	SLA	R1,D2(B2)	RS	8B
- LEFT DOUBLE	SLDA	R1,D2(B2)	RS	8F
- RIGHT SINGLE	SRA	R1,D2(B2)	RS	8A
- RIGHT DOUBLE	SRDA	R1,D2(B2)	RS	8E
Note:	In SLDA and SRDA, R1 must be an even number.			

SEMANTICS		CC	INTRPTS
SLA:	$C(R1)$ shifted left $D2+C(B2)$ places	2	8
SLDA:	$C(R1\&R1+1)$ shifted left $D2+C(B2)$ places	2	68
SRA:	$C(R1)$ shifted right $D2+C(B2)$ places	1	0
SRDA:	$C(R1\&R1+1)$ shifted right $D2+C(B2)$ places	1	6
Note:	In SLDA and SRDA, R1 points to an Even/Odd pair of registers.		

---

represents either multiplying or dividing by two, not ten. Also, the conditions for overflow on a left shift must be considered. Since the sign bit does not participate in a shift operation, an overflow during a left shift is indicated by the shifting of a bit different from the sign bit out of the high-order magnitude position of the register. On left shifts, zeros are fed into the low-order end of the register. On right shifts, bits equal to the sign bit are fed into the left end of the register. Therefore two's-complement notation is properly maintained at all times.

Notice that, in the shift instructions, the value of D2+C(B2) is not the address of a main storage address but rather a shift count representing the number of binary places to shift. Only the low-order six bits are used for the shift amount; thus 63 is the maximum value that is effective. The component of C(B2) that enters into the shift count allows the programmer to specify a shift count indirectly to be determined at execution time. If B2 is zero, no indirect specification of the shift count is indicated, just as in the case of an address computation. Another interesting note is that a SRDA or SLDA instruction, which specifies a zero shift count, is actually a double-length sign and magnitude test, in that the condition code is set but no shifting occurs.

5.3   A MORE COMPREHENSIVE EXAMPLE

To avoid discussing at this point the complex concepts of input and output operations at the assembly-language level, we use a Fortran IV program. Input and output can be accomplished in the normal fashion within the Fortran language, and an exercise with assembly language can be carried out as a subroutine to the Fortran main program. We need to learn the conventions of linking the two types of programs, but this turns out to be much easier than doing basic input and output in assembly language. The following paragraphs describe these linkage conventions.

Within a Fortran program, the method of calling an assembler subroutine is identical to the method of calling either a Function or Subroutine subprogram written in Fortran. Thus entry to an assembly-language subroutine is accomplished through the use of either a functional reference in an arithmetic statement or the CALL statement. The former is used here, since it is slightly easier to understand and use. Suppose the function $F(J) = J^2 + 2J$ is to be implemented as an assembler subprogram. Figure 5.7 shows a Fortran program that calls such a function subprogram for various values of the argument and prints out a table containing J and F(J). An integer type statement is included to inform the Fortran system that the function name, F, is to be an integer function. Thus, the result of the function call is an integer value.

```
C        A FORTRAN PROGRAM TO EXERCISE AN ASSEMBLER SUBPROGRAM
C        FOR THE IMPLEMENTATION OF F(J) = J ::: 2 + 2 :: J
C        WITH J GOING FROM -10 TO +10 IN STEPS OF 1
         INTEGER F
         WRITE (6, 1)
     1   FORMAT('1', 5X, 'J', 5X, 'F(J)'/)
         DO 2 I = 1, 21
         J = I - 11
         K = F (J)
     2   WRITE (6, 3) J, K
     3   FORMAT(2I8)
         STOP
         END
```

FIGURE 5.7   Fortran Service Program

The following conventions and requirements must be satisfied by the assembly-language subprogram to link with the Fortran program shown in Figure 5.7.

1. The name of the subprogram is F. This requires that the symbol F must appear in the location field of the START instruction of the subprogram.

2. Upon entry to the subprogram, certain registers conventionally contain specific information. These registers and their respective contents are listed below.

Register	Contents
1	Contains address of argument address list
2–12	Contains information pertinent to the Fortran program; thus it must be protected
13	Contains address of a save area
14	Contains return address to calling program
15	Contains entry point of called program

3. If one or more registers between 2 and 12 are needed for the assembly subprogram, their original contents must be saved and restored at the completion of the subprogram operation.

4. The Fortran program expects the functional result to be returned in general-purpose register 0. (Floating-point results are returned in floating-point register 0.)

Under conventional subroutine linkage conditions, each calling program supplies the address, in register 13, of an eighteen-word save area in which the called program can store registers and other information in a specified format. However, for the purpose of this simple exercise, only those registers which are needed for the function computation are saved. A local save area is provided in

LOC	OBJECT CODE	ADDR1	ADDR2	STMT		SOURCE STATEMENT	
000000				1	F	START 0	SET LOCATION CNT TO 0
000000				2		USING *,15	BASE REGISTER IS 15
000000	9024 F020		00020	3		STM 2,4,SAVE	STORE REGISTERS 2, 3, AND 4
000000	5821 0000		00000	4		L 2,0(1)	LOAD ARGUMENT ADDRESS
000008	5842 0000		00000	5		L 4,0(2)	LOAD ARGUMENT
00000C	1834			6		LR 3,4	COPY ARGUMENT
00000E	1C23			7		MR 2,3	SQUARE ARGUMENT
000010	8B40 0001		00001	8		SLA 4,1	DOUBLE ARGUMENT
000014	1A34			9		AR 3,4	ADD TERMS
000016	1803			10		LR 0,3	MOVE ANSWER
000018	9824 F020		00020	11		LM 2,4,SAVE	RESTORE REGISTERS
00001C	05FE			12		BALR 15,14	RETURN TO CALLING PROGRAM
000020				13	SAVE	DS 3F	RESERVE 3 WORDS
000000				14		END F	

FIGURE 5.8   Assembly-Language Subprogram for F(J) = J**2+2*J

the assembly-language subprogram for the purpose of saving three registers. Linkage conventions, along with the proper use of save areas, are discussed in more detail in Chapter 11. The subprogram source and object coding is shown in Figure 5.8.

Since the entry point of the subprogram is found in register 15 upon entry to the subprogram, the programmer can take advantage of this fact and use register 15 as the base register for the subprogram. This works properly only if the contents of register 15 remain unchanged during the course of executing the subprogram. This holds true for the example under consideration. Thus, only a USING is required to specify the base register to the assembler.

Let us analyze the subprogram on a statement-by-statement basis. Statement 1 supplies the subprogram name, which is linked with the function call in the Fortran program at linkedit time. This statement also sets the assembler location counter to zero. Statement 2 informs the assembler that register 15 is the base register and will contain relative address zero. Notice that a BALR is not needed, since register 15 will contain the entry point, relative address zero, of the subprogram upon entry. Statement 3, the first machine instruction in the program, stores registers 2, 3, and 4 into the three words reserved at location SAVE. Statement 4 loads into register 2 the address of the function argument from the argument address list, the address of which is in register 1 upon entry to the subprogram. Statement 5 then loads register 4 with the actual argument. Statement 6 copies the argument into register 3. Register 4 continues to contain the same value. Statement 7 causes the machine to multiply the contents of register 3 (odd register of even/odd pair) by the contents of register 3, thereby obtaining the square of the argument. Statement 8, by shifting the contents of register 4 left one binary place, doubles the original argument. Statement 9 adds the squared term to the doubled term, yielding the result required. Statement 10 moves the result into register 0 for transfer back to the calling Fortran program. Statement 11 reloads registers 2, 3, and 4 from the three words containing their original contents. Statement 12 uses the rather unorthodox yet effective method of returning to the calling program with the BALR instruction. The operation loads register 15, no longer needed, with the address of the next instruction (actually data in this case) and branches to the return address contained in register 14. Statement 13 reserves the three full words in which the contents of registers 2, 3, and 4 are saved. Finally, statement 14 indicates the end of the subprogram. Figure 5.9 shows the results obtained from running the Fortran and assembler subprogram in a single run.

Special JCL cards are required for running a job containing both Fortran and assembly-language programs. Again, the contents of these cards may vary from one computing center to another. Figure 5.10 illustrates a set of cards for handling this type of job. This is a four-step job similar to the one in Figure 1.2 of Chapter 1. Notice the special procedure indicated in the EXEC card.

J	F(J)
-10	80
-9	63
-8	48
-7	35
-6	24
-5	15
-4	8
-3	3
-2	0
-1	-1
0	0
1	3
2	8
3	15
4	24
5	35
6	48
7	63
8	80
9	99
10	120

FIGURE 5.9   Output from Programs of Figures 5.7 and 5.8.

```
JOB CARD
PASSWORD CARD
// EXEC FGALPCXS
//FORT.SYSIN DD ::
   FORTRAN PROGRAM APPEARS HERE
/::
//ASM.SYSIN DD ::
   ASSEMBLY-LANGUAGE PROGRAM APPEARS HERE
/::
.//GO.SYSUDUMP DD SYSOUT=A
```

FIGURE 5.10   JCL Layout for Fortran and Assembly Programs

FGALPCXS indicates a cataloged procedure for compiling and executing a Fortran and assembly-language program combination. Since this procedure is not a standard one supplied by IBM, a listing of such a procedure is included in Appendix 12 for possible incorporation into the reader's computing system. Minor adjustments of the operands within the procedure may be required. Even though a core dump is not expected, the SYSUDUMP card must be included in case an error is made and a dump is needed for debugging purposes.

PROGRAMMING EXERCISE

Program and run a job similar to the one discussed in this chapter with the functional relationship defined as follows:

$$F(J) = 2J^2 - 4J + 10$$

STUDY EXERCISES

1. Describe and name the two major methods of storage referencing. Give examples of each method.
2. Discuss the concept of indexing.
3. What is address adjustment?
4. Which general-purpose registers cannot be used as base or index registers?
5. What is the difference between L and LA?
6. Using one instruction, add the contents of registers 2 and 5 plus the constant 25 and leave the result in register 3.
7. How is the EQU instruction useful?
8. Show the operand syntax for each of the five instruction formats. Remember that variations exist for some.
9. Describe the differences between syntax and semantics.
10. Discuss each and every machine instruction presented in Definitions 5.3 through 5.10, including their syntax, semantics, possible interrupts, and their effect on the condition code.

Chapter six

The Concepts of Branching and Indexing

No computer could approach the sophistication of modern machines without the capabilities of decision making and branching. The ability to detect unusual or error conditions while a program is executing and to take corrective and adaptive action is, of course, invaluable. However, the fundamental operations of taking an alternative path, branching to and from subroutines, and forming loops that repeat have become indispensable tools to the programmer. Basic to all of these operations is the branching operation.

Since most machines, System/360 included, operate on the assumption that instructions appear in memory in sequential locations, branching operations usually take the form of either causing a branch at a point in a program or alternatively allowing the machine to proceed with the next instruction in sequence. Besides four variations on this basic concept of branching, System/360 has other, more sophisticated methods of causing a branch to occur within a program, such as in the interrupt system discussed in Chapter 3. A much more detailed presentation of this system is forthcoming in Chapter 11. This chapter is concerned primarily with the basic four variations of branching.

The first variation is a type of branch that provides a record of where the branch occurred. This provides the programmer the information needed to return to the branch point and continue processing as if no branch had occurred. This mode of branching is referred to as branching and linking.

The second variation of branching is based on a countdown. Each time a branch is taken, a register value is reduced by one. Branching continues until the count reaches zero.

The third variation provides the conditional type of branch using the status of the condition code. Thus, the programmer is able to instruct the computer to take one of two alternative paths, depending on specific conditions at the time the program is under execution. This same type of instruction can be used as an unconditional branch or even as a NOP, the mnemonic code representing no operation in older machines.

The fourth variation of branching operations is coupled with the concept of indexing. One set of instructions provides a means of altering the contents of a register by a given amount and branching according to the value of the result. Thus, an index register used for indexing one or more RX type instructions in a loop can be placed under control of an instruction whose behavior is similar to a DO statement in Fortran. An initial value, an increment, and an upper limit can be specified; thus a progression of index values can be controlled by such an instruction.

In order to fully appreciate the behavior of the machine under branching conditions, we need the concepts of the program status word (PSW) and the instruction address counter (IAC). Since the condition code is also part of the PSW, part of the concept has already been discussed in previous chapters. In fact, the concepts involved in program status extend throughout several chapters of this text.

6.1   THE INSTRUCTION ADDRESS COUNTER

Within System/360, a certain collection of pertinent program status information is referred to as the PSW. Sufficient information is contained in this status word to represent the progress of a given program at any given time. If a program must be interrupted temporarily to service a second program, the current contents of the PSW provide the information required to pick up the first program at the point of interruption. Thus, the operating system saves the PSW each time an interruption occurs for the purpose of returning control to the program at the proper time. These supervisory operations fall into the general category of machine status switching and are the subject of Chapter 11. At this point, only a part of the PSW is pertinent to the topic of branching. The total PSW, a double word of 64 bits in length, is discussed in detail at a later time. Of concern here is a 24-bit portion of the PSW called the Instruction Address Counter, abbreviated IAC.

The IAC appears in the right half of the PSW, as shown in Figure 6.1. Three other kinds of information also appear within this half. The Instruction Length Code (ILC), a two-bit number, represents the length of the current instruction being executed. Under normal conditions the value of the ILC is simply the length of the instruction in half words. The Condition Code (CC), also a two-bit number, has been discussed in preceding chapters. The program mask, a four-bit number, is used to mask off the four program interrupts that can be ignored. This group of bits is discussed along with status switching. The remaining 24 bits represent the Instruction Address Counter (IAC).

ILC	CC	Mask	Instruction Address Counter

Bits   2   2   4   24

FIGURE 6.1   Right Half of Program Status Word (PSW)

The reader will remember from Chapter 3 the discussion of fundamental machine cycles. Under normal conditions the computer alternates between two basic cycles, *fetch* and *execute*. During the fetch cycle, the machine retrieves from main storage an instruction to be executed. During the execute cycle, the fetched instruction is interpreted and executed. The contents of the IAC portion of the PSW determine the location in main storage from which the next instruction is to be fetched.

For the purpose of discussion, suppose the machine is in the fetch cycle and the contents of the IAC are 1F000. Further suppose the machine fetches an RX type of instruction from location 1F000. After the machine has determined that the instruction is of RX type and is four bytes in length, the value 4 is added to the IAC portion of the PSW. The contents of the IAC is now 1F004, and representing the updated instruction address of the next instruction to be fetched during the next fetch cycle. Thus, as each new instruction is fetched and interpreted, a value of 2, 4, or 6 is added to the IAC, depending on the length of the instruction just fetched.

By providing a means of altering the contents of the IAC, through the use of various branch instructions, the machine designer has taken care of the need to alter the path of control within a program. During subsequent discussions involving the different branch instructions, reference is made to the IAC and its contents. The shorthand notation of C(IAC), meaning the contents of the IAC, should be considered in the same manner as previous uses of the notation.

6.2   BRANCHING AND LINKING OPERATIONS

Two instructions, BAL and BALR, provide a means of branching, while recording the location at which the branch takes place. These instructions are used to branch to a point outside the sequence of instructions being executed. After executing one or more instructions at this new location, the linkage information can be used to return to the original point of the branch to continue processing as though no branch had even occurred. This technique is extremely valuable in the context of calling subroutines and returning to the calling program.

In the following definition, any reference to the contents of the IAC is made by the machine after the current instruction length has been added to the IAC, called the updated instruction address. While the contents of the IAC are shown being replaced by general-purpose register contents, note that only the low-order 24 bits of the register are replacing the IAC. The contents of the rest of the PSW, such as the ILC, CC, and MASK, are not changed.

6.1 Machine Instructions BRANCH AND LINK -

NAME	SYNTAX	TYPE	CODE
- REGISTER	BALR R1,R2	RR	05
-	BAL R1,D2(X2,B2)	RX	45

SEMANTICS		CC	INTRPTS
BALR: CRH(PSW) $\longrightarrow$ C(R1); if R2$\neq$0, then			
CR3B(R2) $\longrightarrow$ C(IAC)		0	0
BAL: CRH(PSW) $\longrightarrow$ C(R1),			
C(X2)+C(B2)+D2 $\longrightarrow$ C(IAC)		0	0
Note: R3B = right 3 bytes, RH = right half.			

It should now be clear that the use of the BALR to load the base address at the beginning of a program is a special application of the instruction. In normal use, the second register designation is not zero, and it does represent a register that contains a branch address. Notice that no such option is possible with the BAL operation. As an example of how the BALR instruction can be used, consider the case of calling a subroutine from within a given program. Assume the conventions of subroutine calling presented in Chapter 5 hold. Also assume register 15 has been previously loaded with the address of the entry point of the subroutine being called. The following instruction could be used to branch to the subroutine and at the same time provide a return address in register 14.

BALR   14,15

The reader should note that register R1 after execution of either BAL or BALR contains not only the linkage address but also the values of the ILC, CC, and MASK at the time the instruction is executed. Under a few special situations, the programmer must take this fact into consideration to avoid problems.

6.3   BRANCH AND COUNTING OPERATIONS

Quite often the programmer is faced with the need to branch to a certain location for a fixed number of times. For example, a program loop may need repeating for a given number of times. The branch-on-count instructions, BCT and BCTR, provide the simplest method of accomplishing such operations.

6.2 Machine Instructions BRANCH ON COUNT -			
NAME	SYNTAX	TYPE	CODE
- REGISTER	BCTR R1,R2	RR	06
-	BCT R1,D2(X2,B2)	RX	46

SEMANTICS	CC	INTRPTS
BCTR: $C(R1) - 1 \longrightarrow C(R1)$; if $C(R1) \neq 0$, and $R2 \neq 0$, then $CR3B(R2) \longrightarrow C(IAC)$	0	0
BCT: $C(R1) - 1 \longrightarrow C(R1)$; if $C(R1) \neq 0$, then $C(X2)+C(B2)+D2 \longrightarrow C(IAC)$	0	0

The branch address is determined before the counting operation in case register R1 is also taking part in the branch address as the index or base register. The counting operation is carried out in all 32 bits of the register and the condition code is unaffected, even when overflow occurs while going from the largest negative number to the largest positive number. An initial count of one results in zero, and no branch is taken. An initial count of zero results in a minus one, and branching does occur. If R2 in the RR form is zero, counting occurs but no branch is ever taken.

The following problem involving the summation of several values illustrates the BCT instruction. Suppose 50 full-word values beginning with the symbolic location X are to be added to produce a sum. A program segment that solves this problem is shown in Figure 6.2. Do not be concerned with the origin of the contents of the 50 words. Within this program segment, register 5 is being used to count the number of iterations of the add loop. Register 6 maintains the address of each full word being added. Notice that this address is increased by 4 in each iteration of the loop. Register 7 is being used to develop the sum;

```
LOCATION OP.    OPERAND          ... COMMENTS          ...
      .       .        .
      .       .        .
              LA     5,50              INITIALIZE REG 5 TO 50
              LA     6,X               INITIALIZE REG 6 TO A(X)
              LA     7,0               INITIALIZE REG 7 TO 0
LOOP          A      7,0(6)            ADD X(I) TO SUM
              LA     6,4(6)            BUMP INDEX BY 4
              BCT    5,LOOP            BCT ON REG 5 TO LOOP
      .       .        .
      .       .        .
X             DS     50F               RESERVE 50 FULL WORDS
      .       .        .
```

FIGURE 6.2   Example of Branch on Count

initially, therefore, it must be set to zero. At the completion of the loop, register 5 is zero and machine control is said to "fall through" the branch to the next sequential instruction.

This technique could be applied within the context of a subroutine to a Fortran calling program as shown in Figure 6.3. Suppose within the Fortran program, a one-dimensional subscripted variable called LIST is to be summed over its contents. Furthermore, suppose the number of elements in LIST is specified by the variable N. If the sum is to be returned in the variable ISUM, the following Fortran statement could be used to invoke the subroutine.

CALL SUM(LIST, N, ISUM)

The linkage convention between a Fortran program and a subroutine states that register 1, upon entry to the subroutine, points to a list of argument addresses. Thus, in this case, register 1 will contain the address of a word that in turn contains the address of the first word in the variable LIST. The contents of

```
LOCATION OP.    OPERAND          ... COMMENTS          ...
SUM           START  0                NAME SUB & SET LOCA CNT TO 0
              USING  *,15             REG 15 TO BE BASE REGISTER
              STM    5,7,SAVE         SAVE REGS 5, 6, AND 7
              L      6,0(1)           LOAD ADDRESS OF LIST
              L      5,4(1)           LOAD ADDRESS OF N
              L      5,0(5)           LOAD N
              LA     7,0              CLEAR SUM REG
LOOP          A      7,0(6)           ADD LIST(I) TO REG 7
              LA     6,4(6)           BUMP INDEX BY 4
              BCT    5,LOOP           BCT ON REG 5 TO LOOP
              L      5,8(1)           LOAD ADDRESS OF ISUM
              ST     7,0(5)           STORE SUM INTO ISUM
              LM     5,7,SAVE         RESTORE REG 5, 6, AND 7
              BALR   15,14            RETURN TO CALLING PROG
SAVE          DS     3F               RESERVE THREE WORDS
              END    SUM              END OF PROGRAM
```

FIGURE 6.3   Summation Subroutine Using Branch on Count

register 1 plus 4 is the address of a word containing the address of the variable N. The contents of register 1 plus 8 is the address of the address of the variable ISUM. The assembly-language program of Figure 6.3 accomplishes the desired result. Notice that for the CALL statement, the result is stored into a variable before returning to the calling program, rather than returning the result in a register as in Chapter 5. Registers 5, 6, and 7 play the same roles in both the program segment of Figure 6.2 and the subroutine in Figure 6.3.

6.4   BRANCHING-ON-CONDITION OPERATIONS

Two instructions are provided for decision-making operations based on the state of the condition code. These are the RR and RX variations of the branch-on-condition instruction. In these two instructions, the four-bit number within the instruction format, usually interpreted as the first operand register number, is called the mask. During execution of the instruction, the mask is used to determine whether or not a branch is to be taken. The sixteen possible values of the mask correspond to the sixteen possible combinations of condition-code settings. Since, in the writing of the assembly-language program, the mask is usually specified by a decimal number, Table 6.1 provides a simple rule for determining the proper mask for the desired condition-code combination on which to branch. The mask bit number is obtained by counting the bits from left to right. The mask value is simply the decimal value of a binary one in each of the four positions. The desired mask is then computed by adding together the mask values corresponding to each condition code setting that is to be tested for branching purposes. For example, if condition-code settings 1 or 3 are to cause branching, the mask corresponding to this case should be 4 plus 1 or 5. To fully illustrate the meaning of the mask, Table 6.2 shows all sixteen possible mask and code relationships. A third column illustrates the relationship between the general code settings and the specific settings following an add operation. The settings caused by the add operation are given by reference 2 in Table 5.5.

TABLE 6.1   Mask and Condition-Code Correspondence

Mask Bit	Mask Value	Condition Code
1	8	0
2	4	1
3	2	2
4	1	3

TABLE 6.2   All Possible Mask and Code Settings for Addition

Mask Value	Condition-Code Settings	Meaning for Addition Operation
0	none	none
1	3	overflow
2	2	$R > 0$
3	2, 3	$R > 0$, overflow
4	1	$R < 0$
5	1, 3	$R < 0$, overflow
6	1, 2	$R < 0, R > 0$
7	1, 2, 3	$R < 0, R > 0$, overflow
8	0	$R = 0$
9	0, 3	$R = 0$, overflow
10	0, 2	$R = 0, R > 0$
11	0, 2, 3	$R = 0, R > 0$, overflow
12	0, 1	$R = 0, R < 0$
13	0, 1, 3	$R = 0, R < 0$, overflow
14	0, 1, 2	$R = 0, R < 0, R > 0$
15	0, 1, 2, 3	$R = 0, R < 0, R > 0$, overflow

We shall now look at the formal definitions of the branch-on-condition instructions, then consider specific examples of how to use Tables 6.1 and 6.2 for certain branching operations.

6.3 Machine Instructions BRANCH ON CONDITION -

NAME	SYNTAX		TYPE	CODE
- REGISTER	BCR	M1,R2	RR	07
-	BC	M1,D2(X2,B2)	RX	47

SEMANTICS		CC	INTRPTS
BCR:	If M1 : CC, and R2 ≠ 0, then		
	CR3B(R2) ⟶ C(IAC)	0	0
BC:	If M1 : CC, then		
	C(X2)+C(B2)+D2 ⟶ C(IAC)	0	0
Note:	: means matches, R3B = right 3 bytes.		

For purposes of illustration, suppose a programmer wishes to test for the possibility of the occurrence of both an overflow and a zero result after an addition operation. Referring to Table 6.1 and remembering that a zero result sets the condition code to zero and overflow sets the code to three, the programmer would add a mask value of 8, for CC = 0 to a mask value of 1, for

CC = 3, to obtain a final mask value of 9. Looking at Table 6.2, the reader will see that a mask value of 9 does correspond to both a zero result and the overflow condition. Thus, the programmer could code the following instruction to implement the desired test.

BC   9,OVRFORZR

The machine, upon executing this instruction, checks the setting of the condition code. If the setting is either 0 or 3, a branch is taken to the location specified by the symbolic location OVRFORZR.

Notice that if a mask of zero is specified, no branch is ever taken, since the condition-code setting has no effect on the branch. Likewise, if a mask of 15 is specified, a branch is always taken, since, regardless of the condition-code setting, a mask and code match occurs. Thus, in System/360, a NOP (no-operation) is obtained with a BC instruction with a mask of zero. An unconditional branch is obtained with a BC instruction with a mask of 15.

The program in Figure 6.2 is presented again in Figure 6.4 with a BC instruction in the place of the BCT. The program becomes a little less efficient in

```
LOCATION OP.   OPERAND          ...  COMMENTS         ...
      .      .       .
      .      .       .
             LA    5,50              INITIALIZE REG 5 TO 50
             LA    6,X               INITIALIZE REG 6 TO A(X)
             LA    7,0               INITIALIZE REG 7 TO 0
LOOP         A     7,0(6)            ADD X(I) TO REG 7
             BC    1,OVERFLOW        CHECK FOR OVERFLOW
             LA    6,4(6)            BUMP INDEX BY 4
             S     5,ONE             COUNT DOWN ONE
             BC    2,LOOP            LOOP ON NONZERO
      .      .       .
      .      .       .
OVERFLOW  ...                        OVERFLOW RECOVERY ROUTINE
      .      .       .
      .      .       .
ONE          DC    F'1'              CONSTANT ONE
X            DS    50F               RESERVE 50 FULL WORDS
      .      .       .
      .      .       .
```

FIGURE 6.4   Examples of Branch-on-Condition Instruction

the process. A second BC instruction is also inserted to illustrate how one might check for overflow after each addition operation. The first BC instruction in Figure 6.4 tests for condition-code setting 3, the code that represents an overflow during addition. If the code setting is 3, a branch is taken to the symbolic location OVERFLOW, where presumably a routine would attempt to recover from the overflow. The second BC instruction tests for the condition-code setting 2, the code setting for a result greater than zero after a subtract operation. Provided the result is greater than zero, a branch is taken to the location called LOOP. Notice that in order to use the BC in this application, a subtract instruction had to be added to subtract one from the count in register 5. Therefore, in this particular case, the two instructions of S and BC can be replaced by the BCT as shown before.

Neither of these two applications of the BC instruction takes advantage of a multiple test of the condition code. Both instructions here test for only one condition-code setting. However, either of the following three instructions could replace the second BC in the above program.

$$
\begin{array}{ll}
\text{BC} & \text{3,LOOP} \\
\text{BC} & \text{6,LOOP} \\
\text{BC} & \text{7,LOOP}
\end{array}
$$

The reason, in each of the three cases, is that a condition-code setting of 1 or 3 does not occur in the context of this program example. The value in register 5 remains above zero, without overflow, until it reaches zero. Thus, neither overflow nor a result less than zero occurs. The test made by the first BC instruction could not be made broader, since either of the three conditions—less

TABLE 6.3   Extended Mnemonic Instruction Codes

Extended Code		Machine Instruction		Meaning
General				
B	D2(X2,B2)	BC	15,D2(X2,B2)	Branch unconditionally
BR	R2	BCR	15,R2	Branch unconditionally
NOP	D2(X2,B2)	BC	0,D2(X2,B2)	No operation
NOPR	R2	BCR	0,R2	No operation (RR)
After Compare Instructions (A:B)				
BH	D2(X2,B2)	BC	2,D2(X2,B2)	Branch on A high
BL	D2(X2,B2)	BC	4,D2(X2,B2)	Branch on A low
BE	D2(X2,B2)	BC	8,D2(X2,B2)	Branch on A equal B
BNH	D2(X2,B2)	BC	13,D2(X2,B2)	Branch on A not high
BNL	D2(X2,B2)	BC	11,D2(X2,B2)	Branch on A not low
BNE	D2(X2,B2)	BC	7,D2(X2,B2)	Branch on A not equal B
After Arithmetic Instructions				
BO	D2(X2,B2)	BC	1,D2(X2,B2)	Branch on overflow
BP	D2(X2,B2)	BC	2,D2(X2,B2)	Branch on plus
BM	D2(X2,B2)	BC	4,D2(X2,B2)	Branch on minus
BZ	D2(X2,B2)	BC	8,D2(X2,B2)	Branch on zero
BNP	D2(X2,B2)	BC	13,D2(X2,B2)	Branch on not plus
BNM	D2(X2,B2)	BC	11,D2(X2,B2)	Branch on not minus
BNZ	D2(X2,B2)	BC	7,D2(X2,B2)	Branch on not zero
After Test-Under-Mask Instructions				
BO	D2(X2,B2)	BC	1,D2(X2,B2)	Branch if ones
BM	D2(X2,B2)	BC	4,D2(X2,B2)	Branch if mixed
BZ	D2(X2,B2)	BC	8,D2(X2,B2)	Branch if zeros
BNO	D2(X2,B2)	BC	14,D2(X2,B2)	Branch if not ones

than zero, equal to zero, or greater than zero—could be a natural consequence of adding a sequence of numbers.

The assembler provides a set of extended mnemonic codes that produce BC instructions with particular mask values. Table 6.3 lists all of the available extended mnemonics. The Test-Under-Mask instruction, referred to in Table 6.3, is discussed in Chapter 8.

One final example of the branch-on-condition instruction should be given. In most subroutine applications, as in the subroutines of Figures 5.8 and 6.3, the proper final instruction used to return to the calling program would be

$$\text{BCR} \qquad 15,14$$

instead of the BALR used in previous examples. Note that BCR 15,14 causes an unconditional branch to the address in register 14, the desired result. The following extended mnemonic could be used to obtain the same instruction.

$$\text{BR} \qquad 14$$

Thus, with this approach, no register contents are changed because of the linking function of the BALR instruction.

6.5   BRANCHING AND INDEXING OPERATIONS

System/360 provides two instructions that combine branching with the simultaneous alteration of the contents of a general-purpose register by adding to it the contents of a second register. At the same time, control is provided to determine when the process of addition and branching is to end. This combined operation is referred to as branching on index.

6.4 Machine Instructions BRANCH ON INDEX -

NAME	SYNTAX	TYPE	CODE
- HIGH	BXH R1,R3,D2(B2)	RS	86
- LOW OR EQUAL	BXLE R1,R3,D2(B2)	RS	87

SEMANTICS	CC	INTRPTS
BXH: $C(R1) + C(R3) \longrightarrow C(R1)$; if $C(R1) >$ $C(RC)$, then $C(B2)+D2 \longrightarrow C(IAC)$	0	0
BXLE: $C(R1) + C(R3) \longrightarrow C(R1)$; if $C(R1) \leqslant$ $C(RC)$, then $C(B2)+D2 \longrightarrow C(IAC)$	0	0
Note: RC = R3 if R3 is odd, RC = R3+1 if R3 is even.		

In this definition, register R1 is the index register under modification and test. This is the same register that is used to modify a storage reference, such as register 3 in the following example.

$$A \qquad 7,X(3)$$

Either the BXH or the BXLE can be used to modify the contents of an index register by an amount contained within a second register. This second register is called the increment register and is R3 in Definition 6.4. If register number R3 is odd, then this register is also used as a comparand register. If register number R3 is even, then register R3+1 is used as a comparand register. In either instruction, the increment is added to the index and the sum is compared to the comparand. If the instruction is BXH and the resulting sum is greater than the comparand, a branch is taken to the branch address specified by B2 and D2; otherwise no branch occurs. In the case of the BXLE instruction, the increment is added to the index and the sum is compared to the comparand as before. However, the branch is taken only if the resulting index sum is less than or equal to the comparand.

To fully illustrate these two instructions, we investigate further the example used in Figures 6.2, 6.3, and 6.4. The object in the examples was to add 50 full words to form a sum. The BXH or BXLE instructions can be used to advantage to shorten the loop in which the sum is formed. Several approaches can be taken to the problem, but only three are basic. One approach involves a positive increment; thus the sum is formed by progressing through the table of values in a natural forward manner. In a second approach a negative increment can be used to progress through the table in the reverse sequence; this method readily shows how the increment register and the comparand register can be one and the same. A third method can be devised to use a positive increment while also combining increment and comparand registers.

The first method, perhaps the most straightforward, involves a positive increment and a separate comparand register. In this example register 7 is used as the summation register, register 3 as the index, register 4 as the increment, and register 5 as the comparand. The various registers must be properly initialized to

```
LOCATION OP.    OPERAND          ... COMMENTS          ...
         .      .        .
         .      .        .
         LA     7,0                   CLEAR SUMMATION REGISTER
         LA     3,0                   SET INDEX TO ZERO
         LA     4,4                   SET INCREMENT TO 4
         LA     5,196                 SET COMPARAND TO 196
LOOP     A      7,X(3)                ADD X(I) TO SUM
         BXLE   3,4,LOOP              BRANCH ON INDEX TO LOOP
         .      .        .
         .      .        .
X        DS     50F                   RESERVE 50 FULL WORDS
         .      .        .
```

FIGURE 6.5   Example of BXLE with Separate Comparand

their respective values before the loop is entered. The loop then reduces to the one add instruction and the BXLE instruction.

The information in Table 6.4 provides an analysis of the contents of the index register and the second operand address for the addition operation for each of the first three and last three passes through the loop of Figure 6.5.

The following rule can be stated for determining the initial values for the index, increment, and comparand registers. The index is set to zero. The increment is set to the size of each element in the table being indexed. In this case, the element size is four bytes. The comparand should be set to the total length of the table minus one element. Thus, for this problem, the table size of 200 bytes less four bytes yields 196 bytes.

TABLE 6.4   Program Analysis for Figure 6.5

Pass	Index Value	Operand Address
1	0	X
2	4	X+4
3	8	X+8
.	.	.
.	.	.
48	188	X+188
49	192	X+192
50	196	X+196

The method of using a negative increment with a reverse sequence is shown in Figure 6.6. In this method, the increment and comparand both are set to −4 in register 5. The index initially is equal to 196. The BXH instruction is used for control.

```
LOCATION  OP.    OPERAND        ...  COMMENTS          ...
    .      .        .
    .      .        .
          LA     7,0                 CLEAR SUMMATION REGISTER
          LA     3,196               SET INDEX TO 196
          L      5,INCRMENT          SET INCRMT & CMPRND TO -4
LOOP      A      7,X(3)              ADD X(I) TO SUM
          BXH    3,5,LOOP            BRANCH ON INDEX TO LOOP
    .      .        .
    .      .        .
INCRMENT  DC     F'-4'               CONSTANT -4
X         DS     50F                 RESERVE 50 FULL WORDS
    .      .        .
```

FIGURE 6.6   Example of BXH

The progression of index values and operand addresses for the first and last three passes through the loop is shown in Table 6.5.

TABLE 6.5   Program Analysis for Figure 6.6

Pass	Index Value	Operand Address
1	196	X+196
2	192	X+192
3	188	X+188
.	.	.
.	.	.
.	.	.
48	8	X+8
49	4	X+4
50	0	X

In order to increment in the positive direction and still combine increment and comparand functions, the basic reference to the table by the add instruction must be suitably modified. The program segment shown in Figure 6.7 illustrates this case. Here, the index is initially set to −192. Thus, the reference to X must be adjusted by 192. The increment and comparand are jointly set to 4.

```
LOCATION OP.    OPERAND          ...  COMMENTS         ...
        .           .
        .       .   .
        .       .   .
        LA      7,0                CLEAR SUMMATION REGISTER
        L       3,INDEX            SET INDEX TO -192
        LA      5,4                SET INCRMT & CMPRND TO 4
LOOP    A       7,X+192(3)         ADD X(I) TO SUM
        BXLE    3,5,LOOP           BRANCH ON INDEX TO LOOP
        .       .   .
        .       .   .
INDEX   DC      F'-192'            CONSTANT -192
X       DS      50F                RESERVE 50 FULL WORDS
        .       .   .
```

FIGURE 6.7   Example of BXLE with Combined Increment and Comparand

The progression of index values and operand addresses for this program can be obtained from Table 6.4 if 192 is subtracted from the indicated index values. The operand addresses remain unchanged.

6.6   THE EXECUTE INSTRUCTION

A special instruction is included in System/360, called Execute, which allows the execution of a single instruction outside the sequence of instructions containing the Execute. This operation can be thought of as a branch to the single instruction with an immediate return to the original sequence, unless the external instruction causes a branch. The second operand address of the Execute instruction specifies the address of the subject instruction to be executed out of sequence. The first operand register can be used to *effectively* modify the instruction being executed. The modification is performed by logically ORing (see Definition 8.1) the second byte of the subject instruction with the right-most byte of the first operand register. This is very useful in applications involving variable immediate operands in SI instructions and variable length specifications in SS instructions. A strong justification exists for the Execute instruction in reentrant program applications. This subject is investigated in Chapter 11. The formal definition of the Execute instruction follows.

6.5 Machine Instruction EXECUTE

NAME	SYNTAX	TYPE	CODE
EXECUTE	EX R1,D2(X2,B2)	RX	44

SEMANTICS	CC	INTRPTS
EX: Instruction at C(X2)+C(B2)+D2 is executed modified by RB(R1) *Notes:* RB = rightmost byte, * = CC may be affected by the subject instruction.	*	3456

PROGRAMMING EXERCISE

Program and run a Fortran and assembly-language program combination to add a set of values similar to the one shown in Figure 6.3. Use either the BXH or BXLE approach to controlling the index and looping operation. Use a table of integer values containing a variable number of elements. Add the values within the Fortran program and print the result along with the result obtained by the subroutine. Note that this problem involves one of the methods shown in Figures 6.5 through 6.7 cast in the framework of Figure 6.3. Note in particular that the actual table of values is not within the subroutine itself. The following statements can be used to generate 100 random values.

```
DIMENSION IX(100)
CALL RSEED(500.0)
DO 1 I = 1, 100
1 IX(I) = RNDMF(1000.0)
```

These statements imply the existence of a library subroutine for producing pseudo random numbers. The routine being used here contains two entry points.

The first, called RSEED, supplies a seeding value to the generator. The same seed value yields the same sequence of random numbers. The second entry, called RNDMF, supplies a maximum value on the range of random numbers. The result of RNDMF is a random number between zero and the indicated maximum. Such a pseudo random number generator routine is used as an example at the end of Chapters 10 and 11.

STUDY EXERCISES

1. What is the fundamental operation common to decision making, choosing alternative paths, subroutine linkage, and program loops?
2. Describe in general the four variations of branching in System/360.
3. What are the IAC and the PSW?
4. What is the effect of BALR 7,0?
5. What is the effect of BALR 7,7?
6. What is the effect of BAL 7,0(7)?
7. What is the effect of BCTR 12,0?
8. If register 8 contains zero, what is the effect of BCT 8,LOOP?
9. What is the effect of BC 10,EXIT if the condition code is currently set to 2?
10. What BC mask value is required to test for a *valid* nonzero result after an add operation?
11. What is an extended mnemonic?
12. Revise the programs of Figures 6.5, 6.6, and 6.7 to add a table of 500 half-word integers.

Chapter **seven**
Character Operations

Until now only the basic data representation of binary integers has been discussed. System/360 provides the capability for representing several other types of data. This chapter is primarily concerned with the data type referred to as character or zoned decimal representation. The various machine operations provided within the computer's repertoire pertaining to this data type are also presented. The remaining forms of data called logical, packed decimal, and floating-point and their associated operations are the subjects of Chapters 8, 9, and 10.

Basic to some System/360 operations, particularly input and output, is the character-oriented data representation. Within this mode of interpretation the computer recognizes each eight-bit byte as representing a particular character of a basic set of alphabetic, numeric, and special characters. Several code-sensitive operations deal with two entirely different standard character sets on a mutually exclusive basis. These two character sets are called the Extended Binary Coded Decimal Interchange Code (EBCDIC) and the United States of America Standard Code for Information Interchange (USASCII). A special bit in the PSW determines which code is currently active.

The packed decimal data representation, which is useful primarily in data processing operations, is introduced in this chapter to complete the discussion of data conversion operations. In packed decimal form, each eight-bit byte of a field is used to represent two decimal digits. Each digit is its four-bit binary equivalent and takes up one-half of a byte. The low-order or rightmost four bits of the field are used to represent the sign of the number. Instructions are provided, in an optional instruction set, for performing arithmetic on these binary-coded decimal numbers; this instruction set is presented in Chapter 9. Instructions are also provided for converting EBCDIC or USASCII codes to packed decimal and vice versa. In addition, instructions are provided for converting packed decimal numbers to binary integers as well as the reverse. All of these conversion operations are discussed in Section 7.4. Generalized code translation applications are discussed in Section 7.5.

7.1   STANDARD CHARACTER CODES

Two standard character sets are provided in System/360 computer systems. These are the EBCDIC and USASCII-8 standard sets; both are eight-bit codes. The set being used by the machine at any given time is determined by the setting of a special bit in the Program Status Word (PSW). Therefore, the two codes are mutually exclusive, and only one character set is active at any given time.

Historically, character codes have gone through several stages of development in recent years. The first code was associated with the first punched-card systems in use at the turn of the century. This code served very adequately until the mid-1950s when a more comprehensive code was required. This, the Binary-Coded Decimal (BCD) code, was used extensively on first- and second-generation equipment. It was a six-bit code, allowing only 64 different characters—the upper case of alphabetic characters, the ten numeric digits, and a few special characters. The designers of third-generation equipment found it necessary to increase the range of characters that could be coded, and so a seven-bit code was devised, called USASCII. IBM also introduced an eight-bit code called EBCDIC. To provide more compatibility, System/360 includes both. Which code is used the most in a given installation depends on its operating environment; however, the EBCDIC code seems to predominate in most systems.

The seven-bit USASCII code is embedded in the eight-bit byte as shown in Figure 7.1. Also shown in this figure is the bit-position numbering system for the eight-bits in all three codes, the EBCDIC, USASCII, and USASCII-8.

		X	X	X	X	X	X	X
USASCII		7	6	5	4	3	2	1
USASCII	7	6	7	5	4	3	2	1
USASCII-8	8	7	6	5	4	3	2	1
EBCDIC	0	1	2	3	4	5	6	7
	X	X	X	X	X	X	X	X

FIGURE 7.1   Bit Sequence for Standard Codes

The character coding for the USASCII–8 code is shown in Appendix 3. The corresponding character coding for EBCDIC is shown in Appendix 2. It can be seen from either chart that all 256 possible codes do not have printable graphics. However, there is an IBM card punch code for each of the 256 EBCDIC code values. Those codes that correspond to characters in the older BCD representations, with only a few exceptions, use the same card punch code that has been in use for many years. Also given in this same chart are the older BCD graphics and seven-track tape codes. All machine-instruction mnemonics are also given for those hex codes that represent machine instructions.

Most input and output devices manufactured by IBM for use with System/360 transmit data to and from the system using the EBCDIC coding conventions. Thus, most input and output information must be converted from and to EBCDIC to and from the desired internal format for processing. The actual input or output operation is discussed in a later chapter. The discussion in this chapter is centered on the manipulation of the data after reading, during processing, and before the writing of the output data.

The name *zoned decimal* is also used to refer to character codes, whether it be in EBCDIC or USASCII–8. For example, the reader's attention is called to the EBCDIC codes for the ten numeric digits and the 26 capital letters. The rightmost four bits of these codes repeat for the four groups of characters: 0–9, A–I, J–R, and S–Z. These low-order four bits are usually called the *digit* or *numeric* part of the character. The left half of the byte, called the *zone,* is different for each of the four groups of characters listed above.

Several machine instructions are provided that cause the movement of characters, zones, or digits among fields of variable length. Field lengths of 1 to 256 bytes can be accommodated. The actual data interpretation or representation is inconsequential to the movement. These operations are presented in Section 7.3.

7.2   PACKED DECIMAL REPRESENTATION

Certain special operations performed by the machine assume a type of data representation called the *packed decimal* form. Here the ten decimal digits are represented by their four-bit binary equivalents. The remaining six values that can be assumed by a four-bit number are used to represent sign codes. These various representations are shown in Figure 7.2. Notice that there are four acceptable codes for the plus sign and two for the negative sign. However, the code for a sign produced by the machine during an arithmetic operation depends on the currently active character set indicated by the PSW. These particular sign codes are called the preferred codes under the EBCDIC or USASCII–8 character sets.

DIGITS		SIGNS		PREFERRED	
Binary	Digit	Binary	Sign	EBCDIC	USASCII−8
0000	0	1010	+		plus
0001	1	1011	−		minus
0010	2	1100	+	plus	
0011	3	1101	−	minus	
0100	4	1110	+		
0101	5	1111	+	zone	
0110	6	0101			zone
0111	7				
1000	8				
1001	9				

FIGURE 7.2   Digit and Sign Codes in Packed Decimal

In normal operation, packed decimal fields are made up of bytes, each containing two binary-coded decimal digits, except for the rightmost byte which contains the binary-coded sign in the right half of the byte. Instructions are provided in all System/360 machines that convert from the zoned decimal to packed decimal as well as in the opposite direction. Two additional instructions are provided to convert packed decimal numbers into binary integers and vice versa.

Heavy users of data processing applications, those producing a high volume of input and output but low demand on computing, can buy an optional instruction set called the decimal instruction set. These instructions allow arithmetic operations on packed decimal fields without the necessary conversion to binary integer form for computation using the integer operations. The eight instructions provided in this optional set are discussed in Chapter 9.

7.3   CHARACTER-ORIENTED OPERATIONS

System/360 provides a set of five move operations, one SI and four SS instructions. Two additional RX operations to load and store single characters into and from general-purpose registers are also provided. The move instructions allow the programmer to cause data fields of from 1 to 256 bytes to be moved from one point in storage to another. This type of operation is particularly useful in decomposing and composing strings of data for input, output, and intermediate storage purposes.

Each move instruction is formally defined as follows.

7.1 Machine Instructions MOVE -			

NAME	SYNTAX	TYPE	CODE
- IMMEDIATE	MVI D1(B1),I2	SI	92
- CHARACTERS	MVC D1(L,B1),D2(B2)	SS	D2
- NUMERICS	MVN D1(L,B1),D2(B2)	SS	D1
- ZONES	MVZ D1(L,B1),D2(B2)	SS	D3
- WITH OFFSET	MVO D1(L1,B1),D2(L2,B2)	SS	F1

SEMANTICS	CC	INTRPTS
MVI: $I2 \longrightarrow C(C(B1)+D1)$	0	45
MVC: $CL(C(B2)+D2) \longrightarrow CL(C(B1)+D1)$	0	45
MVN: $CNL(C(B2)+D2) \longrightarrow CNL(C(B1)+D1)$	0	45
MVZ: $CZL(C(B2)+D2) \longrightarrow CZL(C(B1)+D1)$	0	45
MVO: $CL2(C(B2)+D2) \ \& \ CN(C(B1)+D1+L1-1)$		
$\longrightarrow CL1(C(B1)+D1)$	0	45
Notes: L = L bytes, N = numeric part,		
Z = zone part.		

The Move Immediate instruction is used where a particular character or eight-bit number between 0 and 255 is to be placed at some given address. Such an operation might be useful for placing a fixed character into a given position in a line of output, for setting control flags, or for other purposes involving a single byte of known data.

The Move Characters instruction provides a means of moving a number of consecutive bytes from one set of storage locations to other locations. Since only one set of data is involved in the transfer, only one length code is required. Since the computer is designed and built in such a way that all length codes in object-code language must always be one less than the actual data lengths, the assembler automatically subtracts one from lengths specified by the programmer. This is true for all length codes in all operations. Thus, an eight-bit length code can specify an actual length between 1 and 256 bytes by object-code values between 0 and 255.

All move operations, except MVO, cause the data fields to be moved one byte at a time, moving from the left to the right in the fields. Since the sending and receiving fields may overlap in any way, interesting effects can be obtained. For example, if a particular field is to be cleared to all EBCDIC blanks, the program segment in Figure 7.3 would accomplish the desired result.

```
LOCATION OP.    OPERAND          ... COMMENTS          ...
    .        .        .
    .        .        .
             MVI     AREA,C' '
             MVC     AREA+1(79),AREA
    .        .        .
    .        .        .
AREA         DS      80C
    .        .        .
    .        .        .
```

FIGURE 7.3   Example of MVI and MVC Instructions

The effect of the program segment in Figure 7.3 is as follows. The MVI instruction stores the hex number 40, the EBCDIC code for a blank, into the first byte of the 80-byte field called AREA. The MVC instruction then essentially causes the blank in the first byte to be propagated throughout the balance of the 80-byte field. The first or leftmost byte of the second operand, the blank, is moved to the leftmost byte of the first operand, the second byte of the field called AREA. Thus, by the time the second byte of the second operand is fetched, a blank has already been stored in that location. Thus a blank is moved throughout the entire 80-byte field, leaving blanks in each byte position.

Several additional points should be made concerning these two operations. The immediate operand in the MVI instruction could be specified in several ways. All of the following statements are equivalent.

MVI	AREA,C' '	CHARACTER FORM
MVI	AREA,X'40'	HEXADECIMAL FORM
MVI	AREA,B'01000000'	BINARY FORM
MVI	AREA,64	DECIMAL FORM

Any of the 256 bit configurations can be specified by any one of these four methods. Even though printable graphics do not exist for most of the EBCDIC codes, a keypunch code does exist for all 256 codes; therefore even the character-form method is applicable. A second point is the address adjustment used in the MVC instruction. The adjustment of +1 causes the first operand to overlap the second operand except for one byte on each end of the field. The length value of 79 shown in parentheses is an actual length. The assembler will subtract one from this value, leaving an object-code length of 78. An actual length of 79 is used, since the MVI fills the first byte of AREA with a blank, and only 79 bytes remain to be filled. Figure 7.4 shows the relationship between the 80-byte field called AREA and the first and second operand fields of the MVC instruction.

A third point is that the actual data moved by these instructions are not inspected by the machine during the movement operation for any special group of codes. Thus, any of the 256 values for a byte can appear within each byte of a

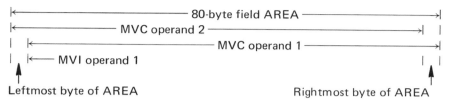

FIGURE 7.4   Diagram of Overlapping Fields

field being moved. A fourth point is that the data within the second operand field are not altered unless overlapping produces an effect similar to the example above.

The MVN and MVZ instructions behave in precisely the same way as the MVC instruction, except MVN moves only the right half of each byte and MVZ moves only the left half of each byte. Otherwise, all of the various points discussed about the MVC apply also to both MVN and MVZ.

The MVO instruction differs from the other move instructions in two ways. First, the bytes are fetched and stored from right to left in the fields rather than from left to right. Second, the right half of the rightmost byte of the first operand field is *effectively* added to the right end of the second operand field before movement starts. The second operand field is then moved to the first operand field, producing an offset action involving a half byte. If $L1 > L2$, the second operand is effectively extended with high-order zeros. If $L1 < L2$, the high-order $L2-L1$ bytes of the second operand are ignored. This instruction is primarily useful in providing a shift operation for the packed decimal data representation for shift counts of odd amounts.

The two RX character-oriented instructions IC and STC are defined as follows.

7.2 RX Machine Instructions for Characters				
NAME	**SYNTAX**		**TYPE**	**CODE**
INSERT CHARACTER	IC	R1,D2(X2,B2)	RX	43
STORE CHARACTER	STC	R1,D2(X2,B2)	RX	42
SEMANTICS			**CC**	**INTRPTS**
IC:	$C(C(X2)+C(B2)+D2) \longrightarrow CRB(R1)$		0	45
STC:	$CRB(R1) \longrightarrow C(C(X2)+C(B2)+D2)$		0	45
Note:	RB = rightmost byte.			

The Insert Character and Store Character instructions cause a single byte to either be loaded into the rightmost byte position of a register from a storage location or stored from the rightmost byte position of a register into a storage location. In both cases the remaining 24 bits of the register are unchanged. No expansion or contraction of data occurs between the register and storage. The operation involves only an eight-bit replacement. These operations are useful for making arithmetic and logical modifications to single characters or for the analysis or synthesis of characters.

Let us consider an example involving character analysis. The problem is one of converting zoned decimal or character codes for the ten decimal digits into binary integer form. Even though a route of conversion is provided by the conversion instruction from the EBCDIC to packed decimal and the conversion instruction from packed decimal to integer, this example is still highly instructive and in some cases might be a preferred method of conversion. The program segment, shown in Figure 7.5, assumes that a string of EBCDIC digit characters exist in a field called DATA. The field is known to be six bytes long, and the decimal number contained therein is right adjusted, is an integer, and has leading zeros if the number is less than 100000. The object is to convert this six-digit decimal number directly from the EBCDIC form to a pure binary integer wholly contained within register 6.

```
·LOCATION OP.    OPERAND          ... COMMENTS          ...
     .          .        .
     .          .        .
              LA      4,0              CLEAR REGISTERS 4
              LR      5,4              AND 5
              LR      6,5              AND 6
              LA      7,6              SET COUNT TO 6
              LA      8,DATA           SET POINTER REGISTER
   LOOP       IC      4,0(8)           PICK UP CHARACTER
              SRDA    4,4              CLEAN OFF
              SRA     4,4              ZONE ON
              SLDA    4,4              CHARACTER
              MH      6,TEN            MPY SUM BY 10
              AR      6,4              ADD NEW DIGIT TO SUM
              LA      8,1(8)           BUMP POINTER
              BCT     7,LOOP           BRANCH ON COUNT TO LOOP
     .          .        .
     .          .        .
   TEN        DC      H'10'            HALFWORD CONSTANT 10
   DATA       DS      6C               SIX BYTE FIELD FOR DATA
     .          .        .
     .          .        .
```

FIGURE 7.5   EBCDIC-to-Binary Conversion

In this EBCDIC-to-binary conversion routine, registers 4 and 5 are used to strip off the zone from the EBCDIC character. Register 6 is used to develop a sum that represents the number after conversion is complete. Register 7 is used as a count register for determining when to terminate the loop. Register 8 is a pointer to the character currently being converted. The Insert Character instruction loads into register 4 the character to be converted next. By shifting the digit portion of the character into register 5, clearing register 4, and shifting the digit back into register 4, the zone is stripped from the character, leaving only the digit. The routine then takes advantage of the fact that this partial result is the binary equivalent of the EBCDIC digit character. At this point, in actual practice, a test should be made to determine if the digit is actually less than ten. Also, the zone should be checked for the hex value F. These extra checks will be added in a later example, after more instructions have been introduced. The next step is to multiply the sum, representing the digits so far converted, by ten and then add the new digit just obtained. The pointer register is then bumped by one and the branch to LOOP is taken if the count is still greater than zero. If the initial contents of the DATA field appeared as

$$F0F0F3F8F2F5$$

in hex, representing the decimal number 003825 in EBCDIC character codes, the final result left in register 6 by the routine would be the binary equivalent of the decimal number 3825.

7.4   CONVERSION INSTRUCTIONS

Four instructions are included within the standard instruction set of System/360 for the express purpose of converting one data representation to another. Two additional instructions provide code-conversion capability in generalized translation applications. The PACK instruction converts a zoned decimal field to a packed decimal field. The UNPK instruction converts a packed decimal field to a zoned decimal field. Data are not checked for valid decimal or sign codes during packing or unpacking operations. The Convert to Binary instruction causes a packed decimal field to be converted to a binary integer and placed in a general-purpose register. The Convert to Decimal instruction causes a binary integer in a general-purpose register to be converted to a packed decimal number and placed in storage. If, during converting from decimal to binary, an invalid decimal code is encountered, a data interrupt occurs. If the decimal number is too large to be contained by a 32-bit register, a fixed-point divide interrupt occurs.

The formal definitions for the packing and unpacking operations are as follows.

7.3 Machine Instructions PACK and UNPACK

NAME	SYNTAX	TYPE	CODE
PACK	PACK D1(L1,B1),D2(L2,B2)	SS	F2
UNPACK	UNPK D1(L1,B1),D2(L2,B2)	SS	F3

SEMANTICS	CC	INTRPTS
PACK: CL2(C(B2)+D2) IS PACKED		
$\longrightarrow$ CL1(C(B1)+D1)	0	45
UNPK: CL2(C(B2)+D2) IS UNPACKED		
$\longrightarrow$ CL1(C(B1)+D1)	0	45
Note: Li = Li bytes.		

Several additional comments must be made regarding the effect of both the PACK and UNPK instructions. Both instructions ignore the actual contents of the fields being packed or unpacked. Thus, no checking is made for valid zone or digit codes. Both instructions process the fields from right to left. Field overlap may occur. However, each result byte is stored immediately after the necessary operand bytes have been fetched.

In the case of the PACK instruction, the zone of the rightmost byte of the second operand field becomes the sign of the packed decimal number in the first operand field. In other words, the zone and digit of the rightmost byte are interchanged. The remaining zones of the second operand are ignored. If the first operand field is longer than required for the packed number, zeros are used to fill the remaining portion. If the first operand field is too short to contain the packed number, the remaining significant digits of the second operand are ignored. No interrupt occurs under this condition. Except for the rightmost byte of the result field, which is stored immediately upon fetching the byte, two second operand bytes must be fetched for each result byte.

In the case of the UNPK instruction, the sign of the packed decimal operand becomes the zone for the rightmost byte of the result field. Thus, the zone and digit parts of the rightmost byte of the field are again interchanged. All remaining bytes in the result field are automatically supplied with zones equal to 1111 for EBCDIC and 0101 for USASCII−8. If the first operand field is longer than necessary to hold the result, the second operand is effectively extended with zeros. If the first operand field is too short for the result, the remaining significant digits of the second operand are ignored. Again, no interrupt occurs for this condition. After the first operand byte is fetched and stored, two result bytes are stored for each additional byte fetched from the second operand field.

Figure 7.6 indicates how data are converted from packed decimal to zoned decimal. The opposite conversion is obtained by reversing all arrows. EBCDIC coding is assumed. Various letters represent variable binary data and also show the movements of digit and zone parts involved in the conversion.

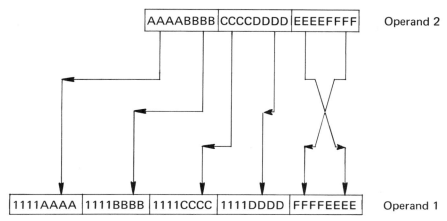

FIGURE 7.6   Illustration of Unpacking Operation

Next we have the formal definitions for the decimal-to-binary and the binary-to-decimal conversion instructions.

7.4 Machine Instructions CONVERT -			
NAME	SYNTAX	TYPE	CODE
- TO BINARY	CVB R1,D2(X2,B2)	RX	4F
- TO DECIMAL	CVD R1,D2(X2,B2)	RX	4E

SEMANTICS	CC	INTRPTS
CVB: CDW(C(X2)+C(B2)+D2) BASE 10		
$\longrightarrow$ C(R1) BASE 2	0	45679
CVD: C(R1) BASE 2		
$\longrightarrow$ CDW(C(X2)+C(B2)+D2) BASE 10	0	456
Note: DW = double word.		

In both the CVB and CVD instructions, the first and second operands are treated as signed right adjusted integers before and after conversion. Also, the second operand in both cases is a double word in storage and must appear on a double-word boundary.

The CVB instruction changes the radix of the second operand from 10 to 2 and places the result in the general-purpose register specified by R1. In the process of conversion, the packed decimal field is checked for valid sign and digit codes. If an invalid code is found, a data interrupt occurs. Since a double word can contain 15 decimal digits plus sign in packed decimal form, it is possible to attempt to convert a number too large to be held by a single 32-bit register. If such an attempt is made, a fixed-point divide interrupt occurs. It is important to note that the binary result is in terms of two's-complement notation. Thus, a positive number is in true form; a negative number is in two's-complement form.

The CVD instruction causes the radix of the first operand to be converted from 2 to 10 and the result to be stored in packed decimal form at the second operand location. Since the double-word field can contain the largest 32-bit binary number, no overflow is possible. The binary-coded sign for the result for EBCDIC coding is 1100 for plus and 1101 for minus. The USASCII−8 sign is 1010 for plus and 1011 for minus.

Let us look at an example of how to use the conversion instructions. The problem is stated in the same way as the example shown in Figure 7.5. A six-character field, called DATA, containing an EBCDIC string of digits is to be converted to a binary integer and left in register 6 as before. The required program segment is shown in Figure 7.7.

```
LOCATION OP.    OPERAND          ...  COMMENTS          ...
     .      .        .
     .      .        .
            PACK  DBLEWORD,DATA        PACK INPUT DATA
            CVB   6,DBLEWORD           CONVERT TO BINARY
     .      .        .
     .      .        .
DBLEWORD DS   D                        RESERVE DOUBLE WORD
DATA     DS   CL6                      6 BYTE INPUT DATA FIELD
     .      .        .
     .      .        .
```

FIGURE 7.7   Application of Conversion Instructions

The PACK instruction causes the EBCDIC contents of the field called DATA to be converted into packed decimal form and stored in the double word called DBLEWORD. The six-digit number is effectively extended with high-order zeros to fill out the eight-byte receiving field. The zone of the rightmost byte in the DATA field, 1111, becomes the sign of the packed decimal number. However, this sign code is acceptable as a representation of the plus sign. Thus, the second operand of the CVB instruction is considered as a signed number and in this case would be positive. If a sign character, outside the six-byte field containing the digits, is to be considered, the sign code of the packed decimal operand should be adjusted for a negative value. The CVB instruction then changes the base of its second operand from ten to two, and the result is loaded into register 6. If the number is negative, the two's complement would be computed. Thus, the desired result is obtained. This method appears quicker than the previous method, but the time required to execute the PACK and CVB instructions on some models of System/360 may actually make the second method slower.

This example also illustrates a feature of the assembler not yet discussed. The PACK operation here is an SS type of instruction in which length codes are required, yet no explicit length-code values are specified in this example for either operand. The lengths of the operands are determined implicitly, in that the assembler obtains the lengths from the statements defining the operand fields themselves. In the case of the first operand, called DBLEWORD, the length is supplied by the standard length attributed to the double-word field being specified by the D type code. Thus, the letter D, used as the operand of the DS assembler instruction, is said to have a length *attribute* of 8. Since the length attribute of the type code C is 1, something extra is required to cause the length of the field called DATA to actually be six bytes. The solution is provided by adding an L6 constant *modifier* to the type code C. This is one of three types of constant modifier, that part of a constant specification which was not defined in Definition 4.4. Notice here that a duplication factor of 6 appearing in front of the type code as 6C is not equivalent to CL6. The case of 6C defines six one-byte character fields, each having an implied length of 1. The use of CL6 defines one character field six bytes in length.

As further illustration of several points, this PACK instruction written in object code with register 12 containing the address of DBLEWORD appears as follows.

$$F275C000C008$$

F2 is the operation code. The 7 indicates that the actual length of the first operand is eight bytes. The actual length of the second operand is six, indicated by the length code 5. Since the address of the first operand is assumed to be wholly within register 12, a base register of C and displacement value of 000 correctly specifies the address of DBLEWORD. Similarly, since DATA is eight bytes higher in storage than DBLEWORD, its address specification is correctly indicated by a base of C and displacement of 008.

7.5   GENERALIZED TRANSLATION OPERATIONS

Two additional instructions are helpful in code conversion or translation applications. These are called the Translate and the Translate and Test operations. The former gives the programmer a means of translating either a standard or nonstandard character coding into a second coding or vice versa. The second instruction is highly useful in applications that involve searching an input character string for the occurrence of one or more specific characters. This latter application occurs frequently in compilers, interpreters, or assemblers where routines are searching for certain delimiters in a string of characters.

The operation of either of these two instructions is based upon a data table constructed by the programmer. The address of the table is specified by the second operand address of each instruction. For each code-conversion application, for example, a table of 256 bytes is constructed, containing the corresponding output codes that represent the 256 possible input codes. Each input code, represented by a byte of information and obtained from the first operand field, is called an *argument* of the translate operation. The value of the argument is added to the address of the beginning of the translate table to yield the address of a *function* byte. The contents of the function byte can then be used as the translated character to replace the original argument. Thus, by proper construction of the table, any eight-bit code can be translated to any other eight-bit code.

Whereas the Translate operation proceeds through the entire first operand field from left to right, translating each argument byte into a function byte that replaces the contents of the first operand field, the Translate and Test instruction operates in a different manner. The Translate and Test fetches argument bytes, adds the table start address, and fetches the function bytes as long as the function-byte value is zero. However, when a nonzero function byte is found, the operation terminates by inserting the last argument address into the rightmost three bytes of register 1 and the contents of the last function byte into the rightmost byte position of register 2. The contents of the first operand field remain unchanged. The condition code is set to indicate three possible results. A setting of zero indicates that all bytes of the first operand field were fetched without finding a nonzero function byte. In this case, the contents of registers 1 and 2 remain unchanged. A condition-code setting of 1 indicates that one or more arguments remained to be fetched when the nonzero function byte was found. Finally, a code setting of 2 indicates that the nonzero function occurred on the final argument byte of the first operand field.

Formal definitions are given in Definition 7.5.

The program segment shown in Figure 7.8 illustrates an application of the Translate instruction. In this example, the contents of the 20-byte field called DATA are being translated using the table called TABLE. This table is constructed in such a way that USASCII−8 upper-case letters, lower-case letters, and decimal digits are translated to their EBCDIC equivalents. All other USASCII−8 codes are replaced by hex 00. A complete USASCII−8 to EBCDIC translation could be accomplished by replacing the USASCII−8 code positions in the table that are zero with their correct EBCDIC equivalents. EBCDIC and USASCII−8 code charts can be found in Appendixes 2 and 3.

7.5   Machine Instructions TRANSLATE -

NAME	SYNTAX	TYPE	CODE
-	TR D1(L,B1),D2(B2)	SS	DC
- AND TEST	TRT D1(L,B1),D2(B2)	SS	DD

SEMANTICS	CC	INTRPTS

TR: $C(C(B2)+D2+C(C(B1)+D1+i))$

         $\longrightarrow C(C(B1)+D1+i)$ where $0 \leqslant i < L$ 0   45

TRT: If $C(C(B2)+D2+C(C(B1)+D1+i)) \neq 0$

         while $0 \leqslant i < L$, terminate and

         $C(B1)+D1+i \longrightarrow CR3B$(reg 1), and

         $C(C(B2)+D2+C(C(B1)+D1+i))$.

         $\longrightarrow CRB$(reg 2)   *   45

Note: * CC = 0 if all function bytes zero,

       CC = 1 if one or more argument bytes

         left after nonzero function,

       CC = 2 if last function byte is

         nonzero. R3B = rightmost 3 bytes.

         RB = rightmost byte.

```
LOCATION OP.    OPERAND          ... COMMENTS          ...
   •      •        •
          TR      DATA,TABLE          TRANSLATE DATA FIELD
   •      •        •
   •      •        •
DATA      DS      CL20                   FIELD TO BE TRANSLATED
TABLE     DC      X'00000000000000000000000000000000'   TABLE
          DC      X'00000000000000000000000000000000'   CONTAINING
          DC      X'00000000000000000000000000000000'   EBCDIC
          DC      X'00000000000000000000000000000000'   CODES
          DC      X'00000000000000000000000000000000'   IN THE
          DC      X'F0F1F2F3F4F5F6F7F8F9000000000000'   USASCII-8
          DC      X'00000000000000000000000000000000'   UPPER
          DC      X'00000000000000000000000000000000'   CASE
          DC      X'00000000000000000000000000000000'   AND
          DC      X'00000000000000000000000000000000'   LOWER
          DC      X'00C1C2C3C4C5C6C7C8C9D1D2D3D4D5D6'   CASE
          DC      X'D7D8D9E2E3E4E5E6E7E8E90000000000'   LETTERS
          DC      X'00000000000000000000000000000000'   AND
          DC      X'00000000000000000000000000000000'   DECIMAL
          DC      X'00818283848586878889919293949596'   DIGIT
          DC      X'979899A2A3A4A5A6A7A8A90000000000'   POSITIONS
```

FIGURE 7.8   Example of Translate Operation

If a field of USASCII–8 characters called INPUT is to be scanned for the first occurrence of a lower-case letter, an upper-case letter, or a decimal digit, the following Translate and Test instruction in conjunction with the TABLE in Figure 7.8 would accomplish the desired result.

TRT   INPUT,TABLE

Provided such characters do appear in the field called INPUT, the address of the first such character would appear in register 1 and the EBCDIC code equivalent, the function byte in this case, would appear in register 2. If the decimal digit codes are made zero in this table, the same instruction could be used to detect the first letter in a string of characters. This application could prove useful in such problems as finding the beginning of a variable in a Fortran expression. Other tables could easily be designed to detect other special groups of characters in a similar way.

It should be pointed out that if the value of the argument bytes used in a Translate or Translate and Test instruction is always less than $N < 255$, the table used by the instruction need not be longer than N bytes. Thus, a table does not always have to be 256 bytes in length.

PROGRAMMING EXERCISE

Reading data in Fortran under a FORMAT field specification of A4 causes the contents of the corresponding four card columns to be placed into storage in EBCDIC form, with each card column filling one byte. A one-dimensional subscripted variable with 20 elements can therefore accommodate an entire 80-column card. Thus,

DIMENSION DATA(20)
READ (5, 1) DATA
1 FORMAT(20A4)

will place 80 EBCDIC characters representing the 80 card columns in 80 consecutive bytes. Passing the name DATA to an assembler subroutine provides access to the address of the first or leftmost byte of the 80-byte field.

Write a Fortran and Assembler program combination as in previous exercises with the following specifications. The Fortran main program is to read all 80 columns of cards and print their contents using the A4 field. The Fortran program is to pass to the assembler subprogram the names of three 20-element arrays. The first array is to contain the 80 characters of the input card upon entry to the subprogram. The subprogram is to fill the second and third arrays with the proper information to represent the EBCDIC equivalent of the hexadecimal zone and digit parts of the original 80 characters. The Fortran program is then to print underneath the 80 input characters the second and third arrays.

Thus, the two-digit hexadecimal code for each input character should appear
under each input character on the output sheet. The following three lines give an
example of how output might look.

```
        THIS MESSAGE CONTAINS 35 CHARACTERS
444444444444444ECCE4DCEECCC4CDDE CCDE4FF4CCCDCCE CDE4444444444444444444
00000000000003892045221750365319520350381913335920000000000000000000000
```

This program could be called an EBCDIC-to-hexadecimal conversion routine.
Punch up several data cards containing letter, digit, and special characters to
exercise the program. These data cards must follow a control card following the
//GO.SYSUDUMP card. The new control card appears as follows.

//GO.SYSIN DD *

Several approaches can be used to solve this problem. All methods involve
the Translate operation, but the contents and size of the translate table differ for
each method. For example, one method involving the move with offset, move
zone, and move digit operations yields a table containing only sixteen bytes.

STUDY EXERCISES

1. What is a standard character code? What standard codes are found in
   System/360? What determines which code is active? What is character data
   representation called? Name the parts of a character-code byte.
2. What are packed decimal numbers and how are they represented within
   System/360?
3. Discuss the five move instructions, showing their differences and similarities.
4. Give a two-instruction program segment that will fill a field of length 40
   with EBCDIC zeros.
5. Using either the IC or STC operation, devise a program segment to reverse
   the sequence of bytes found in a double word. A loop based on BCT will
   prove useful as well as a shift instruction. The leftmost byte may be assumed
   to be less than 128 in magnitude.
6. Assuming DATA in Figure 7.5 does contain EBCDIC codes for the decimal
   digits, devise a different method of stripping the zone from the code than
   that used in the example.
7. Describe the action of the packing and unpacking operations PACK and
   UNPK.
8. Describe the action of the conversion instructions CVB and CVD.
9. Discuss the difference between explicit and implicit lengths of operand
   fields.
10. Describe the action of the two translate operations TR and TRT, showing
    their differences.

Chapter **eight**

Logical Operations

Attention is now focused on fundamental concepts, possibly new to the reader, that are invaluable to the assembly-language programmer. These concepts include Boolean algebra operations such as the logical AND and OR. These operations form the basis of efficient analysis and synthesis of data and program instructions. It is through applications involving the decomposition of existing data and instructions and the generation of new data and instructions that the full value of the stored-program principle is really achieved.

The data representation to be discussed in this chapter is the interpretation of pure unsigned binary information called logical data. Several instructions are provided within System/360 for performing the fundamental logical manipulations on this logical data. These operations include the logical AND, OR, and EXCLUSIVE OR and appear in register-to-register, register-to-storage, storage-immediate, and storage-to-storage forms.

8.1   LOGICAL OPERATIONS

All System/360 logical instructions operate upon data that might best be characterized as having no special representation applied to them at all. Logical data consist merely of a string of binary digits. Furthermore, each digit is totally independent from every other. Logical data are not signed and have no positional notation associated with digit position. Logical data within System/360 can appear as full words or variable-length data between 1 and 256 bytes long.

Logical instructions fall within three major categories: the logical AND, OR, and EXCLUSIVE OR. The first two basic operations are known from Fortran IV use. However, for the sake of completeness, all three are defined here. Since each bit in a logical operand is treated in an independent and identical fashion, each operation is defined in terms of single-bit operands. All three operations are binary operations—that is, requiring two operands.

8.1 Logical operations AND, OR, and EXCLUSIVE OR

Within this text, the logical AND, OR, and EXCLUSIVE OR are represented by the signs &, |, and ✕, respectively.

&	0	1
0	0	0
1	0	1

|	0	1
0	0	1
1	1	1

✕	0	1
0	0	1
1	1	0

Four variations of instructions are provided for each logical operation. These are the RR, RX, SI, and SS instruction types. Therefore, there are twelve different logical instructions in all. These are now defined formally.

8.2 Machine Instructions AND -

NAME	SYNTAX		TYPE	CODE
- REGISTER	NR	R1,R2	RR	14
-	N	R1,D2(X2,B2)	RX	54
- IMMEDIATE	NI	D1(B1),I2	SI	94
- CHARACTERS	NC	D1(L,B1),D2(B2)	SS	D4

SEMANTICS		CC	INTRPTS
NR:	$C(R1)$ & $C(R2) \longrightarrow C(R1)$	*	0
N:	$C(R1)$ & $C(C(X2)+C(B2)+D2) \longrightarrow C(R1)$	*	456
NI:	$C(C(B1)+D1)$ & $I2 \longrightarrow C(C(B1)+D1)$	*	45
NC:	$CL(C(B1)+D1)$ & $CL(C(B2)+D2)$		
	$\longrightarrow CL(C(B1)+D1)$	*	45
Note:	* CC = 0 if result is zero,		
	CC = 1 if result is nonzero.		

The logical AND operations are very useful for analysis of compound data and instructions. Whenever it is desirable to separate such information into its

8.3 Machine Instructions OR -

NAME	SYNTAX		TYPE	CODE
- REGISTER	OR	R1,R2	RR	16
-	O	R1,D2(X2,B2)	RX	56
- IMMEDIATE	OI	D1(B1),I2	SI	96
- CHARACTERS	OC	D1(L,B1),D2(B2)	SS	D6

SEMANTICS	CC	INTRPTS
OR: C(R1) │ C(R2) $\longrightarrow$ C(R1)	*	0
O: C(R1) │ C(C(X2)+C(B2)+D2) $\longrightarrow$ C(R1)	*	456
OI: C(C(B1)+D1) │ I2 $\longrightarrow$ C(C(B1)+D1)	*	45
OC: CL(C(B1)+D1) │ CL(C(B2)+D2)		
$\longrightarrow$ CL(C(B1)+D1)	*	45

Note: * CC = 0 if result is zero,
         CC = 1 if result is nonzero.

8.4 Machine Instructions EXCLUSIVE OR -

NAME	SYNTAX		TYPE	CODE
- REGISTER	XR	R1,R2	RR	17
-	X	R1,D2(X2,B2)	RX	57
- IMMEDIATE	XI	D1(B1),I2	SI	97
- CHARACTERS	XC	D1(L,B1),D2(B2)	SS	D7

SEMANTICS	CC	INTRPTS
XR: C(R1) ⊻ C(R2) $\longrightarrow$ C(R1)	*	0
X: C(R1) ⊻ C(C(X2)+C(B2)+D2) $\longrightarrow$ C(R1)	*	456
XI: C(C(B1)+D1) ⊻ I2 $\longrightarrow$ C(C(B1)+D1)	*	45
XC: CL(C(B1)+D1) ⊻ CL(C(B2)+D2)		
$\longrightarrow$ CL(C(B1)+D1)	*	45

Note: * CC = 0 if result is zero,
         CC = 1 if result is nonzero.

constituent parts, a suitable binary number, called a *mask*, can be found to AND with the data to be separated. A second important use for the AND operation is the ease with which selected bits may be set to zero within a group of bits serving as flags, indicators, or switches without disturbing the other bit settings. Examples of these concepts follow all definitions of this section.

The logical OR operations are very useful for the synthesis of compound data and instructions. After the desired constituent parts of the compound information have been properly arranged for combining, all that is required is to OR the parts together into one composite result. A second important application of the OR instructions is the setting of selected bits within a group of bits to one, without disturbing the remaining bits. This is highly useful in setting flags, indicators, or switches to the on position.

The logical EXCLUSIVE OR is a useful operation for inverting the value of selected bits. Thus, it could be used to change the setting of flags, indicators, or switches from whatever their setting to the opposite setting. This operation is also useful for clearing storage fields, since a value entering an EXCLUSIVE OR with itself results in all zeros. Two fields or registers may be exchanged without a buffer area by performing three EXCLUSIVE OR operations between the two fields or registers as follows. A ⋇ B, B ⋇ A, and A ⋇ B causes the two operands A and B to be interchanged or exchanged.

A set of four logical compare operations are also provided. The comparison operation is carried out in binary from left to right within the two operands being compared. All values are unsigned and can be regarded as absolute-magnitude quantities. An unequal compare occurs when the first corresponding bits in the two operands are found to be unlike during the left-to-right scan. If the first operand has a 0 in this position, the condition code is set to 1,

8.5 Machine Instructions COMPARE LOGICAL -

NAME	SYNTAX		TYPE	CODE
- REGISTER	CLR	R1,R2	RR	15
-	CL	R1,D2(X2,B2)	RX	55
- IMMEDIATE	CLI	D1(B1),I2	SI	95
- CHARACTERS	CLC	D1(L,B1),D2(B2)	SS	D5

SEMANTICS		CC	INTRPTS
CLR:	C(R1) : C(R2)	*	0
CL:	C(R1) : C(C(X2)+C(B2)+D2)	*	456
CLI:	C(C(B1)+D1) : I2	*	45
CLC:	CL(C(B1)+D1) : CL(C(B2)+D2)	*	45

Note: * CC = 0 if operands are equal,
CC = 1 if operand 1 is low,
CC = 2 if operand 1 is high.

indicating the first operand is lower in logical value than the second. If the second operand contains the 0 in this position, the condition code is set to 2, indicating the first operand is higher in logical value than the second. If all bit positions in both operands contain like values, the condition code is set to zero, indicating an equal compare. Condition-code setting 3 never occurs.

The uses of the compare operations are many. However, a few might be listed here. The CLI provides a simple tool for checking for the presence at some location of a particular known character or other eight-bit value that might be serving as a group of flags. There need be no concern for field boundaries for the CLI. The same is true of the CLC, which provides a variable-length field compare. With this instruction, two fields of equal length can be checked for collating sequence, making the application of sorting and collating much easier. For example, two alphabetic data fields containing EBCDIC character data could immediately be tested for alphabetic sequence.

Four logical shifting operations are provided for shifting logical data left and right within single- and double-length general-purpose registers. These operations are unlike the integer shift instructions discussed in Chapter 5, in that here all 32 or 64 bits of the register participate in the shift, since no sign bit is involved in a logical number. Unlike the previous shifts, too, the logical shifts do not effect the condition code. As in previous shifts, only the low-order six bits of the second operand address are used for shift counts, and a base register can also be used to contain an indirect shift count.

One final instruction is presented before we consider some examples of

---

8.6 Machine Instructions Logical SHIFT -

NAME	SYNTAX	TYPE	CODE
- LEFT SINGLE	SLL R1,D2(B2)	RS	89
- LEFT DOUBLE	SLDL R1,D2(B2)	RS	8D
- RIGHT SINGLE	SRL R1,D2(B2)	RS	88
- RIGHT DOUBLE	SRDL R1,D2(B2)	RS	8C

Note: In SLDL and SRDL, R1 must be even.

SEMANTICS	CC	INTRPTS
SLL: C(R1) shifted left C(B2)+D2 places	0	0
SLDL: C(R1&R1+1) shifted left C(B2)+D2 places	0	0
SRL: C(R1) shifted right C(B2)+D2 places	0	0
SRDL: C(R1&R1+1) shifted right C(B2)+D2 places	0	0

Note: In SLDL and SRDL, R1 and R1+1 is an even/odd pair of registers.

NAME	SYNTAX	TYPE	CODE

8.7 Machine Instruction TEST UNDER MASK

NAME	SYNTAX	TYPE	CODE
TEST UNDER MASK	TM D1(B1),I2	SI	91

SEMANTICS	CC	INTRPTS
TM: C(C(B1)+D1) is tested under mask I2	*	45

Note: * CC = 0 if selected bits are all zero,
   CC = 1 if selected bits are mixed,
   CC = 2 does not occur,
   CC = 3 if selected bits are all ones.

logical operations. The Test-Under-Mask instruction is a testing operation that is highly useful in decision making involving one-byte data.

To illustrate one use of the logical AND operation, consider again the example shown in Figure 7.5. The three shifting operations that removed the zone from the EBCDIC characters can be replaced by one AND instruction. At the same time, the Test-Under-Mask instruction is used to verify that the zone is actually 1111. If it is not, a branch is taken to an error routine. A test is also inserted to determine if the digit portion of the character is between zero and nine as it should be. The modified program is shown in Figure 8.1.

```
LOCATION OP.    OPERAND      ...  COMMENTS      ...
        .       .       .
        .       .       .
        LA      4,0               CLEAR REGISTERS 4
        LR      6,4               AND 6
        LA      7,6               SET COUNT TO 6
        LA      8,DATA            SET POINTER REGISTER
LOOP    TM      0(8),X'F0'        TEST ZONE FOR F
        BC      14,ERROR1         IF NOT F, GO TO ERROR1
        IC      4,0(8)            PICK UP CHARACTER
        N       4,MASK            STRIP OFF ZONE
        CH      4,NINE            TEST VALUE OF DIGIT
        BC      2,ERROR2          IF > 9, GO TO ERROR2
        MH      6,TEN             MPY SUM BY 10
        AR      6,4               ADD NEW DIGIT TO SUM
        LA      8,1(8)            BUMP POINTER
        BCT     7,LOOP            BRANCH ON COUNT TO LOOP
        .       .       .
        .       .       .
MASK    DC      F'15'             MASK OF HEX 0000000F
NINE    DC      H'9'              HALFWORD CONSTANT 9
TEN     DC      H'10'             HALFWORD CONSTANT 10
DATA    DS      6C                SIX BYTE FIELD FOR DATA
        .       .       .
        .       .       .
```

FIGURE 8.1   Example of AND and Test-Under-Mask Instructions

If, during the execution of the TM instruction, the operand byte contains 1111 in the left half, then the condition code is set to 3. Any other setting causes a branch at the first BC to ERROR1. The mask of the TM, in binary, is 11110000. Therefore, only the four bits in the left half of the operand of the TM are selected and tested for all zeros, mixed, or all ones.

The full-word mask used in the N instruction contains all zeros except for the rightmost or low-order four bits. This mask in conjunction with the N operation causes the information in the low-order four bit positions of register 4 to be preserved, while setting all other register contents to zero including the sign bit. Notice that this application of the AND operation is one of analysis, or the taking apart, of compound data, which are the zone and digit parts of a character.

As an example of how to use the Compare Logical Immediate instruction, the problem of Figure 7.7 is expanded to include the possibility of a negative number's being involved in the conversion process. It is assumed that an EBCDIC plus (hex 4E) or minus (hex 60) is stored in the byte called SIGN before conversion takes place. Two approaches can be taken in the consideration of this sign; Figures 8.2 and 8.3 show the two techniques. One determines the sign before converting the packed decimal number to a binary integer, the other determines the sign after the CVB operation. The first method also provides an example of how to use the SI form of the logical AND and OR instructions to set the sign of the packed decimal number to minus. The second method utilizes the LCR instruction to change the sign of the binary integer if it is to be negative.

```
LOCATION  OP.    OPERAND           ...  COMMENTS           ...
      .          .        .
      .          .        .
                 PACK   DBLEWORD,DATA        PACK INPUT DATA
                 CLI    SIGN,C'+'            TEST SIGN FOR PLUS
                 BE     PLUS                 IF +, GO TO PLUS
                 NI     DBLEWORD+7,X'F0'     ZERO OUT SIGN CODE
                 OI     DBLEWORD+7,X'0D'     SET SIGN TO MINUS
      PLUS       CVB    6,DBLEWORD           CONVERT TO BINARY
      .          .        .
      .          .        .
      DBLEWORD DS   D                        RESERVE DOUBLE WORD
      SIGN     DS   C                        1 BYTE SIGN FIELD
      DATA     DS   CL6                      6 BYTE INPUT DATA FIELD
      .          .        .
      .          .        .
```

FIGURE 8.2   Example of CLI, NI, and OI Instructions

The program segment in Figure 8.2 uses the CLI instruction to test the contents of the byte called SIGN for the presence of an EBCDIC-coded plus sign. If one is present, the BE instruction causes the machine to skip around the next two instructions. This is possible, since the zone that becomes the sign of the packed decimal number, the 1111, is an acceptable code for a plus sign.

However, if a plus sign is not found in location SIGN, the code stored as the sign of the packed decimal number must be changed. This change is accomplished by a two-step process involving the NI and OI instructions. The NI operation first clears the rightmost four bits of the eighth byte of DBLEWORD to zeros. The OI instruction then sets these same four bits to 1101 in binary, one of the two acceptable codes for a minus sign in the packed decimal representation. Therefore, by the time the CVB instruction is executed, the packed decimal field being converted has the proper sign.

```
         .        .        .
   .          .        .
      .          .        .
         PACK   DBLEWORD,DATA      PACK INPUT DATA
         CVB    6,DBLEWORD         CONVERT TO BINARY
         CLI    SIGN,C'+'          TEST SIGN FOR PLUS
         BE     PLUS               IF +, GO TO PLUS
         LCR    6,6                IF -, CHANGE SIGN
PLUS            .        .
         .         .         .
DBLEWORD DS     D                  RESERVE DOUBLE WORD
SIGN     DS     C                  1 BYTE SIGN FIELD
DATA     DS     CL6                6 BYTE INPUT DATA FIELD
      .          .        .
         .          .        .
```

FIGURE 8.3   An Alternate Approach to Figure 8.2

In the program segment of Figure 8.3, the determination of the correct sign of the binary integer is delayed until after the positive number is completely converted to binary. The code in location SIGN is then tested for a plus sign. If the sign code is not plus, the value in register 6 is complemented, leaving it negative; otherwise the complement operation is skipped, leaving the value positive.

As a final example in this section, we consider an entirely different approach to the problem of analyzing EBCDIC information during conversion from EBCDIC to binary. This approach allows the use of the logical shift and the EXCLUSIVE OR instructions. The initial problem is identical to the one shown in Figures 7.5 and 8.1 except that the field called DATA is reduced to four bytes in length to simplify the program. With a slight increase in complexity the technique could be applied to fields of any length. The new version appears in Figure 8.4. This example is also used to illustrate two new features of the assembler.

The major difference in this example is the method of separating the zone and digit parts of the EBCDIC characters. All four of the initial characters are loaded initially into register 5. Then, using the shift-left double logical operation, the zone of the leftmost character in register 5 is shifted into register 4. The EXCLUSIVE OR operation is then used to verify that the zone is actually 1111. Notice the assembler feature that allows the programmer to specify *literal* data at the point in the program where the data is needed. By preceding any constant

```
LOCATION  OP.    OPERAND          ...  COMMENTS          ...

            .       .                    .
            .       .                    .
            .       .                    .
          LA      4,0                  CLEAR REGISTERS 4
          LR      6,4                  AND 6
          LA      7,4                  SET COUNT TO 4
          L       5,DATA               LOAD 4 BYTES OF DATA
LOOP      SLDL    4,4                  SHIFT ZONE INTO REG 4
          X       4,=F'15'             EX OR WITH 15
          BNZ     ERROR1               IF ≠ 15, GO TO ERROR1
          SLDL    4,4                  SHIFT DIGIT INTO REG 4
          CH      4,=H'9'              TEST VALUE OF DIGIT
          BH      ERROR2               IF > 9, GO TO ERROR2
          MH      6,=H'10'             MPY SUM BY 10
          AR      6,4                  ADD NEW DIGIT TO SUM
          LA      4,0                  CLEAR REGISTER 4
          BCT     7,LOOP               BRANCH ON COUNT TO LOOP

            .       .                    .
            .       .                    .
            .       .                    .
          DS      0F                   ALIGN TO A FULL WORD
DATA      DS      4C                   4 BYTE FIELD FOR DATA
            .       .                    .
            .       .                    .
            .       .                    .
```

FIGURE 8.4   Example of Logical Shift and EXCLUSIVE OR

specification with an equal sign, the constant may be written into the operand position of the instruction that uses the constant. The assembler maintains a list of literals defined by the programmer and inserts them as constants at the end of the user's program. The correct addresses are inserted into the operand address specification of each instruction using a literal. Furthermore, if the programmer uses the same literal more than once, only one constant value is assembled with the program for each unique literal.

If the contents of register 4 are 15 during the execution of the EXCLU-SIVE OR, the results are zero and the branch to ERROR1 does not occur. A second logical shift can immediately follow, since under error-free conditions register 4 is zero. After the shift, the digit part of the character is now in register 4 as in the previous methods. Notice how the second and subsequent characters in register 5 appear at the left end of register 5 for further shifting into register 4 as each loop is executed. Register 4 must be cleared before repeating the loop.

The second new feature of the assembler is the ability to force a field to appear on a particular boundary regardless of what boundary the field would normally occupy. The DS statement containing an operand of 0F only serves to force the next field to begin with a full-word boundary. If the boundary is already satisfied, no additional space is reserved. Notice that in cases such as a double-word constant following a 0F specification an additional full word may be skipped by the assembler.

In general, the programmer can save storage and avoid some problems if all double-word constants are defined first at the end of a program. Following the double-word constants would be full-word constants, followed by half-word constants, and finally followed by character-oriented fields.

PROGRAMMING EXERCISE

Reprogram the problem of Chapter 7, using logical operations to decompose the input data, and reconstitute the output data. The basis of this approach is the simple relationships between the 16 hexadecimal digits and the zone and digit parts of the corresponding EBCDIC characters. The relationships are indicated in the following table.

Hex Digit Value X	EBCDIC Zone	Digit
$0 \leqslant X \leqslant 9$	F	X
$A \leqslant X \leqslant F$	C	X-9

STUDY EXERCISES

1. Perform the logical AND, OR, and EXCLUSIVE OR operations between the binary numbers 1010 and 1100.
2. Discuss the major purposes and effects of the AND operations.
3. Discuss the major purposes and effects of the OR operations.
4. Discuss the major purposes and effects of the EXCLUSIVE OR operations.
5. Assuming that the instruction BC 8,ERROR is located at symbolic location BRNCH, devise a program segment that will change the mask from 8 to 13.
6. Devise a program segment to solve Exercise 5, assuming the original mask value is unknown.
7. What one instruction can be used to set to zero a 200-byte field?
8. Devise a two-instruction program segment to determine if the mask of Exercise 5 is truly 8.
9. Show an instruction that will modify the mask of Exercise 5 in such a way that condition-code settings originally causing a branch will not cause a branch and those settings originally not causing a branch will cause a branch. The instruction must be effective regardless of the original mask value.
10. Write various instructions making use of various literal constants as operands. Use full-word, half-word, and byte operands using constant type codes of F, H, X, B, and C.

Chapter **nine**

Packed Decimal
Operations

For those computer installations found within an environment of significant data processing load, special computing requirements exist. Most data processing applications involve massive amounts of input and output with very simple arithmetic transformations in between. It is very inefficient to convert input data to binary in order to perform a single add or subtract operation only to immediately reconvert the result for output purposes. Designers of System/360 recognized this problem and made special provision for its solution.

An optional instruction subset containing eight operations is available on System/360 computers which allows arithmetic and special editing operations to be performed directly on data stored in the packed decimal representation. These operations are highly useful in contending with problems of high input and output load coupled with low computational demands. Owing to the optional nature of packed decimal arithmetic, the reader may, if he wishes, skip this chapter without hindering his further progress through the text.

9.1   PACKED DECIMAL OPERATIONS

Included within the decimal instruction subset are operations to add, subtract, multiply, and divide packed decimal data. An instruction is also provided for clearing a field to zeros while beginning a summation. A special compare operation is also made available for comparing packed decimal data for the purpose of setting the condition code. Two additional editing instructions provide very useful operations in the application of producing account ledgers, payroll checks, and other jobs involving special characters and the printing of monetary amounts. Shifting of packed decimal numbers is achieved with the Move Characters and Move with Offset instructions discussed in Chapter 7.

The formal definition of the five decimal arithmetic operations follows.

9.1 Machine Instructions DECIMAL -

NAME	SYNTAX	TYPE	CODE
ZERO AND ADD	ZAP D1(L1,B1),D2(L2,B2)	SS	F8
ADD DECIMAL	AP D1(L1,B1),D2(L2,B2)	SS	FA
SUBTRACT DECIMAL	SP D1(L1,B1),D2(L2,B2)	SS	FB
MULTIPLY DECIMAL	MP D1(L1,B1),D2(L2,B2)	SS	FC
DIVIDE DECIMAL	DP D1(L1,B1),D2(L2,B2)	SS	FD

SEMANTICS		CC	INTRPTS
ZAP:	CL2(C(B2)+D2) $\longrightarrow$ CL1(C(B1)+D1)	*	1457A
AP:	CL1(C(B1)+D1) + CL2(C(B2)+D2)		
	$\longrightarrow$ CL1(C(B1)+D1)	*	1457A
SP:	CL1(C(B1)+D1) $-$ CL2(C(B2)+D2)		
	$\longrightarrow$ CL1(C(B1)+D1)	*	1457A
MP:	CL1(C(B1)+D1) $\times$ CL2(C(B2)+D2)		
	$\longrightarrow$ CL1(C(B1)+D1),		
	where $L2 \leqslant 7$ and $L1 > L2$	0	14567
DP:	CL1(C(B1)+D1) / CL2(C(B2)+D2)		
	$\longrightarrow$ CL3(C(B1)+D1),		
	R $\longrightarrow$ CL2(C(B1)+D1+L3),		
	where $L3 = L1 - L2$, $L2 \leqslant 7$, and		
	$L1 > L2$.	0	14567B
Note:	* CC = 0 if result is zero,		
	CC = 1 if result is less than zero,		
	CC = 2 if result is greater than zero,		
	CC = 3 if overflow.		

In all of the decimal arithmetic operations, operands are treated as signed integers and the results are determined by ordinary rules of algebra. A zero result is positive unless a zero is produced during an overflow condition. In this case the sign is the sign of the result had overflow not occurred. In addition and subtraction, the shorter operand is effectively extended with high-order zeros. Overflow occurs when the first operand field is too short to hold all significant digits of the sum or when a carry occurs out of the high-order digit position of the first operand field. Operands in all five operations may overlap only if the low-order or rightmost bytes coincide. This allows values to be doubled by addition, zeroed by subtraction, and squared by multiplication. All five instructions also cause the verification that all data bytes contain either valid digit or sign codes within the digit and sign portions of each data field. If an invalid code is detected, a data interrupt occurs.

In the multiply and divide instructions, the length of the second operand is limited to fifteen digits. Also, since the first operand fields are replaced either by the product or quotient and remainder, the first operand field must be longer than the second operand field. In addition, the first operand in multiplication must have as many high-order zeros as the length of the second operand. If this condition is not satisfied, a data interrupt occurs. This provision guarantees that overflow does not occur during multiplication as in the comparable register operations.

In division, the first operand field is replaced by both the quotient and the remainder. The quotient appears in the left part and the remainder appears in the right part of the field. The length of the remainder is equal to the second operand field, the divisor. Thus, the size of the quotient is equal to the difference of the first and second operand fields, or $L1 - L2$. If the quotient is too large for the result field, a decimal divide interrupt occurs.

A decimal compare is provided for the express purpose of comparing two packed decimal fields. This compare is different from all other compare operations in that the compare moves from right to left taking into consideration sign codes as well as digits. Invalid data detected during a compare operation causes a data interrupt. Fields being compared do not need to be of the same length; the shorter is extended with high-order zeros. Formally, the instruction is defined as follows.

9.2 Machine Instruction DECIMAL COMPARE

NAME	SYNTAX	TYPE	CODE
DECIMAL COMPARE	CP D1(L1,B1),D2(L2,B2)	SS	F9

SEMANTICS	CC	INTRPTS
CP: CL1(C(B1)+D1) : CL2(C(B2)+D2)	*	1457

Note: * CC = 0 if operands are equal,
          CC = 1 if operand 1 is low,
          CC = 2 if operand 1 is high.

As an example of packed decimal arithmetic operations, the following problem is presented. A file of data cards representing deposits and withdrawals made to and from checking accounts of a banking organization are to be processed. Contents of the cards are as shown in Figure 9.1.

Card Columns	Contents
1–8	Account number
9–14	Transaction date (month, day, year)
15–24	Check amount or blank
25–34	Deposit amount or blank
35–50	Account balance before transaction
51–66*	Account balance after transaction
67–68*	Overdraft indicator (letters OD)

*Values to be supplied by the processing program

FIGURE 9.1   Data Card Format

The purpose of the processing program shown in Figure 9.2 is to update each account record by subtracting the check amount and adding the deposit amount to the original account balance before the transaction, which appears in card columns 35–50. The original account balance is assumed to be greater than zero. The input card is to be read by a Fortran program as in the exercises of Chapters 7 and 8. The card contents are to be transferred to the assembly-language subprogram by the following call statement:

CALL UPDATE(CARD)

The updated account balance is to be computed and placed in card columns 51–66 within the same input card image. In case the balance is negative, the letters OD (for overdraft) are to be inserted into card columns 67 and 68. The Fortran program could then list and/or punch the updated card image. Money values are presented as right-adjusted integers with cents as units. No decimal point is included in the fields. The required subprogram is shown in Figure 9.2.

Several aspects of this program may need elaboration. Before arithmetic can occur, the three data values from the input card must be converted from zoned decimal to packed decimal representation. In case one or more of the data fields are originally blank, the three OI instructions set the sign of each packed decimal number to plus (hex C). The digits are zero anyway for blank fields. The data is then combined in the following manner:

ACCNT = ACCNT − CHECK + DPSIT

If the result is negative, the letters OD are inserted into card columns 67 and 68. The result is unpacked into card columns 51 through 66. Since the sign of a packed decimal number after decimal arithmetic is either a hex C or D, the zone of column 66 must be set to hex F to obtain a digit character. Notice that all

```
LOCATION  OP.    OPERAND          ...  COMMENTS          ...

UPDATE    START  0                     SET LCTN CNTR TO 0
          USING  ::,15                 DEFINE BASE REGISTER
          L      1,0(1)                PICKUP CARD ADDRESS
          PACK   ACCNT,34(16,1)        PACK ACCOUNT BALANCE
          PACK   CHECK,14(10,1)        PACK CHECK AMOUNT
          PACK   DPSIT,24(10,1)        PACK DEPOSIT AMOUNT
          OI     ACCNT+8,X'0C'         SET SIGN TO PLUS
          OI     CHECK+5,X'0C'         ON ALL THREE
          OI     DPSIT+5,X'0C'         FIELDS
          SP     ACCNT,CHECK           SUBTRACT CHECK
          AP     ACCNT,DPSIT           ADD DEPOSIT
          BNM    PLUS                  TEST FOR NOT MINUS
          MVC    66(2,1),OD            SET OVERDRAFT INDICATOR
PLUS      UNPK   50(16,1),ACCNT        UNPACK NEW ACCOUNT
          OI     65(1),X'F0'           SET UNIT DIGIT ZONE
          BR     14
ACCNT     DS     CL9                   9 BYTE ACCNT FIELD
CHECK     DS     CL6                   6 BYTE CHECK FIELD
DPSIT     DS     CL6                   6 BYTE DPSIT FIELD
OD        DC     C'OD'                 LETTERS OD
          END    UPDATE
```

FIGURE 9.2   Example of Decimal Operations

references to fields within the card image have displacements equal to one less than the starting column number. If the contents of register 1 are reduced by one, displacements will equal starting-column numbers, a trick that might yield more reliable programming in complex problems.

9.2   EDITING OPERATIONS

Also included in the decimal instruction set are two operations that are perhaps the most complicated and comprehensive operations provided in the total System/360 repertoire. They are called the EDIT and the EDIT AND MARK instructions. Not only do the operations cause the second operand field to be converted from packed decimal into zoned decimal, but they also provide control over the destination field, the first operand, as to format. This format control includes deletion of leading zeros, filling various portions of the field with a fill character, such as an asterisk in check protection; special sign symbols, such as a credit symbol; comma and decimal-point insertion, and currency-symbol insertion. Control is implemented by placing an editing pattern into the destination field before the EDIT operation. Patterns may contain four types of characters: digit selectors, significance starters, field separators, and message characters. These control characters, in conjunction with a two-state significance indicator maintained by the machine and a set of editing rules, govern the editing process during the execution of the EDIT operations. During this editing process, each character in the pattern is affected in one of three possible ways:

1. It is left unchanged.

2. It is replaced by the zoned representation of a source digit from the second operand field.

3. It is replaced by the first character in the pattern, called the fill character.

Which of the three options chosen is determined by one or more of the following:

1. The type of the pattern character.

2. The state of the significance indicator.

3. The value of the source digit.

A detailed discussion of the various aspects of editing operations follows the formal definition of the instructions.

9.3   Machine Instructions EDIT -

NAME	SYNTAX	TYPE	CODE
EDIT	ED D1(L,B1),D2(B2)	SS	DE
EDIT AND MARK	EDMK D1(L,B1),D2(B2)	SS	DF

SEMANTICS	CC	INTRPTS
ED: $C(C(B2)+D2)$ edited $\longrightarrow CL(C(B1)+D1)$	*	1457
EDMK: $C(C(B2)+D2)$ edited $\longrightarrow CL(C(B1)+D1)$,		
A(1st sig. digit) $\longrightarrow CR3B$(reg 1)	*	1457
Note: * CC = 0 if last source field zero,		
CC = 1 if last source field $<$ zero,		
CC = 2 if last source field $>$ zero.		

As can be seen from the definition, the effects of the EDIT and EDIT AND MARK are identical, except that the latter loads the rightmost 3 bytes of register 1 with the address of the first significant digit encountered during the editing process unless significance is forced, as discussed below. Both instructions can be used to edit a succession of fields as long as the fields appear in successive storage locations. In editing multiple fields, however, some editing control is lost, since certain conditions at the end of the operation apply only to the last field edited.

Pattern characters can be of four types.

1. A *digit selector* is hex 20. This character causes the machine to examine the next source digit and the state of the significance indicator. The effect is summarized in Table 9.1.

2. A *significance starter* is hex 21. This character causes the machine to examine the next source digit and generally turns on the significance indicator. The effect is summarized in Table 9.1.

3. A *field separator* is hex 22. This character is used to separate fields during a multiple-field editing operation. It is always replaced by the fill character and sets the significance indicator off.

4. *Message characters* are usually printable graphic codes that represent characters to be printed or not according to the state of the significance indicator. See Table 9.1. The *fill* character, usually a message character or a blank, is the very first character in the first operand field.

TABLE 9.1   Summary of Editing Process

Conditions for Each Pattern Character				Results Produced	
Character	Significance Indicator	Source Digit	Plus?	Character	Significance Indicator
Digit selector	off	0	*	fill	off
		1−9	no	source	on
		1−9	yes	source	off
	on	0−9	no	source	on
		0−9	yes	source	off
Significance starter	off	0	no	fill	on
		0	yes	fill	off
		1−9	no	source	on
		1−9	yes	source	off
	on	0−9	no	source	on
		0−9	yes	source	off
Field separator	*	†	†	fill	off
Message character	off	†	†	fill	off
	on	†	†	message	on

*Has no effect on result character or new state of indicator.
†Not applicable because source digit not examined.

As indicated in Table 9.1, fourteen possible combinations of pattern character, significance indicator setting, source digit value, and source field sign are taken into consideration for each byte in the destination field during an edit operation. Each of the fourteen possible combinations has a specific effect on the character stored in the destination field and the state of the significance indicator. Thus, for each of the fourteen condition combinations on the left of Table 9.1 a pair of results is given on the right. The following paragraphs discuss these cause-and-effect relationships.

Note first that at the beginning of an edit operation the significance indicator is turned off, and the first or leftmost character in the result field is retained as the fill character. Thus, if the fill character is a printable graphic, it will always be printed in the first character position of the result field. During editing, the machine scans source and result fields from left to right. We shall refer to the particular pattern character or source digit being edited at any one time as the *current* character or digit.

If the current pattern character is the digit-selector character (hex 20), the next source digit is always obtained and examined. If the significance indicator is off and the source digit is zero, the digit-selector character is replaced by the fill character. The indicator remains off. If the indicator is off and the source digit is nonzero, the digit selector is replaced by the zoned version of the source digit, and the indicator is turned on. If the current source byte contains a plus-sign code, the significance indicator is turned off; otherwise it is left on.

If the current pattern character is a digit selector and the significance indicator is on, the digit-selector character is always replaced by the zoned version of the source digit. If the current source byte does not contain a plus-sign code, the significance indicator is left on; otherwise it is turned off.

If the current pattern character is the significance-starter character (hex 21), the next source digit is always obtained and examined. If the significance indicator is off and the source digit is zero, the significance-starter character is replaced by the fill character. If the current source byte does not contain a plus-sign code, the significance indicator is turned on; otherwise it is left off. If the current source digit is nonzero, the significance-starter character is replaced by the zoned version of the source digit. If the current source byte does not contain a plus-sign code, the significance indicator is turned on; otherwise it is left off.

If the current pattern character is a significance-starter character and the significance indicator is on, the significance-starter character is always replaced by the zoned version of the source digit. If the current source byte does not contain a plus-sign code, the significance indicator is left on; otherwise it is turned off.

A field-separator character always is replaced by the fill character and always causes the significance indicator to be reset to the off state. This then allows a subsequent field to be edited under the control of the same edit instruction. However, the condition-code setting and the contents of register 1 no longer reflect the status of the preceding field. No source digit is obtained or examined for this pattern character.

Message characters are always replaced with the fill character if the significance indicator is off. Otherwise, the message character remains in the destination field. No source digit is obtained or examined for this type of character. The significance indicator is unaffected.

Figure 9.3 contains eight sets of examples of edited output. The left column of numbers represents the contents of the source field. Above each set of corresponding output is the pattern being used for that particular column of output. Within each pattern the letters B, D, and S are used to represent respectively a blank, the digit-select, and the significance-starter characters. All other characters in the patterns can be interpreted as message characters.

SOURCE FIELD	PATTERN 1 BDDDDDDD	PATTERN 3 BD,DDD,DDD	PATTERN 5 BDD,DDS.DD	PATTERN 7 *DD,DDS.DDBCR
1234567C	1234567	1,234,567	12,345.67	*12,345.67***
0123456C	123456	123,456	1,234.56	**1,234.56***
0012345C	12345	12,345	123.45	*** 123.45***
0001234C	1234	1,234	12.34	*** *12.34***
0000123C	123	123	1.23	*** **1.23***
0000012C	12	12	.12	*** ***.12***
0000001C	1	1	.01	*** ***.01***
0000000C			.00	*** ***.00***
0001234D	1234	1,234	12.34	*** *12.34*CR

	PATTERN 2 *DDDDDDD	PATTERN 4 BDD,DDD.DD	PATTERN 6 BDD,DDS.DDBCR	PATTERN 8 BDD,DDS.DDBCR
1234567C	*1234567	12,345.67	12,345.67	$12,345.67
0123456C	**123456	1,234.56	1,234.56	$1,234.56
0012345C	***12345	123.45	123.45	$123.45
0001234C	****1234	12.34	12.34	$12.34
0000123C	*****123	1.23	1.23	$1.23
0000012C	******12	12	.12	$.12
0000001C	*******1	1	.01	$.01
0000000C	********		.00	$.00
0001234D	****1234	12.34	12.34 CR	$12.34 CR

FIGURE 9.3   Examples of Edited Output

All of the examples in Figure 9.3 should be self-explanatory except for the output under pattern 8. The dollar sign ($) in the output is not generated by the edit operation. By use of the EDIT AND MARK instruction and two additional operations, the dollar sign can be inserted after the edit operation is complete. As the definition of the EDIT AND MARK indicates, the address of the first significant digit is inserted into register 1, unless significance is forced by the significance-starter character. Under these conditions register 1 is unchanged. To avoid this difficulty, the programmer should load the address of the significance-starter character plus one into register 1 before executing the EDMK operation. The program segment in Figure 9.4 could be used to produce the results shown in pattern 8.

```
LOCATION  OP.    OPERAND          ...  COMMENTS          ...
    .        .       .
    .        .       .
           LA      1,OUTPUT+7            LOAD REG 1 WITH A(SIG.ST)+1
           EDMK    OUTPUT,INPUT          PERFORM EDIT AND MARK
           BCTR    1,0                   SUBTRACT ONE FROM REG 1
           MVI     0(1),C'$'             INSERT DOLLAR SIGN
    .        .       .
    .        .       .
OUTPUT     DC      XL13'4020206B2020214B202040C3D9'
INPUT      DS      PL4
    .        .       .
    .        .       .
```

FIGURE 9.4   Using EDMK for Floating $ Sign

PROGRAMMING EXERCISE

The problem discussed in this chapter involving checking accounts of a banking organization is to be extended in the following way. Assume that all input data have been presorted on account number. All cards for a particular account will thus be within a single group of consecutive cards. Besides updating each input card, the subroutine, upon detecting a break in account number (two successive input cards with different account numbers), called a control break, is to produce a final summary of the transaction for each account. Two additional arguments should be added to the Fortran CALL statement for this purpose as follows:

CALL UPDATE(CARD, TOTALS, IFLAG)

TOTALS is an array similar to CARD in which the summary information is to be returned. IFLAG is a single unsubscripted variable, which is to be set to zero by the subroutine except when TOTALS contains actual summary data, in which case IFLAG should be set to a nonzero value. The content and format of TOTALS should be as follows:

Card Columns	Contents
1–8	Account number
9–14	Date of last transaction (month, day, year)
15–20	Number of checks posted
21–26	Number of deposits posted
27–46	Balance prior to all transactions
47–66	Balance after all transactions
67–68	Overdraft indicator (letters OD)

Cards within each account group may be assumed to be sorted also by date of transaction. If this assumption is not made, the problem of determining the last date of transaction and the balance prior to all transactions is somewhat more difficult. The Fortran program, upon finding IFLAG nonzero, can print and/or punch the contents of TOTALS. The EDIT or EDIT AND MARK instructions should be used to insert decimal points, dollar signs, and the overdraft indication into the two monetary fields. No overdraft is needed for the previous balance, as it can be assumed to be a positive value. A card will be needed at the end of the data deck, such as a blank card, to close out the last account group. Some storage will need to be set aside as buffer areas to allow overlap of data while processing the control break. Two fields can be interchanged without a buffer, using the EXCLUSIVE OR instruction discussed in Chapter 8.

STUDY EXERCISES

1. List all of the binary codes for decimal digits and signs used in the packed decimal mode of operation. What determines which signs are used by the machine?
2. Show in hexadecimal how the following decimal numbers would appear in four-byte packed decimal fields assuming EBCDIC coding is active. 725, 39572, −5143, and 1234567.
3. Explain the need for special instructions for decimal arithmetic.
4. How is it possible to obtain an interrupt code of 1 when using a decimal operation?
5. How are the quotient and remainder oriented in the result field of decimal divide?
6. Why must a separate decimal-compare operation be provided? Why is it that the compare logical characters instruction can not be used instead?
7. Discuss the behavior of the EDIT operation.
8. What is a primary use for the fill character in the editing operation?
9. What is the difference between EDIT and EDIT AND MARK?
10. Show the appearance of the four packed decimal numbers of Exercise 2 after being edited into eight fields containing patterns like those in Figure 9.3.

Chapter **ten**

Floating-Point
Arithmetic Operations

Many problems solved with modern computers could not be easily done without floating-point arithmetic. The magnitude range of numbers involved in such problems far exceeds the range of either the integer or decimal representations within System/360. The floating-point representation provides for a number range from approximately 5.4×10^{-79} through 7.2×10^{75}. Negative values are also allowed, ranging from -7.2×10^{75} through -5.4×10^{-79}. The value of zero is also included within the range of floating-point numbers. Floating-point arithmetic is used primarily in problems in scientific applications where values vary over very wide ranges.

A unique representation is used for floating-point data within System/360. It is more complicated than other representations in that each floating-point number is made up of three parts: a sign, a magnitude, and an exponent. Thus, as in most modern computers, a form of scientific notation and its associated arithmetic is provided. This concept is discussed in detail in Section 10.1. As mentioned in Chapter 3, the actual floating-point arithmetic is carried out in a special section of the computer containing four floating-point registers, each 64 bits in length and referred to as floating-point registers 0, 2, 4, and 6. There are also 51 special machine instructions available that deal exclusively with floating-point data in association with the four floating-point registers. As some computer installations operate in environments of low demand for scientific problem solution, the floating-point instruction subset and floating-point registers are obtainable on an optional basis. If the reader is not concerned with floating-point operations, he can skip this chapter, which is not a prerequisite for further progress through the text.

10.1   FLOATING-POINT DATA REPRESENTATION

Floating-point data can appear either as a full word or a double word. Each number of either size contains three parts: a *sign*, a *characteristic*, and a *fraction*. Figure 10.1 designates bits corresponding to these three parts by the letters S, C, and F. The leftmost bit of the number is always the sign of the floating-point value. As in the integer representation, a zero indicates plus while a one indicates minus. The next seven bits in the number (of either size) comprise the *characteristic*, representing the exponent of the floating-point value. This exponent is maintained during floating-point arithmetic in a coded form called *excess 64*. The actual exponent being represented is always 64 less than the value stored within the seven bits. Since a seven-bit number can range from 0 to 127, the excess-64 coded exponent can range from −64 through 63. Thus, the sign of the exponent is indicated by the magnitude of the characteristic relative to 64.

The balance of the floating-point data word is called the *fraction* and represents the magnitude of the floating-point value. In a full-word floating-point number the fraction is 24 bits long, in the double-word version 56 bits long. All floating-point arithmetic is performed as though the radix point appeared immediately to the left of the leftmost fraction bit.

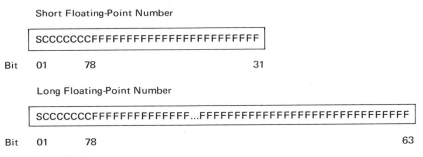

Short Floating-Point Number

```
SCCCCCCCFFFFFFFFFFFFFFFFFFFFFFFF
```

Bit   01   78   31

Long Floating-Point Number

```
SCCCCCCCFFFFFFFFFFFFFFF...FFFFFFFFFFFFFFFFFFFFFFFFFFFFFF
```

Bit   01   78   63

FIGURE 10.1   Full- and Double-Word Floating-Point Numbers

The characteristic, or exponent, of a floating-point number is a power of 16, not 10 or 2. Thus the fraction, although a binary number, can be considered as a hexadecimal fraction to be multiplied by the power of 16 indicated by the characteristic. Therefore, during the process of floating-point arithmetic, various shifting operations involving the fraction must be done in multiples of four bits. If the fraction is shifted left four bits, the characteristic is decreased by one. If the fraction is shifted right four bits, the characteristic is increased by one. The correct magnitude and exponent are therefore maintained for the value being represented.

A floating-point number is said to be *normalized* if the high-order or leftmost hexadecimal digit of the fraction is nonzero. Since a normalized number yields the highest precision or resolution, most floating-point operations are carried out with normalized operands and yield normalized results. However, instructions are provided for performing unnormalized arithmetic for special purposes. If M is the absolute magnitude of a normalized floating-point number, the following relations indicate a more exact measure of the range of such numbers.

$$\text{Short form:} \quad 16^{-65} \leqslant M \leqslant (1 - 16^{-6}) \times 16^{63}$$
$$\text{Long form:} \quad 16^{-65} \leqslant M \leqslant (1 - 16^{-14}) \times 16^{63}$$

In order to provide a better understanding of the composition of a floating-point number, several decimal values are shown in Figure 10.2 with their corresponding floating-point representations. The derivation of each number is also shown. The easiest method of determination is to first convert the decimal number to a hexadecimal number. The hexadecimal number is then written in scientific notation, using base 16 with a pure normalized fraction. The floating-point representation can then be determined by inspection.

Decimal	Hexadecimal	Normalized	Floating-Point Form (Short)
1.0	1.0	0.1×16^1	01000001000100000000000000000000
0.5	0.8	0.8×16^0	01000000100000000000000000000000
12.25	C.4	$0.C4 \times 16^1$	01000001110001000000000000000000
5/256	0.05	0.5×16^{-1}	00111111010100000000000000000000
−19/256	−0.13	-0.13×16^0	11000000000100110000000000000000

FIGURE 10.2   Examples of Specific Floating-Point Values

Floating-point arithmetic is somewhat more complicated than integer or decimal arithmetic. For example, before two floating-point numbers can be added or subtracted, the fraction part of the smaller of the two numbers must be shifted right until the two characteristics are equal. This shift operation is equivalent to the process of aligning the decimal points as one would with pencil and paper. Technically, this operation is called a *preshift* and is performed entirely by the floating-point hardware. No special programming is required. If an instruction is to produce normalized results, a *postshift* may be performed to shift the result in order to make the leftmost fraction digit nonzero. Again, this shifting operation is an automatic function of the floating-point hardware of the machine.

Since decimal points do not need aligning for multiplication or division, a preshift need not occur. However, the operands involved in multiplication or division are always normalized before the operation is performed. No provision is made for doing an unnormalized multiply or divide.

Four types of program interrupt are associated specifically with floating-point operations. These are exponent overflow, exponent underflow, floating-point divide, and significance. The exponent overflow interrupt always occurs if the characteristic attempts to become greater than 127. This interrupt cannot be masked off. Floating-point underflow occurs when the characteristic attempts to go below zero and the PSW bit 38 is one. If PSW bit 38 is zero, the result is forced to a true zero and the interrupt does not occur. A true zero is a floating-point number with zero characteristic and zero fraction. In most cases, the sign of a zero result is positive. A floating-point divide interrupt occurs if an attempt is made to divide by zero. This interrupt cannot be masked off. If significance is lost during floating-point addition or subtraction and PSW bit 39 is set to one, the significance interrupt occurs. If PSW bit 39 is zero and the result fraction is zero, the result is forced to a true zero and no interrupt occurs.

10.2   FLOATING-POINT OPERATIONS

This section presents most of the instructions dealing with floating-point operations. Section 10.3 presents several instructions that were added to the System/360 repertoire at a later date for dealing with extended-precision floating-point data comprised of two double words. Section 10.4 gives a complete example involving floating-point arithmetic and the problem of conversion from fixed- to floating-point representation.

Table 10.1 summarizes condition-code settings. The indicated reference numbers are used throughout this chapter relative to the effect of each instruction on the condition code. As in previous chapters, reference number zero indicates that the code is uneffected by the particular instruction under discussion.

The first set of instructions defined are four RX load and store operations, which provide for loading and storing short and long operands between floating-

TABLE 10.1   Condition-Code Settings for Floating-Point Operations

Reference	Code Settings			
Number	0	1	2	3
0	Unchanged			
1	$R = 0$	$R < 0$	$R > 0$	—
2	$R = 0$	$R < 0$	—	—
3	$R = 0$	—	$R > 0$	—
4	$O1 = O2$	$O1 < O2$	$O1 > O2$	—

Notes: R = result and O = operand.

10.1 Floating-Point RX Loads and Stores

NAME	SYNTAX		TYPE	CODE
LOAD SHORT	LE	R1,D2(X2,B2)	RX	78
LOAD LONG	LD	R1,D2(X2,B2)	RX	68
STORE SHORT	STE	R1,D2(X2,B2)	RX	70
STORE LONG	STD	R1,D2(X2,B2)	RX	60

Note: R1 must be 0, 2, 4, or 6.

SEMANTICS		CC	INTRPTS
LE:	$CF(C(X2)+C(B2)+D2) \longrightarrow CLH(R1)$	0	1456
LD:	$CD(C(X2)+C(B2)+D2) \longrightarrow C(R1)$	0	1456
STE:	$CLH(R1) \longrightarrow CF(C(X2)+C(B2)+D2)$	0	1456
STD:	$C(R1) \longrightarrow CD(C(X2)+C(B2)+D2)$	0	1456

Note: LH = left-half, F = full, D = double.

point registers and main storage. As indicated, indexing capability is provided on all four instructions. As throughout this chapter, symbols R1 and R2 refer to floating-point registers. However, X2 and B2 continue to refer to general-purpose registers as index and base address components.

Ten RR type load instructions are presented in Definition 10.2. Included within this subset are operations that set the condition code while loading, invert signs, and take absolute magnitudes of floating-point values all within floating-point registers. These operations are comparable to those used for integer values in general-purpose registers.

In the addition and subtraction operations (Definitions 10.3–10.6), characteristics or exponents are made equal by a preshift. The fraction of the operand with the smaller characteristic is shifted right until its characteristic is equal to the larger operand. The two fraction parts are then either added or subtracted. In normalized add or subtract, the result fraction may be shifted left in order to normalize the fraction. The result characteristic is adjusted accordingly. In unnormalized add or subtract, the resulting fraction is not shifted left; thus, high-order zeros may remain in the result fraction. In either unnormalized or normalized operations, a carry from the high-order fraction digit causes a right shift in the fraction and a corresponding increase in the characteristic.

Operations involving short operands use only the left half of the register plus one additional guard hexadecimal digit. Thus, seven digits participate in short floating-point arithmetic. Long operands use the entire register plus an additional guard digit, making a total of fifteen-digit accuracy.

10.2 Floating-Point RR Loads - LOAD -

NAME	SYNTAX		TYPE	CODE
REGISTER SHORT	LER	R1,R2	RR	38
REGISTER LONG	LDR	R1,R2	RR	28
AND TEST SHORT	LTER	R1,R2	RR	32
AND TEST LONG	LTDR	R1,R2	RR	22
COMPLEMENT SHORT	LCER	R1,R2	RR	33
COMPLEMENT LONG	LCDR	R1,R2	RR	23
POSITIVE SHORT	LPER	R1,R2	RR	30
POSITIVE LONG	LPDR	R1,R2	RR	20
NEGATIVE SHORT	LNER	R1,R2	RR	31
NEGATIVE LONG	LNDR	R1,R2	RR	21

SEMANTICS	CC	INTRPTS
LER: $CLH(R2) \rightarrow CLH(R1)$	0	16
LDR: $C(R2) \rightarrow C(R1)$	0	16
LTER: $CLH(R2) \rightarrow CLH(R1)$	1	16
LTDR: $C(R2) \rightarrow C(R1)$	1	16
LCER: $-CLH(R2) \rightarrow CLH(R1)$	1	16
LCDR: $-C(R2) \rightarrow C(R1)$	1	16
LPER: $|CLH(R2)| \rightarrow CLH(R1)$	3	16
LPDR: $|C(R2)| \rightarrow C(R1)$	3	16
LNER: $-|CLH(R2)| \rightarrow CLH(R1)$	2	16
LNDR: $-|C(R2)| \rightarrow C(R1)$	2	16

If during the normalization postshift the characteristic underflows, an exponent underflow interrupt occurs if PSW bit number 38 is a one. Otherwise, the result is set to a true zero. No underflow can occur for unnormalized operations.

If the result fraction equals zero, a significance interrupt occurs if PSW bit number 39 is set to one. Otherwise, the result is set to a true zero by making the characteristic and sign also zero.

The sign of the sum or difference is set according to ordinary rules of algebra. The sign of a zero result is always positive.

Four special compare operations are also provided in Definition 10.7 for comparing two floating-point operands. Comparison is algebraic and takes into consideration the sign, fraction, and exponent of the operands. Unequal exponents do not necessarily yield an unequal compare, as the fractions may not be

10.3 Floating-Point Normalized Adds

NAME	SYNTAX		TYPE	CODE
ADD REG SHORT	AER	R1,R2	RR	3A
ADD REG LONG	ADR	R1,R2	RR	2A
ADD SHORT	AE	R1,D2(X2,B2)	RX	7A
ADD LONG	AD	R1,D2(X2,B2)	RX	6A

SEMANTICS		CC	INTRPTS
AER:	CLH(R1) + CLH(R2) $\longrightarrow$ CLH(R1)	1	1 6CDE
ADR:	C(R1) + C(R2) $\longrightarrow$ C(R1)	1	1 6CDE
AE:	CLH(R1) + CF(C(X2)+C(B2)+D2)		
	$\longrightarrow$ CLH(R1)	1	1456CDE
AD:	C(R1) + CD(C(X2)+C(B2)+D2)		
	$\longrightarrow$ C(R1)	1	1456CDE

10.4 Floating-Point Unnormalized Adds

NAME	SYNTAX		TYPE	CODE
ADD REG SHORT	AUR	R1,R2	RR	3E
ADD REG LONG	AWR	R1,R2	RR	2E
ADD SHORT	AU	R1,D2(X2,B2)	RX	7E
ADD LONG	AW	R1,D2(X2,B2)	RX	6E

SEMANTICS		CC	INTRPTS
AUR:	CLH(R1) $\oplus$ CLH(R2) $\longrightarrow$ CLH(R1)	1	1 6C E
AWR:	C(R1) $\oplus$ C(R2) $\longrightarrow$ C(R1)	1	1 6C E
AU:	CLH(R1) $\oplus$ CF(C(X2)+C(B2)+D2)		
	$\longrightarrow$ CLH(R1)	1	1456C E
AW:	C(R1) $\oplus$ CD(C(X2)+C(B2)+D2)		
	$\longrightarrow$ C(R1)	1	1456C E

Note: $\oplus$ denotes unnormalized add.

normalized. An equality is determined by following the rules for floating-point normalized subtract. If the intermediate sum, including the guard digit, is zero, then the operands are said to be equal. Neither operand is changed by the compare operation.

10.5 Floating-Point Normalized Subtracts

NAME	SYNTAX		TYPE	CODE
SUB REG SHORT	SER	R1,R2	RR	3B
SUB REG LONG	SDR	R1,R2	RR	2B
SUBTRACT SHORT	SE	R1,D2(X2,B2)	RX	7B
SUBTRACT LONG	SD	R1,D2(X2,B2)	RX	6B

SEMANTICS		CC	INTRPTS
SER:	$CLH(R1) - CLH(R2) \longrightarrow CLH(R1)$	1 1	6CDE
SDR:	$C(R1) - C(R2) \longrightarrow C(R1)$	1 1	6CDE
SE:	$CLH(R1) - CF(C(X2)+C(B2)+D2)$		
	$\longrightarrow CLH(R1)$	1	1456CDE
SD:	$C(R1) - CD(C(X2)+C(B2)+D2)$		
	$\longrightarrow C(R1)$	1	1456CDE

10.6 Floating-Point Unnormalized Subtracts

NAME	SYNTAX		TYPE	CODE
SUB REG SHORT	SUR	R1,R2	RR	3F
SUB REG LONG	SWR	R1,R2	RR	2F
SUBTRACT SHORT	SU	R1,D2(X2,B2)	RX	7F
SUBTRACT LONG	SW	R1,D2(X2,B2)	RX	6F

SEMANTICS		CC	INTRPTS
SUR:	$CLH(R1) \ominus CLH(R2) \longrightarrow CLH(R1)$	1 1	6C E
SWR:	$C(R1) \ominus C(R2) \longrightarrow C(R1)$	1 1	6C E
SU:	$CLH(R1) \ominus CF(C(X2)+C(B2)+D2)$		
	$\longrightarrow CLH(R1)$	1	1456C E
SW:	$C(R1) \ominus CD(C(X2)+C(B2)+D2)$		
	$\longrightarrow C(R1)$	1	1456C E
Note:	$\ominus$ denotes unnormalized subtract.		

Four instructions are provided in Definition 10.8 for accomplishing multiplications involving floating-point operands. No provision is made for obtaining unnormalized products. Operands are always prenormalized before multiplication, and the resulting product is postnormalized if required.

10.7 Floating-Point Compares

NAME	SYNTAX		TYPE	CODE
COMP REG SHORT	CER	R1,R2	RR	39
COMP REG LONG	CDR	R1,R2	RR	29
COMPARE SHORT	CE	R1,D2(X2,B2)	RX	79
COMPARE LONG	CD	R1,D2(X2,B2)	RX	69

SEMANTICS		CC	INTRPTS
CER:	CLH(R1) : CLH(R2)	4	1 6
CDR:	C(R1) : C(R2)	4	1 6
CE:	CLH(R1) : CF(C(X2)+C(B2)+D2)	4	1456
CD:	C(R1) : CD(C(X2)+C(B2)+D2)	4	1456
Note:	: denotes compare.		

10.8 Floating-Point Multiplies

NAME	SYNTAX		TYPE	CODE
MPY REG SHORT	MER	R1,R2	RR	3C
MPY REG LONG	MDR	R1,R2	RR	2C
MULTIPLY SHORT	ME	R1,D2(X2,B2)	RX	7C
MULTIPLY LONG	MD	R1,D2(X2,B2)	RX	6C

SEMANTICS		CC	INTRPTS
MER:	CLH(R1) $\times$ CLH(R2) $\longrightarrow$ C(R1)	0	1 6CD
MDR:	C(R1) $\times$ C(R2) $\longrightarrow$ C(R1)	0	1 6CD
ME:	CLH(R1) $\times$ CF(C(X2)+C(B2)+D2)		
	$\longrightarrow$ C(R1)	0	1456CD
MD:	C(R1) $\times$ CD(C(X2)+C(B2)+D2)		
	$\longrightarrow$ C(R1)	0	1456CD

The multiplication is carried out by adding characteristics or exponents and multiplying fractions. The sign of the product is determined by ordinary rules of algebra. If the result fraction is zero, the characteristic and sign are also set to zero to produce a true zero. The entire register is used for multiplication of either short or long operands.

10.9 Floating-Point Divides

NAME	SYNTAX		TYPE	CODE
DIVIDE REG SHORT	DER	R1,R2	RR	3D
DIVIDE REG LONG	DDR	R1,R2	RR	2D
DIVIDE SHORT	DE	R1,D2(X2,B2)	RX	7D
DIVIDE LONG	DD	R1,D2(X2,B2)	RX	6D

SEMANTICS		CC	INTRPTS
DER:	CLH(R1) / CLH(R2) $\longrightarrow$ CLH(R1)	0	1 6CDF
DDR:	C(R1) / C(R2) $\longrightarrow$ C(R1)	0	1 6CDF
DE:	CLH(R1) / CF(C(X2)+C(B2)+D2)		
	$\longrightarrow$ CLH(R1)	0	1456CDF
DD:	C(R1) / CD(C(X2)+C(B2)+D2)		
	$\longrightarrow$ C(R1)	0	1456CDF

10.10 Floating-Point Halve

NAME	SYNTAX		TYPE	CODE
HALVE SHORT	HER	R1,R2	RR	34
HALVE LONG	HDR	R1,R2	RR	24

SEMANTICS		CC	INTRPTS
HER:	CLH(R2) / 2.0 $\longrightarrow$ CLH(R1)	0	16D
HDR:	C(R2) / 2.0 $\longrightarrow$ C(R1)	0	16D

Four instructions are provided in Definition 10.9 for performing floating-point division. Again no provision is made for producing unnormalized quotients. Operands are always prenormalized before division. The result never requires normalization by left shifting. A right shift may be needed. No remainder is preserved by the operation.

The division is performed by subtracting characteristics and dividing fractions. The sign of the result is determined by rules of algebra. If the divisor is zero, a floating-point divide interrupt occurs. If the dividend fraction is zero, the sign and characteristic as well as the fraction of the quotient are made zero for a true zero result. No interrupts for exponent overflow or underflow occur in this case. No significance interrupt is ever taken for divide.

Two operations (Definition 10.10) allow a floating-point value to be halved or divided by two. No register-to-storage version exists; both instructions are of the RR type. The operation is performed by shifting the operand fraction right one binary-bit position. The resulting value is then normalized if necessary. If the fraction is or becomes zero, the entire result, including sign and characteristic, is set to zero. Exponent overflow or significance interrupts can never occur.

10.3   EXTENDED-PRECISION AND ROUNDING OPERATIONS

It became apparent to the designers of System/360, after a few months of operation in the field, that the fourteen hexadecimal digits in the long-precision floating-point representation did not offer sufficient accuracy for some problems. Seven additional instructions were designed and implemented to perform addition, subtraction, and multiplication with floating-point data containing 28 hexadecimal digits of accuracy. This type of operand is called an *extended precision* floating-point number and is composed of two standard long-precision floating-point numbers. The two long-precision parts are called the low-order and high-order parts of the extended-precision number.

Operations involving extended-precision data utilize pairs of floating-point registers. Two such pairs are possible; registers 0 and 2 form one pair, registers 4 and 6 a second pair. Thus, a designation of any other pair results in a specification interrupt.

If the high-order part of an extended-precision operand is normalized, the extended operand is normalized. The characteristic of the high-order part is the characteristic of the extended operand. The sign of the high-order part is the sign of the extended operand. The sign and characteristic of the low-order part of extended operands are ignored. In extended-precision results, the sign of the low-order part is set equal to the sign of the high-order part, and the characteristic of the low-order part is set equal to the characteristic of the high-order part less 14. Exponent underflow in the low-order part causes a characteristic 128 greater than its correct value. Exponent underflow for the entire result is indicated only by underflow in the high-order part of the result.

Extending the precision of a long floating-point number can be done by appending a second long-form number whose value is zero. The precision of an extended operand can be reduced to long precision either by truncation or by using a rounding operation provided for the purpose.

Two operations are provided for rounding extended- and long-precision operands down to long- and short-precision operands. Both are RR type instructions. Rounding from long to short precision involves the inspection of bit 32 and the addition, in the absolute sense, of a one to bit 31 of the second operand if indicated. The result replaces the first operand register. The second operand remains unchanged unless both operand registers are the same register. Rounding from extended to long precision involves the inspection of bit 8 of the low-order part and the addition, in the absolute sense, of a one to bit 63 of the high-order part if indicated.

If rounding causes a carry-out of the high-order fraction digit, a right shift is made in the fraction and the characteristic is increased by one. No normalization ever occurs. Exponent underflow and significance interrupts can never occur.

10.11 Floating-Point Load Rounded

NAME	SYNTAX	TYPE	CODE
LOAD ROUNDED -			
LONG TO SHORT	LRER R1,R2	RR	35
Note: R1 and R2 must equal 0, 2, 4, or 6.			
LOAD ROUNDED -			
EXTENDED TO LONG	LRDR R1,R2	RR	25
Note: R1 = 0, 2, 4, or 6. R2 = 0 or 4.			

SEMANTICS	CC	INTRPTS
LRER: C(R2) rounded $\longrightarrow$ CLH(R1)	0	16C
LRDR: C(R2 & R2+2) rounded $\longrightarrow$ C(R1)	0	16C

10.12 Extended-Precision Floating-Point Add, Subtract, and Multiply

NAME	SYNTAX	TYPE	CODE
ADD EXTENDED	AXR R1,R2	RR	36
SUB EXTENDED	SXR R1,R2	RR	37
MPY EXTENDED	MXR R1,R2	RR	26
Note: R1 and R2 must be 0 or 4.			

SEMANTICS	CC	INTRPTS
AXR: C(R1&R1+2) + C(R2&R2+2)		
$\longrightarrow$ C(R1&R1+2)	1	16CDE
SXR: C(R1&R1+2) − C(R2&R2+2)		
$\longrightarrow$ C(R1&R1+2)	1	16CDE
MXR: C(R1&R1+2) × C(R2&R2+2)		
$\longrightarrow$ C(R1&R1+2)	0	16CD

Three instructions, all RR type, are provided in Definition 10.12 for adding, subtracting, and multiplying extended-precision operands to obtain extended-precision results. The procedure and effect of each of the three operations are almost identical to short and long counterpart operations except that all operands and results are in extended precision and involve pairs of floating-point registers. As always, the sign of all results is determined by rules of algebra. All results are normalized. If the result fraction is zero, the entire number is made a true zero. Exponent overflow and underflow may occur for all three operations. Significance interrupts may occur on addition and subtraction only.

Finally, two multiply instructions, one RR and one RX, are provided for multiplying two long-precision operands to obtain one extended-precision result. Comments on procedures and effects of these operations are the same as for prior operations except that operands are long-precision and results are extended-precision floating-point numbers.

10.13 Long- to Extended-Precision Floating-Point Multiplies

NAME	SYNTAX	TYPE	CODE
MULTIPLY LONG TO EXTENDED REG	MXDR R1,R2	RR	27
MULTIPLY LONG TO EXTENDED	MXD R1,D2(X2,B2)	RX	67

Note: R1 must be 0 or 4, R2 is 0, 2, 4, or 6.

SEMANTICS	CC	INTRPTS
MXDR: C(R1) $\times$ C(R2) $\longrightarrow$ C(R1 & R1+2)	0	1 6CD
MXD: C(R1) $\times$ CD(C(X2)+C(B2)+D2)		
$\longrightarrow$ C(R1 & R1+2)	0	1456CD

10.4   AN EXAMPLE USING FLOATING-POINT ARITHMETIC

Figure 10.3 shows an assembly-language subprogram that produces pseudo random numbers similar to those used in the Programming Exercise of Chapter 6. This subprogram is designed to respond to the Fortran function call in the following arithmetic statement:

$$X = RNDMF(XMAX)$$

No provision is given in this example for changing the SEED of the random number sequence. The example at the end of Chapter 11 provides the capability for seed alteration.

LOCATION	OP.	OPERAND	...	COMMENTS	...
RNDMF	START	0		DEFINE ENTRY POINT	
	USING	*,15		DEFINE BASE REGISTER	
	STM	5,7,SAVE		SAVE REG 5 - 7	
	L	5,0(,1)		GET ARGUMENT ADDRESS	
	LE	2,0(,5)		PUT ARGUMENT IN FPR 2	
	L	7,RNDMNMBR		GET LAST RANDOM NMBR	
	M	6,MAGICIAN		MAKE NEW RANDOM NMBR	
	ST	7,RNDMNMBR		SAVE NEW RANDOM NMBR	
	N	7,MASK		ZERO LEFTMOST 8 BITS	
	A	7,CHRCTSTC		SET CHARACTERISTIC 64	
	ST	7,TEMP		STORE TEMPORARILY	
	LE	0,TEMP		LOAD INTO FPR 0	
	MER	0,2		MPY BY MAXIMUM	
	LM	5,7,SAVE		RESTORE REG 5 - 7	
	BR	14		RETURN TO CALLING PGM	
SAVE	DS	3F		GPR SAVE AREA	
RNDMNMBR	DC	X'20000001'		INITIAL RANDOM NMBR	
MAGICIAN	DC	X'0002D403'		MAGIC FACTOR	
MASK	DC	X'00FFFFFF'		MASKING CONSTANT	
CHRCTSTC	DC	X'40000000'		CHARACTERISTIC OF 64	
TEMP	DS	F		TEMPORARY LOCATION	
	END	RNDMF		END OF SUBPROGRAM	

FIGURE 10.3   Pseudo Random Number Generator Subprogram

Let us analyze this routine step by step. The first instruction saves general-purpose registers 5, 6, and 7. The argument address is then loaded into register 5. The actual argument, a floating-point value representing the maximum on the range of the desired result, is loaded into floating-point register 2. The last pseudo random number generated, an integer value, is loaded into general-purpose register 7. This number is then multiplied by a value that yields a new pseudo random value. The multiplying factor is chosen to produce a reasonably random sequence with a low probability of producing a zero. The new value is then returned to location RNDMNMBR. The result is then combined with a mask under the logical AND operation to zero out the high-order 8 bits. A value is then added that inserts a decimal 64 into the relative position of the characteristic of a floating-point value. This result is stored temporarily so that it can be transferred to floating-point register 0. At this point, floating-point registers 0 and 2 are multiplied together, leaving the result in register 0. The original value in register 0 is prenormalized at the beginning of the multiply operation. The final result is then returned to the calling program after general-purpose registers 5, 6, and 7 have been restored.

The secret, if one exists, in the above process lies in the fact that the value transferred to floating-point register 0 is a pseudo random value that lies in the range of 0.0 to 1.0. When this is multiplied by the maximum value, the result is a correspondingly varying number between 0.0 and the maximum value. If the generator is allowed to run long enough, the result either becomes a repeating sequence of numbers or degenerates to zero. The number of nonrepeating nonzero values is one measure of how well the generator works.

PROGRAMMING EXERCISE

Design and write a subprogram to implement a power-series expansion for a function such as e to the x (EXP), sine (SIN), cosine (COS), or other function that is also available in the Fortran library. Expand the series until the ratio between the absolute value of the term and the absolute value of the sum of terms drops below 0.000001. There should be one argument passed to the subprogram, the result being returned in floating-point register 0. By making the entry-point name of your subprogram different from that of the Fortran library routine, comparative results can be obtained with the Fortran supplied function. A Fortran calling program is required to create arguments, call both functions, and print out the results for comparison. Several values of the argument over a wide range should be used for testing. Do not be alarmed if the results do not exactly agree.

STUDY EXERCISES

1. Discuss the appearance of data using the floating-point representation.
2. What is the difference between a normalized and an unnormalized floating-point value?
3. Convert the following values to normalized short-form floating-point numbers and show the results in either binary or hexadecimal: 1.5, 15.75, 201/256, 755/256, −3/16, and 27/4096.
4. What are preshifts and postshifts?
5. What is exponent overflow or underflow?
6. What is the significance of the significance interrupt?
7. Draw comparisons between integer and floating-point instructions.
8. What is a guard digit?
9. What is an extended-precision floating-point number?
10. Some floating-point instructions can cause as many as seven different types of program interrupt. Which instructions are they?

Chapter **eleven**

Status Switching and System Macros

System/360 is designed to operate in several concurrent modes or states of control. The total state of the machine at any one time can be described by four separate substates. Each substate has a set of mutually exclusive alternatives, three of which have only pairs of alternatives. In all of the discussion that follows, the word state is used to mean substate.

One set of mutually exclusive states that describes the current state of the machine is called the Problem/Supervisor state. At any one time, the machine can be in only one of these states. While in the *problem* state, some instructions are invalid and can not be used. While in the *supervisor* state, all instructions are valid.

The second set of mutually exclusive states is called the Wait/Running state. While in the *running* state, instructions are fetched and executed in the normal fashion. While in the *wait* state, no instructions are fetched and executed. However, interruptions may occur in either state.

A third set of mutually exclusive states is called the Stopped/Operating state. While in the *stopped* state, no instructions or interruptions are processed. While in the *operating* state, instructions are executed, if the CPU is not waiting, and interruptions are processed, if their sources are not masked.

The fourth set of mutually exclusive states is called the Masked/Unmasked state. This set of states has several possible states, in that several types of interrupts can be ignored by masking them on an independent basis. While in the *masked* state, certain interrupts either do not occur or they are held pending until the machine state changes to accept the interrupt. While in the *unmasked* state, certain interrupts are accepted as they occur.

This chapter is concerned with the meaning of these various states, how the states change, what the effect of changing states is on the machine, and how the programmer changes and makes use of the various machine states. This study involves the principles of interrupt occurrence and handling. Part of these handling functions are hardware oriented; the rest are a function of software. Several machine instructions are provided for status switching. However, since most of these instructions involve the use of what are called system macro instructions, the concept of macro programming is also discussed in this chapter.

11.1   MACHINE STATES AND THE PROGRAM STATUS WORD

With one exception, all of the states mentioned above are determined by the contents of the current Program Status Word (PSW). The operator initiates the stopped state from the control console by pressing a stop key. Likewise, he initiates the running state from the same console by pressing a start key. There is also a provision for initiating the running state at system start-up time through an Initial Program Load (IPL) key. All other system states are dictated by the setting of particular bits within the PSW. Figure 11.1 contains a diagram of the PSW. The meaning of each part of the PSW is described below.

System Mask	Key	AMWP	Interruption Code

Bit   0   7 8   11 12   15 16   31

ILC	CC	Prog. Mask	Instruction Address

Bit   32–3–4–5 36   39 40   63

FIGURE 11.1   The Program Status Word (PSW)

Bit positions in the PSW are numbered for convenience from left to right with numbers from 0 through 63. We follow this convention throughout the balance of this text.

Bit positions 0–7 of the PSW are called the System Mask. These eight bits are used to indicate whether interrupts associated with input and output channels and other external signals are to be ignored or accepted. When one of these mask bits is zero, the corresponding channel or signal cannot interrupt the central processing unit (CPU). However, the interrupt remains pending until the corresponding mask bit is set to one.

Input and output operations in System/360 are initiated by the CPU under program control by specific instructions. Once started, input and output operations can continue without direct control of the CPU and the program being executed. Thus, computation within the CPU can proceed concurrently with the input or output operations. At the completion of an input or output operation, the particular I/O channel involved causes an input/output interrupt unless the mask bit is set to zero. If an I/O interrupt is masked, no control is lost, since the interrupt is held in suspension until the program is prepared to accept the interrupt. System/360 can support seven I/O channels, but most installations utilize only two or three. The System Mask bits correspond to the channels as shown in Table 11.1.

TABLE 11.1   System Mask-Channel Correspondence

System-Mask Bit	Interruption Source
0	I/O Channel 0 - Multiplexor
1	I/O Channel 1 - Selector[a]
2	I/O Channel 2 - Selector[a]
3	I/O Channel 3 - Selector[a]
4	I/O Channel 4 - Selector[a]
5	I/O Channel 5 - Selector[a]
6	I/O Channel 6 - Selector[a]
7	Timer
7	Interrupt key
7	External signal

[a]May be a multiplexor if desired.

Channel 0, called a multiplexor channel, supports many low-speed input and output devices, such as card readers and punches, printers and terminals. Selector channels, channels 1 through 6, support high-speed input and output devices such as tape drives, disk drives, and magnetic drums.

The timer is a clock that normally decrements 60 units per second and can be set to any value under program control. When it reaches zero, an external interrupt is initiated. This allows the self-timing of program operation with automatic interruption after some fixed length of time determined by the program. The interrupt key located on the operator's console and other external interrupt signals can also be used in special applications.

PSW bits 8 through 11 are called the *protection* key. This key is used in connection with the optional storage-protection feature. If the feature is installed, there is also associated with each block of 2048 bytes of storage an independent *storage* key five bits in length. The values of the *storage* keys may be changed under program control by the supervisor program. During execution of a given program, access to storage can then be controlled by the machine by comparing the *protection* key in the current PSW with the *storage* key associated with the block of storage being used by the program. If the two keys do not match, access can be denied and a protection interrupt initiated. The fifth bit in the key associated with storage is used to distinguish between a store protect only and a combination of store and fetch protect. Fetch protection, an optional variation of the optional protection feature, allows the supervisor program to selectively control fetch access and/or store access by problem programs.

Bit number 12 of the PSW determines the active character code being used by code-sensitive operations. If the bit is set to one, USASCII–8 zones and signs are used. If the bit is set to zero, the EBCDIC zones and signs are used.

The machine-check mask bit is bit number 13. When this bit is set to one, the detection of a machine error causes a machine-check interrupt and allows diagnostic operations to be carried out and possible recovery to be made. If the bit is set to zero, machine-check interrupts are held pending.

Bit number 14 of the PSW is called the wait-state bit. When this bit is one, the CPU is in the wait state and no instructions are fetched or executed. However, interrupts may occur that may change the CPU state. When this bit is zero, the CPU is in the running state and normal instruction execution is occurring.

The problem-state bit, number 15 of the PSW, set to one, indicates that the CPU is operating in the problem mode and certain instructions are unavailable for use. If such an instruction is attempted, a privileged-operation interrupt occurs. If the bit is set to zero, the machine is said to be in the supervisor state and all instructions are valid.

PSW bits 16 through 31 are called the interruption code and are used to identify the exact type of interrupt after an interrupt does occur. A detailed discussion of interrupts, the various types, how they occur, their effects, and the processing of interrupts is presented in the next section.

The Instruction Length Code (ILC) occupies PSW bits 32 and 33. This code indicates the length, in half words, of the last interpreted instruction following a supervisor call interrupt. The code value is unpredictable for all other types of interrupt, including I/O, external, program, and machine-check.

The Condition Code (CC) appears in PSW bit positions 34 and 35. Previous chapters have discussed at length the effect on the condition code of various instructions and how it is used for branching.

PSW bit positions 36 through 39, called the Program Mask, are used for controlling the occurrence of four of the fifteen possible program interruptions that can occur. When a mask bit is one, the interrupt is allowed to occur. When a bit is zero, the interrupt does not occur. The following table identifies the interrupt associated with a given bit position.

Program Mask Bit	Program Interruption
36	Fixed-point overflow
37	Decimal overflow
38	Exponent underflow
39	Significance

The Instruction Address Counter (IAC) occupies bits 40 through 63 of the PSW. This counter contains the address of the next instruction to be executed by the machine. Its contents are increased by the length of each instruction as it is fetched and interpreted in preparation for the next fetch cycle. The contents of the IAC can also be changed by various branch instructions to alter the sequential flow of a program. Since all instructions must appear on a half-word boundary, an odd address in the IAC causes a specification interrupt.

In summary, all pertinent control information concerning a program under execution is contained within the PSW. All machine states, except the stopped state, are determined by the PSW. Therefore, all state changes, except the stopped state, are accomplished by changing the contents of the PSW. The next sections discuss methods and procedures used by the programmer and the machine to change the contents of the PSW.

11.2   THE INTERRUPT SYSTEM

The proper operation of the interrupt system depends on an intimate interaction between a specifically designed hardware subsystem behavior and a set of sophisticated software operating-system routines. Certain functions within the interrupt system are strictly hardware oriented, others strictly software oriented. Successful operation depends on a clear channel of communication between the two separate functions. Central to this requirement is the permanent allocation of certain storage locations for specific uses. All of these locations are at the extreme low end of memory, beginning with address zero. Table 11.2 presents a list of these reserved locations together with their addresses, their lengths, and their purposes.

Five levels or types of interrupt may occur in System/360. These are identified as input/output, machine-check, program, supervisor call, and external interruptions. In order that all five levels can always be distinguished, the procedure followed during an interrupt varies slightly for each level.

If, when an interrupt occurs, the machine is currently executing an instruction, the instruction is either completed, terminated, or suppressed before the interrupt is honored. In any event, the interrupt source must not be masked if the interrupt is to be honored. Thus, if an interrupt condition exists and the source is not masked, at the conclusion of the current instruction the interrupt is

TABLE 11.2   Permanent Storage Allocations

Address	Length	Purpose
0 00000000	Double word	Initial program loading PSW
8 00001000	Double word	Initial program loading CCW1
16 00010000	Double word	Initial program loading CCW2
24 00011000	Double word	External old PSW
32 00100000	Double word	Supervisor old PSW
40 00101000	Double word	Program old PSW
48 00110000	Double word	Machine-check old PSW
56 00111000	Double word	Input/output old PSW
64 01000000	Double word	Channel status word
72 01001000	Word	Channel address word
76 01001100	Word	Unused
80 01010000	Word	Timer
84 01010100	Word	Unused
88 01011000	Double word	External new PSW
96 01100000	Double word	Supervisor call new PSW
104 01101000	Double word	Program new PSW
112 01110000	Double word	Machine-check new PSW
120 01111000	Double word	Input/output new PSW
128 10000000	*	Diagnostic scan-out area

*The size of the diagnostic scan-out area is model dependent.

said to be *taken*. Taking an interrupt is accomplished as a hardware function by causing the current PSW to be stored in the permanently assigned storage location for the *old* PSW associated with the interrupt level causing the interrupt. A code is also stored with the old PSW identifying the specific interrupt condition. The contents of a double word, obtained from the location assigned to the same level for a *new* PSW, are then loaded into control registers, becoming the active PSW. By the introduction of this new PSW, a different program operating under a different machine state can be brought into service through the specification of a new instruction address, condition code, masks, and key. Under normal operating conditions this new program is usually a program module within the operating system written to *service* the interrupt that has just occurred. Thus, servicing an interrupt is performed by a software routine, rather than as a hardware function. Once the interrupt condition has been analyzed and serviced by the interrupt handling routine, either the previous routine or an entirely different one can be reinitiated by the service routine by execution of the LOAD PSW instruction. Since LOAD PSW is a privileged instruction, the interrupt-handler routine must be operating in the supervisor mode.

As a specific example of how the interrupt system operates, consider the following situation. Assume the machine is operating and is in the running state executing a sequence of instructions in the problem state. During the execution of an integer add instruction, an overflow occurs. Bit position 36 of the current PSW contains one. Thus, a fixed-point overflow interrupt occurs. In taking the interrupt, the interrupt hardware causes the current PSW to be stored into the double word at the storage location with decimal address 40, the location reserved for the program old PSW. A value of 8, indicating fixed-point overflow, is stored in the PSW interruption code, bits 16 through 31. The interrupt hardware then loads from decimal address 104, the program new PSW location, the contents of the double word previously stored there, which now becomes the new current PSW. Instruction execution then continues in normal fashion under control of the new PSW. In the process of preparing the machine for proper operation, the operating system will have stored information at location 104 for the specific purpose of servicing program interrupts. The address contained in the Instruction Address Counter part of this new PSW information is the address of the first instruction in an operating-system module that has the prime purpose of analyzing program interrupts. This new PSW-initiated module, by looking at location 40, inspects the old PSW to determine the conditions of the interrupt. Under ordinary conditions, the operating system terminates the offending job, flushes it from execution, and initiates a new job. At the conclusion of interrupt service, the operating system returns control to the new user's program by loading a new PSW with the LOAD PSW instruction, again changing CPU states.

Since interrupts from various sources can occur at the same time, a method of determining which to honor first is needed. Thus, priorities are assigned to the five levels of interrupt. The machine-check interrupt is given first priority. When such an interrupt occurs, the current instruction being executed is terminated and the interrupt is taken if PSW bit number 13 is one. Terminating the current instruction eliminates any possibility of occurrence of a program interrupt. The new PSW loaded at this time has bit 13 set to zero so that no further machine-check interrupts occur while the operating system attempts to recover from the failure. If the System Mask is also set to zero, all other interrupts can be held pending while machine error diagnostic operations are being carried out by the operating system.

The next level of priority is assigned to either a program or supervisor call interrupt. Since the supervisor call interrupt is issued by the problem programmer by executing the supervisor call instruction (SVC), and since no program interrupts can result from this instruction, these two levels of interrupt are mutually exclusive. In other words, a program interrupt can never occur at the same time as a supervisor call interrupt. Thus both types of interrupt have priority two. Normally, when taking one of these interrupts, the new PSW switches the machine state from problem to supervisor mode.

Priority three is assigned to the external interrupt level which includes the timer. The final level of input/output interrupt has priority four.

If several interrupts occur simultaneously, the interrupt hardware stores and fetches a sequence of PSWs until all requests have been honored. The requests are accepted in the priority scheme described above, subject to masking conditions. For example, as indicated above, the machine-check interrupt can be accepted in such a way that no further interrupts can occur. In the absence of a machine-check interrupt, the other three levels of interrupt could cause a sequence of three PSW exchanges. Thus, at the conclusion of the interrupt sequence, the lowest-priority PSW is in control. Therefore, servicing of the interrupts occurs in the reverse order from that in which interrupts are taken. As each interrupt service is concluded, the old PSW for this level can be loaded as the current PSW to initiate service at the higher priority level. Interrupt service order, assuming proper masking, is machine-check, input/output, external, and program or supervisor call.

11.3   INSTRUCTIONS FOR STATUS SWITCHING

Several instructions are provided for switching CPU states. However, only two instructions are available to the problem programmer. These are the Set Program Mask (SPM) and Supervisor Call (SVC) instructions. The first allows the programmer to change the Program Mask, which controls the occurrence of the four maskable program interrupts. The second provides a means for the problem programmer to call for the various services, such as input or output, which are outside the domain of programs operating in the problem state.

Formal definitions are given below for each instruction.

11.1 Machine Instruction SET PROGRAM MASK			
NAME	SYNTAX	TYPE	CODE
SET PROGRAM MASK	SPM R1	RR	04

SEMANTICS	CC	INTRPTS
SPM: C2-7(R1) $\longrightarrow$ CC & Prog. Mask of PSW	*	0
Notes: * CC = bits 2 and 3 of R1,		
C2-7 = contents of bits 2–7.		

11.2 Machine Instruction SUPERVISOR CALL

NAME	SYNTAX	TYPE	CODE
SUPERVISOR CALL	SVC I	RR	0A

SEMANTICS	CC	INTRPTS
SVC I $\longrightarrow$ Interrupt code for old PSW	0	*
Note: * Supervisor Call Interrupt occurs.		

In actual practice the SVC instruction should never be used as a single instruction by a problem programmer. Instead, it is used by means of macros, the subject of the next section.

Of the remaining eight status-switching instructions, all are privileged operations, except TEST AND SET, and must be executed while the CPU is in the supervisor state, otherwise a privileged-operation interrupt results. Four of the eight instructions are standard on all System/360 machines. Three are LOAD PSW, SET SYSTEM MASK, and TEST AND SET. Formal definitions of these three follow.

11.3 Machine Instruction LOAD PSW

NAME	SYNTAX	TYPE	CODE
LOAD PSW	LPSW D1(B1)	SI	82

SEMANTICS	CC	INTRPTS
LPSW: CDW(C(B1)+D1) $\longrightarrow$ PSW except for the interrupt and instruction-length codes	*	2456
Notes: * CC = setting of new PSW, DW = double word.		

Even though the TS instruction is not a privileged instruction, it is useful only in more sophisticated applications encountered by systems programmers. Its primary purpose is for controlled sharing of common storage areas by more than one program. An interlock can be achieved between the two programs, since the setting of the operand byte to all ones occurs in the same storage access as the test for the leftmost bit. Thus, no other program can gain access to the operand byte between the testing and setting operations.

11.4 Machine Instruction SET SYSTEM MASK

NAME	SYNTAX	TYPE	CODE
SET SYSTEM MASK	SSM D1(B1)	SI	80

SEMANTICS	CC	INTRPTS
SSM: C(C(B1)+D1) $\longrightarrow$ System Mask	0	245

11.5 Machine Instruction TEST AND SET

NAME	SYNTAX	TYPE	CODE
TEST AND SET	TS D1(B1)	SI	93

SEMANTICS	CC	INTRPTS
TS: 11111111 $\longrightarrow$ C(C(B1)+D1) after CC is set	*	45

Note: * CC = 0 if leftmost bit = 0,
            CC = 1 if leftmost bit = 1.

11.6 Machine Instructions SET and INSERT STORAGE KEY

NAME	SYNTAX		TYPE	CODE
SET STORAGE KEY	SSK	R1,R2	RR	08
INSERT STOR KEY	ISK	R1,R2	RR	09

SEMANTICS	CC	INTRPTS
SSK: C24-28(R1) $\longrightarrow$ key of block indicated by C8-20(R2), C28-31(R2) must = 0	0	1256
ISK: C24-28(R1) $\longleftarrow$ key of block indicated by C8-20(R2), C28-31(R2) must = 0	0	1256

On machines that have the protection feature installed, the two instructions given in Definition 11.6 are provided for storing and fetching the storage keys associated with each block of 2048 bytes. The instructions are the SET STORAGE KEY and INSERT STORAGE KEY.

In systems involving more than one CPU, a direct read and write feature is available that allows two CPUs to communicate directly. The names of the two associated instructions are READ DIRECT and WRITE DIRECT. Owing to the highly specialized nature of this feature, we shall not discuss it further.

The eighth instruction in the special or privileged category is the DIAG-NOSE instruction. This instruction is provided primarily to help machine and system maintenance engineers locate failing components within the machine.

All System/360 machine instructions have now been discussed or at least mentioned, except for four input and output instructions, which will be discussed in Chapter 12.

11.4   THE CONCEPT OF MACRO PROGRAMMING

Often a programmer is called upon to write the same sequence of instructions repeatedly at several points in a program. The assembler provides a technique by which such a set of instructions can be combined into one new instruction code, called a *macro* instruction. Thus, each time the set of instructions is needed, only the one macro instruction need be written. From a previously entered definition of the macro, the assembler expands the one macro instruction code and operands during the assembly process into the complete and actual sequence of real machine instructions. Macro definitions may be written by the user and used in the same program containing the definitions.

The methods employed by the programmer to define his own macros are the subject of Chapter 15. This section is concerned primarily with a selected few of many *system macros*, those macros that are predefined by systems programmers and provided to the user through a system macro library. Provided the assembler is made aware of this library and the programmer uses the proper mnemonic, the assembler will retrieve the appropriate definition for the macro and replace the macro instruction with its expanded machine-instruction version.

All operating-system services, such as input and output, timer control, interrupt control, job termination, and core management, are obtained by the programmer through the use of specified macro instructions. This approach provides an extra level of error prevention and makes for a much higher reliability in interfacing the user with the operating system. Macros concerning input and output are discussed in Chapters 12 through 14. This chapter presents a few of the most commonly used macros concerned with other aspects of operating-system services.

There are three basic versions of the operating system: the Primary Control Program (PCP), Multiprogramming with a Fixed Number of Tasks (MFT), and Multiprogramming with a Variable Number of Tasks (MVT). Most of the macros to be presented here have slight variations of use between these three operating systems. Each macro discussed in this text is presented in terms of the MFT version; where variations exist, a note is made. To find a discussion of the exact variations as well as a complete listing of all available system macro instructions, the reader is referred to IBM Reference C28-6647.

Macros to be discussed here fall into five general categories of service, including program termination, program linkages, program-interrupt control, timer services, and main storage management. We look first at a sample format for macro definitions.

11.7 Sample Definition for Macro Instructions

The first partition contains the term being defined stated in English. The second partition contains the prototype, or standard form for writing the macro instruction into an assembly-language program. Additional information is given to completely define the syntax involved.

The third partition contains the semantic description of the macro instruction in terms of the effect of the instruction on the operation of the machine and the operating system.

11.5   MACROS FOR PROGRAM TERMINATION

First to be presented is the ABEND macro. This instruction is primarily used to abnormally terminate an assembly language program. However, there is

---

11.8 Macro Instruction ABEND

---

symbol   ABEND   completion code,DUMP

where *symbol* is an optional location reference, the completion code is a decimal number between 0 and 4095, and DUMP is an optional request for a storage dump.

This macro causes the operating system to terminate the program. The completion code is recorded on the output device as a "user completion code" for identification. If a dump is requested, a //SYSABEND or //SYSUDUMP   DD statement must be provided in the JCL of the program in order to obtain a complete dump. If the JCL statement is not included, only an indicative dump of register contents is sent to the output device.

Note: This macro is slightly different for MVT systems.

no reason for not using it for normal termination as well. Provision is made for identifying each ABEND during execution, in case several are to be included in the same program. Thus, different identification numbers, called completion codes, can be used to identify different error or normal terminating conditions, thereby aiding the programmer in checking out and using his program. At the same time, a request may be made for a storage dump for debugging purposes.

As an example of how a macro appears after expansion and replacement by its equivalent sequence of actual machine instructions, Figure 11.2 shows an illustration of the ABEND. The expansion statements of a macro are always identified by plus signs between the statement-number field and the symbolic-location field of the statements making up the expansion. Macro instructions are replaced by their expansions before the actual assembly of the program occurs. Thus, the expansion statements are assembled along with the other ordinary instructions, as if the programmer had written the macro expansion statements himself.

This ABEND macro instruction is replaced by six lines of assembly-language statements taken from the macro library. No object code ever appears on the line with the original macro statement. This particular macro expansion uses the load (L) instruction to load the constant being specified by lines 3 and 4 (statements 8 and 9) of the expansion. Thus, the constant must be placed on a full-word boundary. This is accomplished through the Conditional No-operation (CNOP) instruction appearing on the first line of the expansion. The CNOP forces the assembler to align the next instruction on a full-word boundary by conditionally inserting the half-word BCR instruction with a zero mask. The formal definition of CNOP appears in Definition 11.9. Notice that the location symbol of the macro instruction is repeated on an instruction within the expansion to allow any references to ERROR1 to remain valid.

An unconditional branch instruction is used to branch around the constant being specified by the two DC instructions. These two constants specify the dump option and the completion-code value. Notice how the constants are defined using the Address (A) constant specifications with length modifiers. The first, AL1(128), sets the first byte of the full word to 10000000 in binary, thus making the constant negative. The second, AL3(101), places the completion-code value in the right three bytes, right adjusted, of the full word. Following the constant specification, a load (L) instruction loads into register one the full-word constant for use by the ABEND routine. The final instruction in the expansion, as is true in many macro expansions, is a Supervisor Call (SVC) instruction. This instruction causes the CPU to be interrupted, changing states from the problem mode to the supervisor mode. The operand of the SVC, the value 13, informs the supervisor call interrupt routine that the ABEND operation is being specified. Thus, by looking in register one, the ABEND routine can determine the options chosen by the programmer and can proceed to carry out the indicated operations.

```
LOC  OBJECT CODE  ADDR1 ADDR2  STMT  SOURCE STATEMENT

                                 5 ERROR1   ABEND 101,DUMP
                                 6+         CNOP  0,4
000002 0700                      7+ERROR1   B     *+8 BRANCH AROUND CONSTANT
000004 47F0 500A   0000C         8+         DC    AL1(128) DUMP/STEP CODE
000008 80                        9+         DC    AL3(101) COMPLETION CODE
000009 000065                   10+         L     1,*-4 LOAD CODES INTO REG 1
00000C 5810 5006   00008        11+         SVC   13 LINK TO ABEND ROUTINE
000010 0A0D
```

FIGURE 11.2 Illustration of ABEND Macro Expansion

175

11.9 Extended Mnemonic Machine Instruction Conditional No-operation (CNOP)

CNOP   *b,w*
where *b* is either 0, 2, 4, or 6 and *w* is either 4 or 8.

Causes the assembler to conditionally generate a sequence of 0, 1, 2, or 3 half-word BCR instructions with zero masks. Operand *b* specifies at which byte, on a half-word boundary, in a word or double word, the location counter is to be set. Operand *w* specifies whether byte *b* is in a word or a double word. Table 11.3 gives all valid combinations of *b* and *w*.

The operands of the CNOP instruction may appear in six ways. These six variations and their exact meaning are shown in Table 11.3. The only purpose of the CNOP instruction is to provide boundary alignment in the instruction stream and still produce valid executable code in the area of alignment.

TABLE 11.3   CNOP Instruction Operands

b,w	Specifies
0,4	Beginning of a full word
2,4	Middle of a full word
0,8	Beginning of a double word
2,8	Second half word of a double word
4,8	Middle of a double word
6,8	Fourth half word of a double word

The same ABEND macro is shown in Figure 11.3 without the DUMP request. This time, the macro library produces a different approach for setting up register one with the completion code. Here the code value is loaded into the register as the displacement value in a load address (LA) instruction. The contents of register one remain positive in this case, signifying that no core dump is to be taken. Since a load (L) instruction is not involved in this expansion, the CNOP instruction is not needed.

Most system macros allow a variation in the specification of certain operands, in that a register number may be specified as already containing the operand value before the macro is to be executed. This coding variation is indicated by writing in the operand position a register number enclosed in

```
LOC   OBJECT CODE    ADDR1 ADDR2   STMT   SOURCE STATEMENT

                                   13 ERROR2    ABEND 101
000012 4110 0065             00065 14+ERROR2   LA    1,101(0,0) LOAD PARAMETER REG 1
000016 0A0D                        15+          SVC   13 LINK TO ABEND ROUTINE
```

FIGURE 11.3   ABEND without DUMP Option

```
LOC   OBJECT CODE    ADDR1 ADDR2   STMT   SOURCE STATEMENT

                                   17 ERROR3    ABEND (1)
000018                             18+ERROR3   DS    0H
000018 0A0D                        19+          SVC   13 LINK TO ABEND ROUTINE
```

FIGURE 11.4   ABEND Macro Using Register Variation

parentheses. Thus, if the programmer wishes to indicate that the completion code is already loaded in register one at the time the macro is to be generated, the instruction is written as shown in Figure 11.4. The corresponding expansion is also shown in the figure. Notice that only two statements are produced in the expansion. The first, under normal conditions, causes nothing to happen; it simply provides a statement on which the location symbol may be placed. No storage is skipped, since all instructions are normally on half-word boundaries. If the macro should follow constant specifications, boundary alignment might occur. Under these conditions however, entrance to the macro must be made by branching to the symbolic reference of the macro instruction. The symbolic reference is actually the name of the SVC instruction in this case. Being able to specify a register as the operand allows the programmer to easily change the completion code at execution time.

Figure 11.5 illustrates what occurs to the macro expansion if the statement in Figure 11.4 also specifies the DUMP option. Notice that three new instructions have been added that load 128 into the rightmost byte of register zero, shift left logically 24 places, and logically or register zero with register one, leaving register one negative. Thus, the DUMP option is specified as before.

A register other than register one may be specified as initially containing the completion code. Figure 11.6 illustrates the same macro statement as in Figure 11.4, except that register two is used instead of register one. Notice that a load register (LR) instruction is inserted to copy register two into register one.

Figure 11.7 illustrates the final possible variation of ABEND macro codings. The statement in Figure 11.6 is altered to include the DUMP option. Notice now that the effects of variations in Figures 11.5 and 11.6 are combined into the same expansion.

As these examples demonstrate, registers zero and one are used in various ways by the ABEND macro expansion. This is true of most system macros. Thus, the programmer must remember that the contents of these registers are not protected while system macros are in use. Some system macros also affect registers 13, 14, and 15, as will be seen in the following discussion.

11.6   MACROS FOR SUBPROGRAM LINKAGE

Three macros are provided for specific use in control linkages between subprograms. Two, the SAVE and RETURN macros, are used primarily to save and restore registers at the entry and return points within a called subprogram. The third macro, CALL, is used in a calling program to transfer control to a subprogram. The effect is similar to the results produced by the Fortran CALL statement.

The SAVE and RETURN macros are formally defined on p. 180. Examples appear on pp. 182 and 183.

```
LOC    OBJECT CODE   ADDR1 ADDR2   STMT   SOURCE STATEMENT

                                    21 ERROR4    ABEND (1),DUMP
00001A                              22+ERROR4    DS   0H
00001A 4100 0080         00080      23+          LA   0,128(0,0) PICK UP DUMP/STEP CODE
00001E 8900 0018         00018      24+          SLL  0,24(0) SHIFT TO HIGH BYTE
000022 1610                         25+          OR   1,0 OR IN WITH COMPCODE
000024 0A0D                         26+          SVC  13 LINK TO ABEND ROUTINE
```

FIGURE 11.5   ABEND Macro Using Register Variation with DUMP

```
LOC    OBJECT CODE   ADDR1 ADDR2   STMT   SOURCE STATEMENT

                                    28 ERROR5    ABEND (2)
000026 1812                         29+ERROR5    LR   1,2 LOAD PARAMETER REG 1
000028 0A0D                         30+          SVC  13 LINK TO ABEND ROUTINE
```

FIGURE 11.6   ABEND Using Register Two

```
LOC    OBJECT CODE   ADDR1 ADDR2   STMT   SOURCE STATEMENT

                                    32 ERROR6    ABEND (2),DUMP
00002A 1812                         33+ERROR6    LR   1,2 LOAD PARAMETER REG 1
00002C 4100 0080         00080      34+          LA   0,128(0,0) PICK UP DUMP/STEP CODE
000030 8900 0018         00018      35+          SLL  0,24(0) SHIFT TO HIGH BYTE
000034 1610                         36+          OR   1,0 OR IN WITH COMPCODE
000036 0A0D                         37+          SVC  13 LINK TO ABEND ROUTINE
```

FIGURE 11.7   ABEND Using Register Two with DUMP

11.10 Macro Instruction SAVE

symbol   SAVE   (*reg1*,*reg2*),T,*id name*
where *symbol* is an optional location reference, *reg1* and *reg2* represent the first and last of a sequence of registers (*reg2* is optional), T is an optional code (see below), and the *id name* is an optional sequence of characters with a maximum length of 70.

This macro causes the specified set of registers to be stored in the save area whose address is assumed to be in register 13 upon entry to the save macro. The indicated registers are stored in words 4 through 18 of the save area. If *reg2* is not coded, only the one register indicated by *reg1* is stored. The code T indicates that registers 14 and 15 are to be stored in words 4 and 5 of the save area. If both T and *reg2* are coded, and *reg1* is either 14, 15, 0, 1, or 2, all of registers 14 through *reg2* are stored. If an * is coded in the place of the *id name*, the location symbol of the macro is used as the name. If the name is left blank, the name appearing on the START instruction is used. SAVE must appear at the entry point of the subprogram.

11.11 Macro Instruction RETURN

symbol   RETURN   (*reg1*,*reg2*),T,RC=*n*
where *symbol* is an optional location reference, *reg1* and *reg2* represent the first and last of a sequence of registers (one or both may be omitted), T is an optional code (see below), and RC=*n* is an optional return code with a maximum value of 4095 [may be coded as RC=(15)].

This macro causes registers *reg1* through *reg2* to be restored from the save area pointed to by register 13. If *reg2* is not coded, only the one *reg1* is restored. If neither *reg1* or *reg2* is coded, all registers remain unchanged. The code T may be used to cause a hex FF to be stored in the leftmost byte of word four of the save area, indicating completion of the subprogram. The number supplied for the RC operand is called a return code; if specified, it is loaded right-adjusted in register 15. If RC=(15) is coded, register 15 remains unchanged. Finally, a BR 14 instruction is generated, returning control to the calling program.

11.12 Macro Instruction CALL

symbol   CALL   *sub,(x,y,z,...)*,VL,ID=*n*
where *symbol* is optional, *sub* is an external symbol (see Definition 11.13) [may be coded as (15)], *x,y,z,...* are optional location symbols within the calling program, if arguments are coded, VL may be optionally coded (see below), and an optional ID number less than 65536 may be included.

This macro causes a V type address constant to be created, defining the entry-point name, *sub*, as an external symbol (see Definition 11.13). If (15) is coded instead, the entry-point address must be in register 15 before the macro is executed. The argument reference symbols, *x,y,z,...*, cause an argument-address list to be created, each address requiring a full word. If a list is created, its location is loaded into register 1. If VL is coded, the high-order bit of the last argument-address word is set to one. A BALR 14,15 is then generated. If ID=*n* is coded, a full word containing a NOP instruction with the ID number in the low-order two bytes is generated following the BALR. Thus, register 14 contains the address of this word if it is generated.

Figure 11.8 contains five examples of the SAVE macro statement with five different variations. Notice that the expansion depends on register 15's containing the address of the entry point of the subprogram. Furthermore, for proper operation the entry-point address and the first address of the SAVE macro expansion must coincide. The expansion also depends on register 13's containing the address of the save area provided by the calling program. Notice how the various combinations of registers are specified and the effect caused on the instructions in the expansions.

The RETURN macro is used at the logical end of a subprogram, causing registers to be restored from the save area, optional setting of a return indicator, and optional loading of a return code.

Figure 11.9 contains five variations of RETURN macro statements. Notice that, regardless of the register sequence specified, each register is stored and restored by the SAVE and RETURN macros into and from the same word of the save area. For example, register 5 is always stored in word 11 of the save area.

The CALL macro (Definition 11.12) provides a compact means for linking a calling program with a called subprogram. The statement allows the specifica-

LOC	OBJECT CODE	ADDR1	ADDR2	STMT	SOURCE STATEMENT
				39 ENTRY1	SAVE (14,12),,*
000038	47F0 F00C		0000C	40+ENTRY1	B 12(0,15),, BRANCH AROUND ID
00003C	06			41+	DC AL1(6)
00003D	C5D5E3D9E8F1			42+	DC CL6'ENTRY1' IDENTIFIER
000043	00				
000044	90EC D00C			43+	STM 14,12,12(13) SAVE REGISTERS
				44 ENTRY2	SAVE (14,5),,THISISENTRY2
000048	47F0 F012		00012	45+ENTRY2	B 18(0,15),, BRANCH AROUND ID
00004C	0C			46+	DC AL1(12) LENGTH OF IDENTIFIER
00004D	E3C8C9E2C9E2C5D5			47+	DC CL8'THISISEN' IDENTIFIER
000055	E3D9E8F2			48+	DC CL4'TRY2' IDENTIFIER
000059	00				
00005A	90E5 D00C			49+	STM 14,5,12(13) SAVE REGISTERS
				50 ENTRY3	SAVE (5,10),,*
00005E	47F0 F00C		0000C	51+ENTRY3	B 12(0,15),,* BRANCH AROUND ID
000062	06			52+	DC AL1(6)
000063	C5D5E3D9E8F3			53+	DC CL6'ENTRY3' IDENTIFIER
000069	00				
00006A	905A D028		00028	54+	STM 5,10,40(13) SAVE REGISTERS
				55 ENTRY4	SAVE (5,10),T,*
00006E	47F0 F00C		0000C	56+ENTRY4	B 12(0,15),, BRANCH AROUND ID
000072	06			57+	DC AL1(6)
000073	C5D5E3D9E8F4			58+	DC CL6'ENTRY4' IDENTIFIER
000079	00				
00007A	90EF D00C		0000C	59+	STM 14,15,12(13) SAVE REGISTERS
00007E	905A D028		00028	60+	STM 5,10,40(13) SAVE REGISTERS
				61 ENTRY5	SAVE (5),T,*
000082	47F0 F00C		0000C	62+ENTRY5	B 12(0,15),, BRANCH AROUND ID
000086	06			63+	DC AL1(6)
000087	C5D5E3D9E8F5			64+	DC CL6'ENTRY5' IDENTIFIER
00008D	00				
00008E	90EF D00C		0000C	65+	STM 14,15,12(13) SAVE REGISTERS
000092	505D 0028		00028	66+	ST 5,40(13,0) SAVE REGISTER

FIGURE 11.8 Examples of SAVE Macro Expansions

```
 LOC   OBJECT CODE   ADDR1 ADDR2  STMT   SOURCE STATEMENT

000096                             68 RETURN1   RETURN (14,12)
000096                             69+RETURN1   DS    0H
000096 98EC D00C                   70+          LM    14,12,12(13) RESTORE THE REGISTERS
00009A 07FE                        71+          BR    14 RETURN

00009C                             72 RETURN2   RETURN (14,5)
00009C                             73+RETURN2   DS    0H
00009C 98E5 D00C                   74+          LM    14,5,12(13) RESTORE THE REGISTERS
0000A0 07FE                        75+          BR    14 RETURN

                                   76 RETURN3   RETURN (5,10),T
0000A2                             77+RETURN3   DS    0H
0000A2 985A D028         00028     78+          LM    5,10,40(13) RESTORE THE REGISTERS
0000A6 92FF D00C   0000C           79+          MVI   12(13),X'FF' SET RETURN INDICATION
0000AA 07FE                        80+          BR    14 RETURN

                                   81 RETURN4   RETURN (14,12),T,RC=12
0000AC                             82+RETURN4   DS    0H
0000AC 98EC D00C                   83+          LM    14,12,12(13) RESTORE THE REGISTERS
0000B0 92FF D00C   0000C           84+          MVI   12(13),X'FF' SET RETURN INDICATION
0000B4 41F0 000C   0000C           85+          LA    15,12(0,0) LOAD RETURN CODE
0000B8 07FE                        86+          BR    14 RETURN

                                   87 RETURN5   RETURN (14,12),T,RC=(15)
0000BA                             88+RETURN5   DS    0H
0000BA 58ED D00C   0000C           89+          L     14,12(13,0) RESTORE REGISTER 14
0000BE 980D D014   00014           90+          LM    0,12,20(13) RESTORE THE REGISTERS
0000C2 92FF D00C   0000C           91+          MVI   12(13),X'FF' SET RETURN INDICATION
0000C6 07FE                        92+          BR    14 RETURN
```

FIGURE 11.9   Examples of RETURN Macro Expansions

LOC	OBJECT CODE	ADDR1	ADDR2	STMT	SOURCE STATEMENT	
0000C8				94 CALL1	CALL	SUB1,(X,Y,Z)
0000C8	47F0 50CE		000D0	95+	CNOP	0,4
0000CC	00000000			96+CALL1	B	*+8 BRANCH AROUND VCON
0000D0				97+IHB0022B	DC	V(SUB1) ENTRY POINT ADDRESS
0000D0				98+	CNOP	0,4
0000D0	4510 50DE		000E0	99+	BAL	1,IHB0023A LOAD LIST ADDR IN REG1
0000D4				100+IHB0023	EQU	*
0000D4	00000200			101+	DC	A(X) PROB.PROG.PARAMETER
0000D8	00000204			102+	DC	A(Y) PROB.PROG.PARAMETER
0000DC	00			103+	DC	B'00000000' SET VL SWITCH BIT
0000DD	000208			104+	DC	AL3(Z) PROB. PROG. PARAMETER
0000E0				105+IHB0023A	EQU	*
0000E0	58F0 50CA		000CC	106+	L	15,IHB0022B LOAD 15 WITH ENTRY ADR
0000E4	05EF			107+	BALR	14,15 BRANCH TO ENTRY POINT
				108 CALL2	CALL	SUB2,(X,Y,Z),VL
0000E6	0700			109+	CNOP	0,4
0000E8	47F0 50EE		000F0	110+CALL2	B	*+8 BRANCH AROUND VCON
0000EC	00000000			111+IHB0024B	DC	V(SUB2) ENTRY POINT ADDRESS
0000F0				112+	CNOP	0,4
0000F0	4510 50FE		00100	113+	BAL	1,IHB0025A LOAD LIST ADDR IN REG1
0000F4				114+IHB0025	EQU	*
0000F4	00000200			115+	DC	A(X) PROB.PROG.PARAMETER
0000F8	00000204			116+	DC	A(Y) PROB.PROG.PARAMETER
0000FC	80			117+	DC	B'10000000' SET VL SWITCH BIT
0000FD	000208			118+	DC	AL3(Z) PROB. PROG. PARAMETER
000100				119+IHB0025A	EQU	*
000100	58F0 50EA		000EC	120+	L	15,IHB0024B LOAD 15 WITH ENTRY ADR
000104	05EF			121+	BALR	14,15 BRANCH TO ENTRY POINT
				122 CALL3	CALL	SUB3,(X,Y,Z),ID=1111

```
000106 0700       123+        CNOP  0,4           BRANCH AROUND VCON
000108 47F0 510E  124+CALL3   B     *+8           BRANCH AROUND VCON
00010C 00000000   125+IHB0026B DC   V(SUB3)       ENTRY POINT ADDRESS
000110            126+        CNOP  0,4
000110 4510 511E  127+        BAL   1,IHB0027A LOAD LIST ADDR IN REG1
000114            128+IHB0027 EQU   *
000114 00000200   129+        DC    A(X)  PROB.PROG.PARAMETER
000118 00000204   130+        DC    A(Y)  PROB.PROG.PARAMETER
00011C 00         131+        DC    B'00000000' SET VL SWITCH BIT
00011D 000208     132+        DC    AL3(Z) PROB. PROG. PARAMETER
000120            133+IHB0027A EQU  *
000120 58F0 510A  134+        L     15,IHB0026B LOAD 15 WITH ENTRY ADR
000124 05EF       135+        BALR  14,15 BRANCH TO ENTRY POINT
000126 4700       136+        DC    X'4700' NOP INSTRUCTION WITH
000128 0457       137+        DC    AL2(1111) ID IN LAST TWO BYTES
00012A            138+CALL4   CALL  SUB4,(X,Y,Z),VL,ID=2222
00012A 0700       139+        CNOP  0,4
00012C 47F0 5132  140+CALL4   B     *+8           BRANCH AROUND VCON
000130 00000000   141+IHB0028B DC   V(SUB4)       ENTRY POINT ADDRESS
000134            142+        CNOP  0,4
000134 4510 5142  143+        BAL   1,IHB0029A LOAD LIST ADDR IN REG1
000138            144+IHB0029 EQU   *
000138 00000200   145+        DC    A(X)  PROB.PROG.PARAMETER
00013C 00000204   146+        DC    A(Y)  PROB.PROG.PARAMETER
000140 80         147+        DC    B'10000000' SET VL SWITCH BIT
000141 000208     148+        DC    AL3(Z) PROB. PROG. PARAMETER
000144            149+IHB0029A EQU  *
000144 58F0 512E  150+        L     15,IHB0028B LOAD 15 WITH ENTRY ADR
000148 05EF       151+        BALR  14,15 BRANCH TO ENTRY POINT
00014A 4700       152+        DC    X'4700' NOP INSTRUCTION WITH
00014C 08AE       153+        DC    AL2(2222) ID IN LAST TWO BYTES
```

FIGURE 11.10 Examples of CALL Macro Expansions

185

tion of the entry-point name to the subprogram, any arguments required, an end-of-argument list indicator, and an ID number all within the same macro. The only operand required is the entry-point name; the other three operands are optional. Central to the macro expansion is the setting up of registers and argument list for transfer to a subprogram. Actual transfer of control is accomplished by a BALR 14, 15 instruction.

Figure 11.10 on pp. 184 and 185 contains four examples of CALL macro statements. Notice that special location symbols are generated by the macro under control of the assembler. They are always generated by the assembler in such a way that all are unique. The effect of the V type address constant is to cause the assembler to treat the address represented by the symbol enclosed by parentheses as an external symbol. The same effect can be produced by using an EXTRN assembler instruction. See Definition 11.13. The provision of the special ID number operand allows a called program to verify that a valid linkage has been established between two specific program modules.

Essential to the problem of linking two program modules together is the distinction between location symbols that are external and internal to a program module. The name of a called program is normally external to the calling program. The resolution of external references cannot be made until just prior to execution, when several program modules are *linkedited*, or combined into one load module. However, to make this possible, the assembler must be told which symbols are external to a module during the assembly phase. Two assembler instructions, EXTRN and ENTRY, are provided for the express purpose of indicating which symbols are external to a program. These two instructions are now formally defined.

11.13 Assembler Instruction EXTRN

EXTRN $x,y,z,...$

where $x,y,z,...$ are location reference symbols outside this program module.

This instruction defines the listed symbols as being external to this program module. Thus, they usually do not appear within this module in the location field of any statement. Address resolution is delayed until linkedit time.

A V type address constant, as used in the CALL macro expansion, also defines the symbol enclosed by parentheses as an external symbol. Thus, the effect of the V type address constant is identical to placing the symbol in an EXTRN statement with the added feature of also creating an address constant.

11.14 Assembler Instruction ENTRY

ENTRY *x,y,z,...*

where *x,y,z,...* are location reference symbols within this program module.

This instruction causes the indicated locations within this program module to be made available for external address resolution during linkedit of this module with other modules that refer to the same symbols by EXTRN statements or with V type address constants.

This constant will equal the proper address after address resolution occurs during linkedit.

An application of the ENTRY statement is shown in the comprehensive example given at the end of this chapter.

11.7   MACROS FOR PROGRAMMING INTERRUPT CONTROL

Returning to the discussion of macros, program-interrupt control can be maintained by the problem programmer through the use of the Set Program Interrupt Exit (SPIE) macro. This macro sets up the necessary conditions to allow the problem program to regain control after a program interrupt occurs. Thus, the problem programmer can write programs that recover from any or all

---

11.15 Macro Instruction Set Program Interrupt Exit

---

symbol   SPIE   *exit,(n1,n2,n3,...)*

where *symbol* is optional, *exit* represents the symbolic address of an exit routine, and *n1,n2,n3,...* represent numbers between 1 and 15. A sequence of digits may be coded as (n1,n2), where n1 < n2 and the parenthesis is a second level of parenthesis.

Specifies the address of a problem programmer-provided routine called an interruption exit routine. Also indicates which interrupts are to be returned to the exit routine. If one of the maskable interrupts is involved, its corresponding program-mask bit is set to one. The effect of each SPIE macro issued by a program is to cancel the effect of any previously issued SPIE.

types of program interrupts. The major purpose of the SPIE macro is to inform the operating system which interrupts are to be returned to the problem programmer for analysis, and the address of a routine written by the problem programmer that should receive control after the occurrence of one of the indicated interrupts.

Figure 11.11 contains one example of a SPIE macro expansion. Contained within this expansion are six bytes of constant information called the Program Interrupt Control Area (PICA). The first byte contains 0000XXXX in binary, where XXXX represents the setting of the program mask in the current PSW. Bytes 2, 3, and 4 contain the address of the interrupt exit routine. Bytes 5 and 6 contain fifteen binary switches indicating which of the fifteen possible program interrupts are to be returned to the exit routine. A one bit indicates the corresponding interrupt is to be returned to the exit routine.

During the execution of the SPIE macro, the operating system makes note of the contents of the PICA. In addition, a Program Interrupt Element (PIE) is created in storage. The PIE is a 32-byte area that contains information after an interrupt occurs. The first word of the PIE contains the PICA address. The second and third word contain the old PSW that was in effect when the interrupt occurred. Words four through eight contain the contents of registers 15 through 2 when the interrupt occurred. At the time the operating system returns control to the interrupt exit routine, the general-purpose registers contain the following information.

Reg. 0:   Internal control program information.

Reg. 1:   Address of the PIE currently active.

Reg. 2–12:   Same as when interrupt occurred.

Reg. 13:   Address of save area for main program. Exit routine cannot use this area.

Reg. 14:   Return address. Exit routine must return control to this address.

Reg. 15:   Address of exit routine. May be used as base register during execution of exit routine.

With the information contained in the PIE, pointed to by register 1, the interrupt exit routine can analyze the program interrupt to determine the course of action desired. After appropriate action has been taken, including the possible change of the old PSW in the PIE, control must be returned to the operating system at the address in register 14. A new program address can be introduced by changing the PSW in the PIE before returning to the operating-system control program.

11.8   MACROS FOR TIMER OPERATIONS

Three macros that provide timer services are TIME, Set Timer (STIMER), and Test Timer (TTIMER). The TIME macro allows the programmer to obtain

```
      LOC   OBJECT CODE   ADDR1 ADDR2   STMT   SOURCE STATEMENT

    00014E                              155 SETEXIT SPIE  INRPEXIT,(1,(4,7),10,(13,15))
    00014E  4110 5158                   156+        CNOP  2,4
    000152  0511                0015A   157+SETEXIT LA    1,*+12 LOAD BRANCH ADDRESS
    000154  07                          158+        BALR  1,1 BRANCH AROUND PARAMS.
    000155  00020C                      159+        DC    B'00000111' PROGRAM MASK BITS
    000158  4F                          160+        DC    AL3(INPPEXIT) EXIT ROUTINE ADDRESS
    000159  27                          161+        DC    B'01001111'
    00015A  040E                        162+        DC    B'00100111' INTERUPTION MASK
                                        163+        SVC   14 ISSUE SPIE SVC
```

FIGURE 11.11   Example of SPIE Macro Expansion

```
      LOC   OBJECT CODE   ADDR1 ADDR2   STMT   SOURCE STATEMENT

    00015C  4110 0002          00002    165 TIME1 TIME  DEC
    000160  0A0B                         166+TIME1 LA    1,2(0,0) LOAD 1 TO SPECIFY UNIT
                                         167+      SVC   11 ISSUE TIME SVC
                                         168 TIME2 TIME  BIN
    000162  4110 0001          00001    169+TIME2 LA    1,1(0,0) LOAD 1 TO SPECIFY UNIT
    000166  0A0B                         170+      SVC   11 ISSUE TIME SVC
                                         171 TIME3 TIME  TU
    000168  1B11                         172+TIME3 SR    1,1 ZERO 1 TO SPECIFY UNIT
    00016A  0A0B                         173+      SVC   11 ISSUE TIME SVC
```

FIGURE 11.12   Examples of TIME Macro Expansions

189

the current date and time. STIMER provides the means to set the interval timer to interrupt the program after a specified length of time. Several modes of timing are available. TTIMER can be used to determine the remaining time set by the STIMER. TTIMER can also optionally cancel the timing and proposed interrupt operation.

The formal definition of the TIME macro follows.

11.16 Macro Instruction TIME

symbol   TIME   *option*
where *symbol* is optional and *option* is coded as either DEC, BIN, or TU.

The control program returns the date in register 1 and the time of day in register 0. The date appears as a packed decimal number as 00YYDDDC, where YY is the last two digits of the year, DDD is the day of the year, and C is the plus sign. The time-of-day (24-hour clock) format depends on the option chosen. DEC yields HHMMSSth in packed decimal, where HH is hours, MM is minutes, SS is seconds, t is 0.1 second, and h is 0.01 second. BIN yields a binary number whose units are 0.01 second. TU yields a binary number whose units are timer units (26 microseconds).

Figure 11.12 on p. 189 contains the three variations of the TIME macro. These are the only possible coding variations for the TIME macro.

The STIMER macro allows the programmer to specify an exit routine address to be given control after a specified length of time has elapsed or at a particular time of day. Two modes of timer operation are possible. The first, called REAL time, causes the time interval to be decremented continuously. The second, called TASK time, causes the time interval to be decremented only while the associated task that issued the STIMER macro is active. In a multi-programming environment, such as is normally in operation under MFT, several tasks may be in execution concurrently. Thus, a single task may not be in execution on an exclusive basis. The time interval to be decremented may be specified in decimal, binary, or timer units. The macro can also be used to place the task into a wait condition for the specified length of time.

Upon entry to the timer completion exit routine, the contents of registers are as follows.

Reg. 0–1:   Control program information.

11.17 Macro Instruction Set Timer

symbol   STIMER   *mode,exit,intvl=x*
where *symbol* is optional, *mode* is replaced by REAL, TASK, or WAIT, *exit* is an optional exit routine address for REAL or TASK, *intvl* is replaced by DINTVL, BINTVL, TUINTVL or TOD, and *x* is a location symbol.

This macro causes a program timer to be set to interrupt the program either after a specified length of time or at a specified time of day. The timer interval is decremented continuously for REAL or WAIT mode or only when the task is active for the TASK mode. Upon timer interruption, control is given to the timer completion exit routine if an *exit* address is specified; otherwise, the program is terminated. An exit address can be specified only for REAL or TASK. The symbol *x* specifies the location of either a time interval or a time of day. For DINTVL, *x* is a double word containing unpacked zoned decimal digits in HHMMSSth form. BINTVL indicates a full-word binary number in 0.01 second. TUINTVL is a full-word binary number in timer units. TOD has the same format as DINTVL and specifies the time of day when the interrupt is to occur. If TOD is coded with TASK, TOD is interpreted as DINTVL.

Reg. 2–12:   Unpredictable.
Reg. 13:   Address of a save area provided by control program.
Reg. 14:   Return address to control program.
Reg. 15:   Address of exit routine.

Figure 11.13 contains four examples of STIMER macro codings. The first specifies that the exit routine at address TIMEEXIT is to be given control after the amount of REAL time specified by the zoned decimal number at INTERVAL has elapsed. The second measures only TASK time, and the interval is given in binary (0.01 second). The third causes the program to wait for the indicated number of timer units. No exit routine can be specified for this option. The fourth causes TASK time to be measured, and the program is terminated after the interval given in zoned decimal has elapsed.

The TTIMER macro provides the means of determining how much time is left in an interval set by a STIMER macro. The timer interval can optionally be canceled at the same time by the TTIMER macro.

LOC	OBJECT CODE	ADDR1	ADDR2	STMT	SOURCE STATEMENT		
				175	STIMER1	STIMER	REAL,TIMEEXIT,DINTVL=INTERVAL
00016C	4110 5212		00214	176+STIMER1		LA	1,INTERVAL LOAD PARAMETER REG 1
000170	4100 520E		00210	177+		LA	0,TIMEEXIT LOAD PARAMETER REG 0
000174	41E0 0033		00053	178+		LA	14,51(0,0) LOAD FLAG BYTE
000178	89E0 0018		00018	179+		SLL	14,24(0) SHIFT TO HI-ORDER BYTE
00017C	160E			180+		OR	0,14 AND PACK WITHEXIT ADDR
00017E	0A2F			181+		SVC	47 ISSUE STIMER SVC
				182	STIMER2	STIMER	TASK,TIMEEXIT,BINTVL=INTERVAL
000180	4110 5212		00214	183+STIMER2		LA	1,INTERVAL LOAD PARAMETER REG 1
000184	4100 520E		00210	184+		LA	0,TIMEEXIT LOAD PARAMETER REG 0
000188	41E0 0010		00010	185+		LA	14,16(0,0) LOAD FLAG BYTE
00018C	89E0 0018		00018	186+		SLL	14,24(0) SHIFT TO HI-ORDER BYTE
000190	160E			187+		OR	0,14 AND PACK WITHEXIT ADDR
000192	0A2F			188+		SVC	47 ISSUE STIMER SVC
				189	STIMER3	STIMER	WAIT,TUINTVL=INTERVAL
000194	4110 5212		00214	190+STIMER3		LA	1,INTERVAL LOAD PARAMETER REG 1
000198	4100 0001		00001	191+		LA	0,1(0,0) LOAD FLAG BYTE
00019C	8900 0018		00018	192+		SLL	0,24(0) SHIFT TO HI-ORDER BYTE
0001A0	0A2F			193+		SVC	47 ISSUE STIMER SVC
				194	STIMER4	STIMER	TASK,TOD=INTERVAL
0001A2	4110 5212		00214	195+STIMER4		LA	1,INTERVAL LOAD PARAMETER REG 1
0001A6	4100 0030		00030	196+		LA	0,48(0,0) LOAD FLAG BYTE
0001AA	8900 0018		00018	197+		SLL	0,24(0) SHIFT TO HI-ORDER BYTE
0001AE	0A2F			198+		SVC	47 ISSUE STIMER SVC

FIGURE 11.13 Examples of STIMER Macro Expansions

192

11.18 Macro Instruction Test Timer

symbol   TTIMER   CANCEL where *symbol* is optional and CANCEL is optional.

Causes the control program to return in register 0 the amount of time remaining in the timer interval set by a STIMER. The time is measured in timer units (26 microseconds). If CANCEL is coded, the timer interval and interrupt, if any, is canceled.

Figure 11.14 illustrates the two forms of the TTIMER macro. Cancellation of timer operation is indicated by a nonzero value in register 1.

11.9   MACROS FOR CORE MANAGEMENT

In sophisticated applications, the assembler-language programmer finds it useful to obtain blocks of core storage on a dynamic basis. In other words, rather than reserving storage with DS or other instructions, he can obtain storage areas during execution by requesting the operating system to dynamically allocate a block of storage through the use of the GETMAIN macro. Provision is also made for returning storage on a dynamic basis through the use of the FREEMAIN macro. These two macros are now defined.

11.19 Macro Instruction GETMAIN

symbol   GETMAIN   R,LV=*n* where *symbol* is optional, R indicates the register form (other forms are available but not described here—see IBM Reference C28-6647), and LV=*n* requests *n* bytes of storage. The value of *n* may appear in a register *r* by coding LV=(*r*).

This macro causes the operating system to dynamically allocate *n* bytes of storage to the program issuing the macro. The address of the requested block is returned in register 1. If there is not enough storage to satisfy the request, the job is terminated. The amount of storage requested can appear in a register before entering the macro. *Note:*   This macro varies slightly with MVT.

```
      LOC  OBJECT CODE    ADDR1 ADDR2  STMT   SOURCE STATEMENT

                                        200   TTIMER1  TTIMER CANCEL
0001B0 4110 0001           00001        201+TTIMER1  LA    1,1(0,0) INDICATE CANCEL
0001B4 0A2E                             202+         SVC   46 ISSUE TTIMER SVC
                                        203   TTIMER2  TTIMER
0001B6 1B11                             204+TTIMER2  SR    1,1 NO CANCELLATION
0001B8 0A2E                             205+         SVC   46 ISSUE TTIMER SVC
```

FIGURE 11.14   Examples of TTIMER Macro Expansions

```
      LOC  OBJECT CODE    ADDR1 ADDR2  STMT   SOURCE STATEMENT

                                        207  GETMAIN1 GETMAIN R,LV=1000
0001BA 4100 03E8           003E8        208+GETMAIN1 LA    0,1000(0,0) LOAD LENGTH
0001BE 4510 51C0           001C2        209+         BAL   1,*+4 INDICATE GETMAIN
0001C2 0A0A                             210+         SVC   10 ISSUE GETMAIN SVC
                                        211  GETMAIN2 GETMAIN R,LV=(0)
0001C4 4510 51C6           001C8        212+GETMAIN2 BAL   1,*+4 INDICATE GETMAIN
0001C8 0A0A                             213+         SVC   10 ISSUE GETMAIN SVC
                                        214  GETMAIN3 GETMAIN R,LV=(4)
0001CA 1804                             215+GETMAIN3 LR    0,4 LOAD LENGTH
0001CC 4510 51CE           001D0        216+         BAL   1,*+4 INDICATE GETMAIN
0001D0 0A0A                             217+         SVC   10 ISSUE GETMAIN SVC
```

FIGURE 11.15   Examples of GETMAIN Macro Expansions

194

11.20 Macro Instruction FREEMAIN

symbol   FREEMAIN   R,LV=*n*,A=*a*
where *symbol* is optional, R indicates the register form (other forms are available but not described here—see IBM Reference C28-6647), *n* is the number of bytes being freed, and *a* is the address of the address of the block being freed. Both *n* and the contents of address *a* may be coded as being in a pair of registers before the macro is executed.

This macro causes the operating system to free up the block of *n* bytes at the address specified at address *a* that was previously reserved by a GETMAIN macro. Both the value of *n* and the contents of address *a* may be supplied in registers before the macro is executed.
Note: This macro varies slightly with MVT.

Figure 11.15 contains three examples of GETMAIN macro codings. In the first, 1000 bytes are requested. In the second, the value is to be supplied in register 0. In the third, the value is to be in register 4.

Figure 11.16 contains four examples of FREEMAIN macro statements. The first is explicitly defining the length of the block to be freed as 1000 bytes whose address is at the address called ADDRESS. The second specifies that the length is in register 0 and the address of the block is in register 1. The third specifies that the length is 1000 bytes and the address of the block is in register 4. The fourth specifies the length in register 4 and that the block address is at location ADDRESS.

One of the major uses of the GETMAIN and FREEMAIN macros is in writing reentrant programs. A program is said to be *reentrant* when it can be used by several users at the same time. Before one user completes the use of a reentrant program, a second and subsequent users may start use of the program. This means the program can never modify itself in a user-dependent way. Also, all user-dependent data must be kept separate from those of every other user. This latter problem is solved quite easily by using the GETMAIN macro to reserve storage areas for data for each new user that enters the program. As each user completes service, the block of storage can be released for future use by subsequent users. One or more registers can be used to point to particular blocks of storage that are in use by a given user. If the program is interrupted while serving one user to allow service of another user, register contents are restored by the control program, reflecting the conditions that were in effect at the time when the first user was last interrupted.

LOC	OBJECT CODE	ADDR1	ADDR2	STMT	SOURCE STATEMENT
				219 RELMAIN1	FREEMAIN R,LV=1000,A=ADDRESS
0001D2	4100 03E8		003E8	220+RELMAIN1	LA 0,1000(0,0) LOAD LENGTH
0001D6	5810 5216		00218	221+	L 1,ADDRESS LOAD AREA ADDRESS
0001DA	4111 0000		00000	222+	LA 1,0(1) CLEAR THE HIGH ORDER BYTE
0001DE	0A0A			223+	SVC 10 ISSUE FREEMAIN SVC
				224 RELMAIN2	FREEMAIN R,LV=(0),A=(1)
0001E0				225+RELMAIN2	DS 0H
0001E0	4111 0000		00000	226+	LA 1,0(1) CLEAR THE HIGH ORDER BYTE
0001E4	0A0A			227+	SVC 10 ISSUE FREEMAIN SVC
				228 RELMAIN3	FREEMAIN R,LV=1000,A=(4)
0001E6	4100 03E8		003E8	229+RELMAIN3	LA 0,1000(0,0) LOAD LENGTH
0001EA	1814			230+	LR 1,4 LOAD AREA ADDRESS
0001EC	4111 0000		00000	231+	LA 1,0(1) CLEAR THE HIGH ORDER BYTE
0001F0	0A0A			232+	SVC 10 ISSUE FREEMAIN SVC
				233 RELMAIN4	FREEMAIN R,LV=(4),A=ADDRESS
0001F2				234+RELMAIN4	DS 0H
0001F2	1804			235+	LR 0,4 LOAD LENGTH
0001F4	5810 5216		00218	236+	L 1,ADDRESS LOAD AREA ADDRESS
0001F8	4111 0000		00000	237+	LA 1,0(1) CLEAR THE HIGH ORDER BYTE
0001FC	0A0A			238+	SVC 10 ISSUE FREEMAIN SVC

FIGURE 11.16 Examples of FREEMAIN Macro Expansions

11.10   AN EXAMPLE ILLUSTRATING SEVERAL MACROS

The example of the pseudo random number generator of Chapter 10 is now shown in Figure 11.17, using standard linkage conventions using SAVE and RETURN macros. Means is also provided for altering the seed of the random number sequence through a second entry to the subroutine called RSEED. This second entry is designed to respond to the following Fortran statement:

CALL RSEED (SEED)

The following points should be made concerning this example.

The ENTRY statements are included to designate RSEED and RNDMF as entry points to be linkedited with external symbols of other program modules. Notice the effect of the two SAVE macros at the two entry points. Note their dependence on register 15 containing the address of the entry point and on register 13 containing the address of the save area provided by the calling program. The RETURN macros also depend on registers 13 and 14 containing the save area address and the return address respectively.

The effect of the RSEED entry is to use the corresponding argument to compute an initial value for the pseudo random number sequence. The argument is made positive, large, and odd before being stored into the location called RNDMNMBR.

PROGRAMMING EXERCISE

Write a recursive subroutine to compute the factorial of N. [*Hint*: The subroutine should recursively call itself for $n(i) = n(i - 1) - 1$ until $n(i) = 1$. Then, by setting $1! = 1$, each call can be returned, computing each product in turn.] This subroutine, or function, should make use of the SAVE, RETURN,

Save Area Contents

Word	Contents
1	Used by PL/1 language programs
2	Address of previous save area (stored by calling program)
3	Address of next save area (stored by current program)
4	Register 14 (Return Address)
5	Register 15 (Entry Point Address)
6	Register 0
7–18	Registers 1–12

```
LOC    OBJECT CODE    ADDR1 ADDR2  STMT  SOURCE STATEMENT

000000                                1  DECK    START 0              SET LOCATION COUNTER
                                      2          ENTPY PSEED          DEFINE ENTRY POINT
                                      3          ENTRY RNDMF          DEFINE ENTRY POINT
000000                                4          USING *,15           DEFINE BASE REGISTER
000000 47F0 F00A         0000A        5  RSEED   SAVE  (14,12),*      SAVE REGISTERS
000004 05                             6+RSEED    B     10(0,15),*     BRANCH AROUND ID
000005 D9E2C5C5C4                     7+         DC    AL1(5)
00000A 90EC D00C                      8+         DC    CL5'RSEED'     IDENTIFIER
00000A 90EC D00C         000C         9+         STM   14,12,12(13)   SAVE REGISTERS
00000E 5850 1000         00000       10          L     5,0(,1)        LOAD ARGUMENT ADDRESS
000012 5860 5000         00000       11          L     6,0(,5)        LOAD ARGUMENT
000016 1066                          12          LPR   6,6            SET SIGN PLUS
000018 5660 F060         00060       13          O     6,ODD          MAKE ODD AND LARGE
00001C 5060 F064         00064       14          ST    6,RNDMNMBR     SAVE FIRST RANDOM NMBR
                                     15          RETURN (14,12)       RESTORE REGS AND RETURN
000020 98EC D00C         000C        16+         LM    14,12,12(13)   RESTORE THE REGISTERS
000024 07FE                          17+         BR    14             RETURN
000026                               18          USING *,15           DEFINE BASE REGISTER
000026                               19  RNDMF   SAVE  (14,12),*      SAVE REGISTERS
000026 47F0 F00A         0000A       20+RNDMF    B     10(0,15),*     BRANCH AROUND ID
```

```
00002A 05            21+           DC    AL1(5)
00002B D9D5C4D4C6    22+           DC    CL5'RNDMF'   IDENTIFIER
000030 90EC D00C     23+           STM   14,12,12(13) SAVE REGISTERS
000034 5850 1000     24            L     5,0(,1)      GET ARGUMENT ADDRESS
000038 7820 5000     25            LE    2,0(,5)      PUT ARGUMENT IN FPR 2
00003C 5870 F03E     26            L     7,RNDMNMBR   GET LAST RANDOM NMBR
000040 5C60 F042     27            M     6,MAGICIAN   MAKE NEW RANDOM NMBR
000044 5070 F03E     28            ST    7,RNDMNMBR   SAVE NEW RANDOM NMBR
000048 5470 F046     29            N     7,MASK       ZERO LEFT MOST 8 BITS
00004C 5A70 F04A     30            A     7,CHRCTSTC   SET CHARACTERISTIC 64
000050 5070 F04E     31            ST    7,TEMP       STORE TEMPORARILY
000054 7800 F04E     32            LE    0,TEMP       LOAD INTO FPR 0
000058 3C02          33            MER   0,2          MPY BY MAXIMUM
                     34            RETURN (14,12)     RESTORE REGS AND RETURN
00005A 98EC D00C     35+           LM    14,12,12(13) RESTORE THE REGISTERS
00005E 07FE          36+           BP    14 RETURN
000060               37            DS    0F           ALLIGN TO FULL WORD
000060 20000001      38 ODD        DC    X'20000001'  LARGE ODD CONSTANT
000064 20000001      39 RNDMNMBR   DC    X'20000001'  INITIAL RANDOM NMBR
000068 0002D403      40 MAGICIAN   DC    X'0002D403'  MAGIC FACTOR
00006C 00FFFFFF      41 MASK       DC    X'00FFFFFF'  MASKING CONSTANT
000070 40000000      42 CHRCTSTC   DC    X'40000000'  CHARACTERISTIC OF 64
000074               43 TEMP       DS    F            TEMPORARY LOCATION
000026               44            END   RNDMF        END OF SUBPROGRAM
```

FIGURE 11.17   Extended Pseudo Random Number Generator

CALL, GETMAIN, and FREEMAIN macros. Note that within a recursive subroutine an external reference symbol may actually be internal to the subprogram. An eighteen-word save area should be obtained for each recursive call and then released when the call is returned. The standard way of using a save area is shown in the table on p. 197.

STUDY EXERCISES

1. What is the difference between the following states?
    (a) Problem-supervisor.
    (b) Running-waiting.
    (c) Stopped-operating.
    (d) Masked-unmasked.
2. What are the PSW, its components, and their purposes?
3. How are interrupts taken?
4. How are interrupts serviced?
5. What are the various interrupt levels?
6. What are privileged operations?
7. What is a macro instruction?
8. Discuss the ABEND macro instruction.
9. Discuss the macros useful in subroutine linkage.
10. Discuss the SPIE macro instruction.
11. Discuss the macros for timer services.
12. Discuss the macros for core management.

Chapter **twelve**
The Concepts of Input and Output

Input and output in System/360, as in most modern computing systems, is a relatively complex topic. The main reason is that input and output equipment and the central processing unit must operate simultaneously. A second complicating factor is the wide variety of input and output devices and the need for providing a common interface between this equipment and the central processor. Compounding the complexity is a vast software structure of a highly generalized operating system.

Basic to all input and output operations is a sophisticated set of hardware features and functions that carry out the desired operations. However, the operating system effectively isolates the ordinary user from these hardware characteristics and operations; only very experienced systems programmers become completely familiar with them. For practical reasons, then, this chapter dwells only briefly on the hardware concepts of input and output operations. Primary emphasis is placed on the organization and management of input and output data within the framework of the data management features of the operating system. The bulk of this chapter is devoted to the OS features that are common to all data management operations. Future chapters are devoted to specific methods of performing input and output operations.

12.1 INPUT/OUTPUT DEVICES, CONTROL UNITS, AND CHANNELS

As described in Chapter 11, up to seven I/O channels may be attached to a single System/360 CPU. Most systems, however, have only two or three channels. A channel is the major communication link between the computer and its environment. A channel communicates with the computer through the main storage unit. Data being read or written do not flow through the central processing unit. The CPU is involved in input or output only at the initiation and conclusion of the I/O operations. Thus, a system with three channels can be performing three input and/or output operations in the three channels while the CPU is also executing instructions carrying out computations.

Channels operate independently, once started by the CPU, by fetching and executing what is called a *channel program* made up of channel *commands*. Channel commands are similar to machine instructions in that they also are made up of operation codes and operands. However, they are all a double word in length, and there are only six different commands. Commands may be grouped into a channel program, called command chaining, much as CPU instructions are grouped into programs.

Channels provide a standard interface between main storage and various input and output devices. Since most devices have significant design differences in speed, capacity, and access mechanisms, some kind of adapter is usually required to interface the common channel interface with each I/O device. This adapter is called a control unit. Sometimes the control unit is physically housed in the device it is interfacing, other times it is in a separate cabinet. Some devices can share the same control unit, such as tape drives. Other devices require a stand-alone control unit. In most cases, the presence of the control unit between the channel and an I/O device does not concern the computer programmer.

Input and output devices appear in a great many varieties. Device characteristics vary over wide ranges. Low-speed devices, such as remote typewriter terminals, operate in the range of 10 to 15 characters per second. High-speed devices, such as disk drives and magnetic drums, operate in the range of 250,000 to 1,300,000 characters per second. Capacities of various devices run almost in inverse proportion to their respective speeds of operation. Cost of input and output devices runs proportional (nonlinearly) to speed. Some devices, such as tape drives, can do some operations independently of the control unit or the channel to which they are connected. This frees the channel and control unit to perform other operations. Operations that devices can perform include, for example, rewinding tapes and seeking a particular recording track on a single disk drive. Operations such as these are specified by *orders*, as opposed to instructions and commands. In other words, the CPU executes instructions, channels execute commands, and devices execute orders.

Returning to channels, two types are available, multiplexor and selector. Multiplexor channels have the capability of supporting many low-speed I/O devices through the use of separate subchannels for each. Selector channels can support only one device at a time regardless of its speed. Therefore, only high-speed devices are usually placed on a selector channel. Selector channels always operate in what is called the *burst* mode. Multiplexor subchannels operate normally in the *multiplex* mode, but if an I/O device on a particular subchannel demands service for longer than 100 microseconds, the entire multiplexor channel reverts to the burst mode as if it were a selector channel.

Upon installation, each I/O device is assigned a permanent I/O device address. This address is a sixteen-bit number consisting of two parts. The leftmost eight bits represent the channel on which the particular device is connected. The rightmost eight bits represent the particular I/O device and control unit being addressed on the indicated channel. Since only seven channels can be installed on a single system, any channel address higher than 00000110 is invalid. Devices that are shared by more than one channel have a unique address for each distinct path from the CPU to the device. This allows an alternate path to a device if one path is busy with other operations.

12.2   INPUT AND OUTPUT INSTRUCTIONS

The risk of committing the sin of oversimplification must now be taken. It is no exaggeration to state that full disclosure of details of the I/O subsystem within System/360 would yield another volume equal in size to the present one. Even after such disclosure, the beginning programmer would be no closer to being able to actually perform I/O operations under the standard System/360 programming environment. Thus, the following discussion is necessarily abridged. Formal definitions for I/O instructions are dropped in favor of prose presentation.

All four I/O instructions are privileged and are of the SI format, except that no immediate operands are specified or used. The names of the instructions and their mnemonics are Start I/O (SIO), Test I/O (TIO), Halt I/O (HIO), and Test Channel (TCH). In all four instructions, bit positions 16 through 23 of the sum of C(B1) and D1 specify a particular channel number. In all except TCH, bit positions 24 through 31 of this sum specify a particular device on the indicated channel. The only program interrupt that can occur for any of the four instructions is the privileged operation interrupt. If an I/O instruction is executed while in the problem state, the instruction is suppressed before any action is taken by the I/O subsystem.

The Start I/O instruction is used to initiate either a read, write, read-backward, control, or sense operation on the indicated channel and device. The particular I/O operation initiated is determined by the first Channel Command Word (CCW), whose address must be made available by the programmer in the

Channel Address Word (CAW) that is stored in the permanently allocated storage location 72. The CAW also specifies in its leftmost four bits a protection key to be used during the associated I/O operations for storage protection.

If the channel and device addressed by the SIO instruction is not first tested to determine its availability, the SIO may not actually initiate the desired I/O operation. The exact result of the instruction is posted in the condition code as follows:

CC = 0:   I/O operation successfully initiated
CC = 1:   CSW stored (see next paragraph)
CC = 2:   channel or subchannel busy
CC = 3:   device or channel not operational

The only condition-code setting not self-explanatory is CC = 1. For a multitude of reasons, it may be that the I/O device is not busy and is operational, yet the I/O operation does not begin. Under these conditions, a Channel Status Word (CSW) is created reflecting the status of the addressed channel, control unit, and I/O device and is stored into the CSW location at address 64. Determination can then be made as to why the operation failed to start.

Since SIO, TIO, and HIO all may cause a CSW to be stored, all I/O interrupts should be masked off prior to executing SIO, TIO, or HIO to avoid loss of CSW information owing to a subsequent I/O interrupt that also stores CSW information.

The Test I/O instruction is used to determine the status of a particular device and channel. The condition code is set as in the following list:

CC = 0:   available
CC = 1:   CSW stored
CC = 2:   channel or subchannel busy
CC = 3:   not operational

Again, each condition-code setting is understandable except perhaps CC = 1. In this case, either the addressed device and channel had an I/O interrupt pending or some unusual or error condition existed. In either case, the stored CSW can be used to determine the cause of the condition. In most cases, a pending I/O interrupt is cleared by the TIO operation. Since most I/O devices on a given channel have a permanent set of interrupt priorities associated with them, the TIO instruction provides the programmer with a method of accepting and clearing interrupts in nonpriority sequence. Priority between channels can be controlled by proper masking in the system mask of the PSW.

The Halt I/O instruction causes the current I/O operation being performed on the addressed channel and device to be terminated. The final state of the channel depends on the type of channel involved in the operation. The resulting condition codes are as follows:

CC = 0:   interruption pending in subchannel

CC = 1:   CSW stored

CC = 2:   burst operation terminated

CC = 3:   not operational

Condition 0 corresponds to an interrupt condition that cannot be cleared by the Halt I/O. Condition 1 occurs when the channel is either available or with a pending interrupt. At the same time, the subchannel can be either available or working in the multiplex mode while the device is either available, working, or with a pending interrupt. Condition 2 occurs only for a selector channel, which is always operating in the burst mode. Condition 3 occurs when the addressed channel and/or device is not operational. This instruction causes a working channel to immediately become free for a higher-priority operation.

The Test Channel instruction allows the programmer to determine the status of the indicated channel. No I/O device is addressed by the operation. Thus, the condition-code setting is determined only by the status of the channel. The settings are as follows:

CC = 0:   channel available

CC = 1:   interruption pending in channel

CC = 2:   channel operating in burst mode

CC = 3:   channel not operational

Notice that no pending interrupts are cleared by storing CSW information by the TCH. Condition-code settings are fairly straightforward.

12.3   CHANNEL COMMANDS

Channels execute six commands called read, write, read backward, control, sense, and transfer in channel. Each command except transfer in channel can be used as the first channel command indicated by the CAW in the execution of SIO by the CPU. Each of the commands except transfer in channel cause a particular operation to be performed by the channel and the associated I/O device. The format of a CCW is shown in Figure 12.1.

CC code	Data address	Flags	000	/ / / / / /	Count

Bits: 0   7   8   31–2 36–7–9 40   47 48   63

FIGURE 12.1   Format of CCW (Double Word)

The Channel Command (CC) code is given in bit positions 0 through 7 of the CCW. The codes and their meanings are given in the accompanying table. Bits indicated by x are ignored; bits indicated by m are used as modifier bits and sometimes represent orders to be executed by the I/O device.

CCW Code Table

Code	Command
x x x x 0 0 00	Invalid CC Code
mmmm0 1 00	Sense
x x x x 1 0 00	Transfer in channel
mmmm1 1 00	Read backward
mmmmmm01	Write
mmmmmm10	Read
mmmmmm11	Control

Bit positions 8 through 31 of the CCW specify an address in main storage that is to be used in conjunction with the I/O operation. For example, during a read operation, this address indicates the main storage area in which the data being read are to be stored. For read and write operations, the CCW address indicates the low-order address of the affected area. In read backward, the CCW address indicates the high-order address of the affected area.

The five flags in bit positions 32 through 36 have the following purposes:

Bit 32, the Chain-Data (CD) flag, indicates that data chaining is to take place. When this flag is on, the next CCW in the channel program is to be fetched and its data address is to be used in conjunction with the current CCW. This allows a data stream to be read into or written from a set of noncontiguous areas of main storage.

Bit 33, the Chain-Command (CC) flag, indicates that command chaining is to occur. When this flag is on, and the CD flag is off, the next CCW is to be fetched from the channel program and used as the next channel command after normal completion of the current CCW.

Bit 34, the Suppress-Length-Indication (SLI) flag; when on causes the system to ignore any incorrect data-length indication detected by the device or channel. When the SLI bit is one and the CD flag is zero in the last CCW executed, the incorrect length indication is suppressed. When both the CC and SLI flags are one, command chaining occurs regardless of the presence of an incorrect length condition.

Bit 35, the skip flag, when on causes the suppression of data transfer during a read, read-backward, or sense operation.

Bit 36, the Program-Controlled-Interruption (PCI) flag, when on causes the channel to generate an interruption condition when this CCW takes control of the channel.

Bit positions 48 through 63, the count field, indicate to the channel how many bytes of data are involved in the current I/O operation. In operations involving data transfer, this count is decremented by one for each byte of data transferred. The point at which the count reaches zero is the signal indicating completion of the current CCW operation.

Bit positions 37 through 39 should always be zero, except in the transfer-in-channel command, and bit positions 40 through 47 are ignored.

The command codes have the following characteristics. The two low-order bits—or, when these two bits are 00, the four low-order bits of the code—identify the operation desired. Commands that initiate I/O operations (read, write, read backward, control, and sense) cause all eight bits of the command code to be transferred to the I/O device. In these codes, the high-order bits are used as modifiers to specify how the particular command is to be executed. The meanings of the modifier bits depend on each individual type of I/O device.

When a transfer-in-channel command is encountered during command chaining, the channel fetches the next CCW from the main storage location indicated in the data address field of the transfer in channel command. Thus, it is quite possible to place a channel under the operation of a channel command program containing a loop. Also, the provision is made to allow the channel to fetch the next CCW from sixteen bytes higher than the current CCW conditionally based on conditions present in the channel and device. Thus, not only are loops possible, but also branching to entirely different channel programs can occur.

The sense-channel command allows the obtaining of status information concerning the status of particular devices, and the transfer of this information to main storage.

The control-channel command allows special operations to be specified for execution by a device, such as backspacing or rewinding tape or seeking an address on disk. Most control functions can be specified by the modifier bits of the CCW code. However, some operations require that data from storage at the address indicated by the CCW be sent to the device as control information rather than as data.

It probably is obvious, even from this cursory discussion, that the I/O subsystem is a highly complex one and that it holds fantastic possibilities. This fact is being proven everyday by the many sophisticated installations in which real-time interactive time-sharing applications are in operation. At this point we conclude our discussion of the various aspects of hardware, turning now to the data management features of the operating system.

12.4 DATA MANAGEMENT SERVICES

In general, the Operating System can be broken into four major divisions. The first, called Job Management, is concerned with the analysis of Job Control Language (JCL) and the subsequent management and control of the job as it passes through the system from one job step to another. A second, called Task Management, sometimes referred to as Supervisor Services, involves such services as were discussed in Chapter 11. A third, called System Generation and Maintenance, is used by the systems programmer to initially configurate the Operating System to match the hardware configuration and the needs of the users of a particular installation as well as to maintain the system beyond initial generation. The fourth and final division, called Data Management, provides generalized I/O services for all aspects and types of data. Data Management provides an interface between an executing program and all associated input and output data. All Data Management services and functions are obtained by the programmer through the use of selected system macro instructions. Very few users ever program their own input and output instructions while running under the Operating System.

The purpose of Data Management is threefold: (1) to permit the user to store, retrieve, and modify programs and data using the various storage devices, such as the direct-access disk drive, without being concerned with the specific hardware configuration of a system; (2) to permit the free interchange of programs and data between various users at their discretion; (3) to provide a systematic method of identifying and locating programs and data within a system as well as systematic methods for referring to the data after it is located.

Central to Data Management is a library in which programs and data are maintained by the system. The library consists of collections of programs or data called *data sets*. A data set is made up of logically related information. Each data set may be given a name, which is placed in a catalog of all data-set names. Means are provided for easily entering and deleting data sets into and from the library and entering and deleting data-set names into and from the catalog. No distinction is made between various types of data within the library. Data are cataloged in the same way regardless of whether they are a collection of Fortran statements, an object program, a load module, or data to be processed by an object program. The only distinction among the various types of data is in the user's interpretation of them and in the way they are used.

The data-set cataloging system uses a hierarchial classification similar to the Dewey decimal library system. However, data-set names can be alphabetical rather than just numeric. Each data-set name may be up to eight characters in length, but several levels of classification are possible. For example, a data set might have the following name:

COURSES.ISE450.SN0023

This name implies to the catalog system that the data set in question can be found under the major heading of COURSES, an intermediate heading of ISE450, and a minor heading of SN0023. Thus, the same name replacing 23 by 24 would represent an entirely different data set, but it would be filed under the same major and intermediate headings. In most installations, the first major heading name refers to a particular disk pack or other storage-medium unit.

A complete set of utility programs is available for manipulation of data sets. Some are programs that can be used to create new data sets, renaming or deleting catalog entries for data sets, reorganizing and rearranging data sets within the library, and dumping the contents of data sets onto the printer or another I/O device.

Finally, a comprehensive set of I/O routines is provided within the Operating System to provide access to a user's data sets while his program is executing. These routines, called access routines, fall into categories called *access methods*. They automatically provide for overlapping of I/O operations with computation, checking and preparing descriptor labels for data sets, and other useful operations. In general, input and output routines are available for the following operations:

1. Processing logical or physical records stored on I/O devices in sequential order.

2. Processing logical or physical records stored on I/O devices in non-sequential order.

3. Processing messages received from remote locations at unpredictable intervals of time.

The operating system is designed so that once a program is written it need not be changed in order to make changes in the I/O device containing the data sets in question. In other words, the system provides a device independence in I/O operations. Likewise, the description of a data set is stored along with the data set, so that the programmer need not redescribe it each time it is used. Means are provided however, to allow certain changes to be made in the description of the data set and the processing operations involving that data set without any change in the processing program. These changes are usually made through Job Control Language statements at the time the program is run.

12.5   FUNDAMENTALS OF I/O OPERATIONS

In order for the access routines to be able to process a data set, much information must first be supplied to them about the data. This information can be supplied from several sources. Some is supplied when the data set is originally recorded and is stored with the data set. Other information is supplied during assembly time through the use of a Data Control Block (DCB) macro. This macro generates a variable-length area of storage containing various constants that indicate characteristics of the data set. A DCB macro must be specified for every data set used by a program. Additional information can be supplied at execution time through the use of Data Definition (DD) cards in the JCL associated with a job. This allows the programmer to delay making some decisions concerning the data set until the actual execution of the program. Another source of information is from the problem program itself during execution.

Before any data can be accessed during execution, the data set in question must be *opened* through the use of an OPEN macro instruction. At OPEN time, the access routines pull together all of the information supplied from the various sources, the data-set label contained within the data set, the DD statements, and the original contents of the DCB, and completes the setting up of the DCB. The programmer may delay, until the point of opening a data set, the complete definition of all the characteristics of the data set and the methods to be used for processing that data set.

Before discussing the DCB and OPEN macros, we need to define and discuss a few terms.

A *data set* is a logically related collection of data that has been named and described to the operating system.

The structure of a data set, in general, is made up of *records*. A record is a logical collection of information. A *block* is a physical collection of information. Blocks are separated on the recording medium by physical space that is machine sensible. A block is usually made up of one or more logical records. Records may be of fixed, variable, or undefined length. The length of fixed-length records is constant throughout the entire data set. A variable-length record contains its length in the first four bytes of the record. Specifying this information causes the system to check the lengths at recording time and reading time. The system can automatically block and deblock fixed- and variable-length records. Undefined-length record specification allows the processing of records that do not conform to the fixed- or variable-length conventions. In this case, the programmer must block and deblock the records.

When data sets are stored on direct-access or magnetic tape devices, the data sets are said to be on *volumes*. Examples of volumes are a reel of tape, a disk pack, a data cell, or a drum.

The name of a data set is referred to during the programming of input and output macros by the key word parameter DSNAME. The name of a DD card, the characters immediately following the initial // of the DD card, is referred to during programming by the key word parameter DDNAME. These two names are different and should not be confused.

A data-set *label*, which can be either a standard or nonstandard description of a data set, is stored at the beginning of the data set. A nonstandard label is created by, and must be analyzed by, the user. A standard label can be created and analyzed by either the user or the access-method routines.

Access techniques are of two forms. The *queued-access* technique is a method of I/O service whereby the access routines anticipate the needs of the programmer. By the time the programmer requests a new I/O record, the access routines will have already read it from the data set. The programmer does not need to be concerned about waiting for the record to be read before processing can continue. Likewise, on output, the access routines collect output records until a sufficient number of records can be collected and blocked before writing them into the data set. *Buffers*, areas of main storage, are used by the access routines to buffer the reading and writing of records. The queued-access technique is the easiest to use from the standpoint of the programmer.

The second access technique is called *basic access*. This method reads and writes blocks only, not logical records. Thus, the programmer must block and deblock the records. This method is also unlike the queued-access technique in that automatic synchronization between program processing and I/O operations does not occur. In other words, under the basic-access methods, the programmer must be concerned about whether the requested input block has actually been read before proceeding to process the block. For this reason, the basic-access technique is somewhat harder to deal with. However, many applications cannot be handled by the queued-access technique, and so the programmer must resort to the basic-access methods.

Data-set content can be organized in five different ways. In the *Sequential* organization all records of the data set are stored in a consecutive fashion, and the location of a record does not depend on its contents. This organization is common to and must be used for magnetic tape, card readers and punches, and line printers. The sequential organization may also be used on other devices as well. Normally, a particular record in a sequential data set must be obtained by reading all records appearing ahead of the desired record. Likewise, if a particular record is to be made shorter, longer, or deleted, all successive records must be rewritten. Either the queued- or basic-access techniques may be used with the sequential organization. The resulting access methods are referred to as the Queued Sequential Access Method (QSAM) and the Basic Sequential Access Method (BSAM).

Partitioned data-set organization is a useful method of arranging several sequential sets of data within one data set placed on a direct-access storage device. Each subset of the total data set forms a partition of the data set, is called a *member,* and has an associated name in the data-set directory. The directory contains the starting location for each member of the data set. The queued-access technique cannot be used for the partitioned organization; the only access method for this form of data is the Basic Partitioned Access Method (BPAM).

Indexed Sequential organization means that the contents of the data set are sorted on a particular field within the records and the records are stored in this order. Knowing where the key is in the record, the access routines can locate a particular record in a more direct way than by searching the entire data set for the record as in the sequential organization. The system maintains a directory of where certain key values are stored within a direct-access device. Therefore, a particular record location can be determined more easily than without the key. Both access techniques can be used with this organization; the access methods are called the Queued Indexed Sequential Access Method (QISAM) and the Basic Indexed Sequential Access Method (BISAM).

The *Direct* form of data-set organization allows the access routines to read and write specific blocks of data directly without searching for the block location. Given knowledge of the starting location of the data set and the length of each block, the exact address of the record can be computed prior to access. The programmer can specify the actual record address or can specify a relative block number from the first block in the data set. This organization can be used only on direct-access devices; the queued-access technique is not applicable. Thus, the only access method here is the Basic Direct Access Method (BDAM).

The fifth and final data-set organization is the *Telecommunications* organization, designed for the transmission of data to and from telecommunications devices. The actual transmission of the data is considerably different from I/O operations with local equipment. However, once an input message has been received, or up until an output message is transmitted, the messages appear as ordinary data and can be operated upon by both access techniques. The two access methods are the Queued Telecommunications Access Method (QTAM) and the Basic Telecommunications Access Method (BTAM).

Table 12.1 summarizes the various access methods which are available within the Data Management division of the Operating System.

TABLE 12.1   Access Methods

Data-Set Organization	Access Technique	
	Basic	Queued
Sequential	BSAM	QSAM
Partitioned	BPAM	
Indexed Sequential	BISAM	QISAM
Direct	BDAM	
Telecommunications	BTAM	QTAM

12.6   COMMON I/O MACRO INSTRUCTIONS

This section describes the system macro instructions that must always appear within a user's program regardless of the access method being employed to access data. For every data set being used by a program, the user must provide a Data Control Block (DCB). The DCB macro instruction is used for this purpose. This macro is rather large and may contain many operands, depending on the application of the macro. It is unlike most other macro instructions, in that the expansion contains no executable instructions, only data and constants that describe the data set involved, the access method being used, and the locations of the various service routines used by that access method.

A second macro instruction that must always appear in a program involving I/O operations is the OPEN. The OPEN macro causes the action called *opening* a data set. The same OPEN macro may be used to open several data sets with the same instruction. The OPEN causes the Data Management routines to complete the contents of the DCB using the various sources discussed in the previous section. The OPEN also assures that all service routines needed for processing the data set are loaded into main storage.

A third macro that usually appears in a program involving I/O operations is the CLOSE macro. This macro causes the indicated data sets to be closed and logically removed from under control of the program. If either a CLOSE is not issued or the program abends before the CLOSE can be executed, the Operating System usually is successful in closing the associated data sets without damaging them.

12.1 Macro Instruction Data Control Block (DCB)

---

symbol   DCB   *operands*
where *symbol* is a required symbolic reference to the DCB macro statement and the *operands* include two or more key-word operands (see Table 12.2) separated by commas and written in any order.

This macro causes allocation of an area of storage containing various constants describing the characteristics of an associated data set and the various parameters that define the access method to be used in operating on the data set. The length of the DCB area depends on the particular access method being specified for use with the associated data set. (See Table 12.2 for a list of the key-word operands possible for the DCB macro.)

Table 12.2 contains the list of possible key-word operands that can be used in the DCB macro statement. Notice that each access method uses a different subset of the total set of operands. Two operands must appear in every DCB macro statement, the DSORG and MACRF operands. Where *code* or capital letters appear within Table 12.2, either the given letters or some other letter defined later must be used. Symbols must appear where *symbol* is written. The entry *address* must be replaced by either a location symbol or other relocatable address reference. The entry *number* is replaced by some absolute expression yielding a value. Some of the more important key-word parameters are discussed below.

A major portion of the DCB operands can be omitted for simple I/O applications. Therefore, the descriptions that follow are somewhat abridged. For a complete description the reader may consult IBM Reference C28-6647. The first line of each of the paragraphs below contains the key word being discussed and the access methods in which the key-word parameter may be used. Several

TABLE 12.2   DCB Key-word Operands

Operand	Access Method					
	BDAM	BISAM	BPAM	BSAM	QISAM	QSAM
BFALN=	F or D	F or D	F or D	F or D	F or D	F or D
BFTEK=	–	–	–	–	–	S or E
BLKSIZE=	number	–	number	number	number[a]	number
BUFCB=	address	address	address	address	address	address
BUFL=	number	number	number	number	number	number
BUFNO=	number	number	number	number	number	number
CYLOFL=	–	–	–	–	number[a]	–
DDNAME=	symbol	symbol	symbol	symbol	symbol	symbol
DEVD=	–	–	–	code	–	code
DSORG=	DA or DAU	IS	PO or POU	PS or PSU	IS or ISU	PS or PSU
EODAD=	–	–	address	address	address	address
EROPT=	–	–	–	–	–	code
EXLST=	address	address	address	address	address	address
KEYLEN=	number	–	number	number	number[a]	–
LIMCT=	number	–	–	–	–	–
LRECL=	–	–	number	number	number[a]	number
MACRF=	code	code	code	code	code	code
MSHI=	–	address	–	–	–	–
MSWA=	–	address	–	–	–	–
NCP=	–	number	number	number	–	–
NTM=	–	–	–	–	number[a]	–
OPTCD=	code	–	code	code	code[a]	code
RECFM=	code	–	code	code	code[a]	code
RKP=	–	–	–	–	number[a]	–
SMSI=	–	number	–	–	–	–
SMSW=	–	number	–	–	–	–
SYNAD=	address	–	address	address	address	address

[a]Allowed only when creating the data set.

of the parameters are used for only one or two access methods. In such cases that do not involve QSAM or BDAM, the description of the parameter is severely abridged.

BFALN=(BDAM, BISAM, BPAM, QISAM, and QSAM). This parameter specifies whether buffers used by the access routines are to be on full- or double-word boundaries. In this case, the full-word boundary means one that is not also a double-word boundary. This parameter can be specified by the DCB, the DD statement, or by the problem program before data-set opening is completed. It can also be omitted, in which case double-word boundaries are assumed. For BPAM, the data-set label is also a source. For QSAM, the source must be the same as for the BFTEK source or both omitted.

BFTEK=(QSAM). This parameter specifies the type of buffering to be used by the access routines. S indicates simple buffering while E specifies exchange buffering. The differences between these two types of buffering are discussed in Chapter 13 with the development of the QSAM access method. Track overflow cannot be specified for RECFM if exchange buffering is used. The source of BFTEK can be the DCB, the DD statement, the problem program, or omitted. The source must be the same as for BFALN or both omitted. If BFTEK is omitted, simple buffering is assumed.

BLKSIZE=(BDAM, BPAM, BSAM, QISAM (Output only), and QSAM). This parameter specifies the maximum length, in bytes, of a block. For fixed-length records, the block size must be an integral multiple of the record length (LRECL). For variable-length records, the block size must be as large as the largest block encountered in an application, and must include the four-byte block-length field. The maximum length that can be used is 32,760. For QISAM, the block size specified must be at least ten bytes less than the number of available data bytes on one track of the direct-access device being used. When creating a new data set, the block size may be specified by the DCB, the DD statement, or by the problem program. For existing data sets the source is normally the data set label. With the exception of QISAM and BISAM, the DCB or DD statement can be used to override the label specification.

BUFCB=(BDAM, BISAM, BPAM, BSAM, QISAM, and QSAM). This parameter specifies the address of the buffer-pool control block. This operand is normally omitted, as this address is supplied by the access routines under most access methods and applications. The only time the address must be supplied by the DCB is when the problem program controls buffering and uses the BUILD macro. This is not used when buffering is automatic under BSAM, QISAM, and QSAM or for dynamic buffering under BDAM and BISAM. If the problem program controls all buffering, this parameter should be omitted.

BUFL=(BDAM, BISAM, BPAM, BSAM, QISAM, and QSAM). This parameter specifies the length of each buffer in the buffer pool. Maximum length is 32,760 bytes. The source of this parameter is either the DCB, the DD statement, or the problem program. Requirements depend on access method. For BDAM, BUFL is required only with dynamic buffering. If S is specified for the key-address operand of the READ or WRITE macro instructions, the length must include the key length. For BPAM, BSAM, and QSAM, buffer length is optional. If it is omitted and buffers are obtained automatically, the block-size and key-length parameters are used to establish the buffer length. For BISAM and QISAM the buffer length must be specified only if BUILD or GETPOOL macros are used to obtain a buffer pool. If all buffering is controlled by the problem program, the length should be omitted.

BUFNO=(BDAM, BISAM, BPAM, BSAM, QISAM, and QSAM). This parameter determines the number of buffers assigned to the buffer pool associated with the DCB. The maximum number is 255. When required, the source may be the DCB, the DD statement, or the problem program. Requirements depend on the access method. If the BUILD macro is used, the number must be specified. If GETPOOL is used, the number is provided in the GETPOOL macro. The number must be specified under BPAM and BSAM if buffers are automatically obtained. Under QISAM and QSAM or for dynamic buffering under BDAM and BISAM, the number is optional. If omitted, two buffers are assumed. If the problem program controls all buffering, this parameter should be omitted.

CYLOFL=(QISAM Output). This parameter is too specialized for discussion here.

DDNAME=(BDAM, BISAM, BPAM, BSAM, QISAM, and QSAM). This parameter specifies the name of the corresponding DD statement used to describe the associated data set. This operand must be supplied either in the DCB or by the problem program before the OPEN macro is issued.

DEVD=(BSAM and QSAM). This parameter specifies the type of device on which the data set can or does reside. The following table lists the devices and the codes used to indicate them.

Device	Code
Direct access	DA
Magnetic tape	TA
Paper tape	PT
On-line printer	PR
Card punch	PC
Card reader or card reader/punch	RD

The codes are given in the order of device independence. Thus, for a given code, the data set can reside on any device of lower or equal level in the list. If omitted, DA is assumed. No other source is available. If DEVD is coded, additional operands not given in Table 12.2 are available for specific devices. These include density (DEN=) specifications for magnetic tape, recording technique (TRTCH=) for seven-track tape, paper-tape code (CODE=), line spacing for printer (PRTSP=), card-reader mode (MODE=) of operation, and card-stacker bin (STACK=) selection. All of these optional operands are useful only in special applications and may be specified either by the DCB, the DD statement, or the problem program. See IBM Reference C28-6647 for details.

DSORG=(BDAM, BISAM, BPAM, BSAM, QISAM, and QSAM). This parameter specifies the organization of the data set and whether the data set contains any location-dependent information that would prohibit moving the data set (specified by the letter U). The following list provides the code letters for each organization.

Organization	Code
BDAM	DA or DAU (PS or PSU when creating data set)
BISAM	IS
BPAM	PO or POU
BSAM	PS or PSU
QISAM	IS or ISU (ISU only for creating data set)
QSAM	PS or PSU

The only source for this parameter is the DCB, and it must be specified.

EODAD=(BPAM, BSAM, QISAM, and QSAM). This parameter specifies the address of the routine to be given control when the end of the data set is reached. The source is either the DCB or the problem program. If the operand is omitted, and the end of data set is reached, the program is terminated.

EROPT=(QSAM). This parameter is used to indicate the options to be taken when an uncorrectable input or output error occurs. Details are given in Chapter 13.

EXLST=(BDAM, BISAM, BPAM, BSAM, QISAM, and QSAM). This parameter specifies the problem program exit list. This list must be provided only if special label or data control block exits are required for processing the data set. If provided, the list must begin on a full-word boundary. The format and content of the exit list can be found in IBM Reference C28-6646. The source is either the DCB or the problem program before the exit routines are needed.

KEYLEN=(BDAM, BPAM, BSAM, and QISAM Output). This parameter specifies the length, in bytes, of the keys used in the data set. Except for QISAM, the keys are associated with blocks on direct access devices. For QISAM, the keys are associated with records. The maximum key length is 255 bytes. The source can be the DCB, the DD statement, or the problem program. The key length must be defined before the completion of the data control block exit routine when creating a data set. If, under BDAM, standard labels are used, the key-length information can be supplied by the data-set label of an existing data set. If a key length is not given while using BDAM, no input or output requests may be issued that require a key. For BPAM and BSAM with standard labels, the key length may be supplied by an existing data-set label. If no key length is given before the OPEN macro is issued, a length of zero is assumed. For QISAM using existing data sets with standard labels, the key length can be supplied only from the data-set label.

LIMCT=(BDAM). This parameter is used to specify the extent of the search when the extended-search option is requested under BDAM. Details appear in Chapter 14. The source is either the DCB, the DD statement, or the problem program.

LRECL=(BPAM, BSAM, QISAM Output, and QSAM). This parameter specifies the length of logical records contained in the data set. For variable-length records, the maximum length should be specified. The logical record length usually does not exceed the block size (BLKSIZE). In spanned records, a subject not discussed in this text, the logical record length may exceed the block size. The source is either the DCB, the DD statement, or the problem program. Standard labels in existing data sets can also provide this parameter. Under BPAM, only fixed-record-length specification is required. Under BSAM, the logical record length can be omitted; if so, it is set equal to the block size. For QISAM, with unblocked records with a relative key position of zero, the record length includes only the data portion of the record.

MACRF=(BDAM, BISAM, BPAM, BSAM, QISAM, and QSAM). This parameter is required and must appear in the DCB macro instruction. The purpose of this operand is to specify the macro instructions and facilities to be used by the programmer in processing the associated data set. Each access method utilizes a different set of macros for reading and writing the data set. However, options also exist within each set. Thus, the programmer must indicate choices from among a list of possible code letters, each representing a particular macro or facility. QSAM choices are discussed in Chapter 13. BDAM choices are presented in Chapter 14. The other access-method macro choices can be found in IBM Reference C28-6647.

MSHI=(BISAM). This parameter is too specialized for discussion here.

MSWA=(BISAM). Also too specialized for discussion.

NCP=(BISAM, BPAM, and BSAM). This parameter indicates the maximum number of READ and WRITE macro instructions that can be issued before a CHECK macro instruction is issued. The maximum number allowed is 99. The source is either the DCB, the DD statement, the problem program, or omitted. If omitted, the value assumed is one.

Character	Meaning
A	The record contains USASI control characters.
B	The records are blocked.
F	The records are fixed in length.
M	The records contain machine-code control characters.
S	The records are written in standard blocks for fixed-length records. A record may span more than one block for variable-length records.
T	The records may be written onto overflow tracks if required. Exchange buffering cannot be used.
U	The records are of undefined length.
V	The records are of variable length.

NTM=(QISAM Output). This parameter is too specialized for discussion here.

OPTCD=(BDAM, BPAM, BSAM, QISAM Output, and QSAM). This parameter is used to code various optional services that can be performed by the access routines. Again, each access method has a separate set of options coded by various letters. QSAM choices are given in Chapter 13, BDAM choices in Chapter 14. The source for these codes can be either the DCB, the DD statement, the problem program, or omitted. All options must be indicated by the same source.

RECFM=(BDAM, BPAM, BSAM, QISAM Output, and QSAM). This parameter is used to specify the format and characteristics of the records in the data set. Letter characters used in the specification are listed on p. 218.

The following combinations of characters are possible for the indicated access methods. Information in parentheses represents optional specifications. Only one or none of the codes can be chosen from among those between one pair of parentheses. The parentheses are omitted in actual codings.

BDAM: U, V, F, or FT
QISAM: F or FB
BPAM: Option 1: U(T)(A or M)
         Option 2: V(B, T, or BT)(A or M)
         Option 3: F(B, T, or BT) (A or M)
BSAM: Option 1: U(T)(A or M)
         Option 2: V(B, T, or BT)(A or M)
         Option 3: F(B, S, T, BS, BT, ST, or BST)(A or M)
QSAM: Same three options as for BSAM

This information can be supplied either by the DCB, the DD statement, the standard data-set labels, the problem program before issuing the OPEN macro, or may be omitted. If omitted, undefined-length records are assumed without any further optional features. All information must be supplied by the same source.

RKP=(QISAM Output). This parameter is too specialized for discussion.

SMSI=(BISAM). Too specialized for discussion.

SMSW=(BISAM). Too specialized for discussion.

SYNAD=(BDAM, BPAM, BSAM, QISAM, and QSAM). This parameter specifies the address of an error routine that is to be given control upon detecting an uncorrectable I/O error. For details concerning this operand and the contents of registers upon entry to the error routine, see Chapters 13 and 14 and IBM Reference C28-6647. The source of this operand can be either the DCB, the problem program, or omitted. If omitted, the action indicated by the EROPT= operand is taken for QSAM; otherwise the program is terminated.

This completes the discussion of the various DCB key-word operands. The definition of the OPEN macro instruction is now presented.

12.2 Macro Instruction OPEN

symbol   OPEN   (*dcb*,(*options*),...)
where *symbol* is optional, *dcb* is a required symbolic reference to a
DCB macro statement, and *options* are optional operands taken from
Table 12.3. Several different DCBs may be listed in the same statement.

This macro causes the indicated DCBs to be completed in preparation
for processing the associated data sets. Any required access routines not
in main storage are loaded at OPEN time. The indicated data sets are
opened and prepared for the type of processing specified by the options
associated with each DCB address. Table 12.3 contains the various
possible options. If option 1 is omitted, INPUT is assumed. If option 2
is omitted, DISP is assumed. Option 1 must be coded if option 2 is
coded. BISAM ignores coded options. OUTPUT or OUTIN must be
coded when creating a data set.

TABLE 12.3   Open Macro Options

Access-Method Name	Device Type					
	Magnetic Tape		Direct Access		Other Types	
	Optn. 1	Optn. 2	Optn. 1	Optn. 2	Optn. 1	Optn. 2
QSAM	INPUT OUTPUT RDBACK	,REREAD ,LEAVE ,DISP	INPUT OUTPUT UPDAT	,REREAD ,LEAVE ,DISP	INPUT OUTPUT	—
BSAM	INPUT OUTPUT INOUT OUTIN RDBACK	,REREAD ,LEAVE ,DISP	INPUT OUTPUT INOUT OUTIN UPDAT	,REREAD ,LEAVE ,DISP	INPUT OUTPUT	—
QISAM	—	—	INPUT OUTPUT	—	—	—
BPAM BDAM	—	—	INPUT OUTPUT UPDAT	—	—	—
Note: Optionally select one choice from vertical stacks.						

The following statements describe each of the options given in Table 12.3

and the implications for the data set under the control of the OPEN macro.

Option	Meaning
INPUT:	Input data set only
INOUT:	Input data set first and then, without reopening, output data set
OUTPUT:	Output data set only (OUTPUT is equivalent to UPDAT for BDAM)
OUTIN:	Output data set first and then, without reopening, input data set
RDBACK:	Input data set, positioned to read backward
UPDAT:	Data set to be updated in place, or blocks to be added, or both
LEAVE:	No repositioning performed at volume switching
REREAD:	Position current volume to reprocess the data set when volume switching occurs
DISP:	Perform volume positioning implied by the DISP parameter of the DD statement, as follows:

DISP Parameter	Action
PASS	Forward-space to end of data set
DELETE	Rewind current volume
KEEP, CATLG, or UNCATLG	Rewind and unload current volume

12.3 Macro Instruction CLOSE

symbol   CLOSE   (*dcb,option*,....),TYPE=T
where *symbol* is optional, *dcb* is the symbolic reference to a DCB statement, *option* is either REREAD, LEAVE, or DISP, and TYPE=T is optional. Several DCBs can be listed in the same CLOSE macro statement.

This macro instruction logically disconnects or repositions the associated data sets for access by the problem program. The specified options have the same meanings as the options of the same name discussed for the OPEN macro. If the option is omitted and TYPE=T is coded, LEAVE is assumed. If TYPE=T is not coded, DISP is assumed. TYPE=T can be coded for BSAM only. TYPE=T indicates that labels are created and volumes are positioned, but the contents of the DCB are not altered. The BSAM data set can then be processed without issuing another OPEN macro.

After the OPEN macro instruction has been executed by the supervisor routines, bit 3 of the DCBOFLGS field in the data control block is set to 1 if the DCB has been opened successfully, otherwise the bit is set to 0. Thus, the programmer can check to see if the DCB has been successfully opened before beginning to process the associated data set. Symbolic references to fields within the DCB can be obtained by using a macro called DCBD. For details of this macro instruction see IBM Reference C28-6647.

Several specific examples of DCB, OPEN, and CLOSE macros are presented and discussed in Chapters 13 and 14 in connection with input and output operations using QSAM and BDAM access methods.

STUDY EXERCISES

1. What are I/O channels, channel commands, and channel programs?
2. What are multiplex and burst modes of channel operation?
3. Describe briefly the four CPU instructions for input and output operations.
4. Describe briefly the Channel Address Word, the Channel Status Word, and Channel Command Words.
5. Distinguish between command and data chaining.
6. How does the programmer accomplish loops and branches within a channel program?
7. What are the four divisions of the Operating System and their purposes?
8. What are the five data-set organizations?
9. What are the two access techniques?
10. What are the eight access methods?
11. What is the data control block and its purpose?
12. What are data sets, data records, data blocks, buffers, volumes, and data-set labels?
13. Why and how are data sets opened and closed?
14. Which DCB operands must be coded in every DCB macro? What are their purposes?

Chapter **thirteen**

Queued Sequential-Access Method

The Queued Sequential-Access Method (QSAM) of input and output (I/O) is perhaps the easiest of the access methods to learn and use. By providing a maximum of automatic processing facilities, QSAM relieves the problem programmer of several details that he must otherwise deal with when doing I/O in assembly language. However, QSAM can be used only to process data sequentially. For nonsequential access, other more complicated methods are required, such as the Basic Direct-Access Method (BDAM) to be discussed in Chapter 14.

Major simplifying functions provided by QSAM are automatic synchronization of I/O operations with computations and the automatic deblocking and blocking of physical and logical records. Given advance knowledge that access is to be sequential, QSAM input routines can read input records ahead of those requested by the processing program. At the same time, input composed of physical blocks is deblocked into logical records for use by the processing program. Concurrently, QSAM output routines can collect logical records created by the processing program, block them into physical blocks, and, when sufficient records have been collected, write a block into the output data set. Thus, overlap of I/O and computation can be maintained without concerning the problem programmer about problems of synchronization and blocking.

I/O operations under QSAM, as in other access methods, involve the use of a particular set of operational macros in addition to the required DCB, OPEN, and CLOSE. Section 13.1 presents and discusses the GET and PUT macros. How they are used in reading and writing operations involving sequential data sets and the queued technique is discussed in Section 13.2. Section 13.3 discusses specific requirements of the DCB, OPEN, and CLOSE macros in conjunction with QSAM. Finally, Section 13.4 presents examples of programs designed for performing complete I/O operations using QSAM.

13.1   THE GET AND PUT MACROS

Input under QSAM is accomplished with the GET macro. In general, the execution of this macro causes the next logical record from the indicated data set to be made available to the requesting program. The exact method by which the record is made available is determined by the MACRF operand of the DCB associated with the indicated data set. Three possible methods of presentation are the locate, move, and substitute modes.

The locate mode causes the address of the buffer area containing the input record to be returned in register 1 at the conclusion of the GET macro. The move mode causes the input record to be physically moved into an area, called the work area, specified by the GET macro. The substitute mode resembles the locate mode but replaces the input buffer by a new area specified by the GET macro. This latter mode of operation is somewhat specialized and sophisticated and is used only with the exchange buffering technique, a subject not discussed in this text. For a discussion of exchange buffering and the substitution mode of operation, refer to IBM Reference C28-6646. Only the technique of simple buffering is involved in this presentation.

The GET macro is formally defined in Definition 13.1.

The operation of the PUT macro, essentially the reverse of the GET, causes an output record provided by the problem program to be blocked and buffered as output to a specified data set. Again, the same three modes of operation are possible: the locate mode, the move mode, and the substitute mode. Only the locate and move modes are discussed here. Refer to IBM Reference C28-6646 for a discussion of the substitute mode and exchange buffering. With the locate mode of operation, an address is returned in register 1, which indicates the buffer location for the next output record. This method of operation requires that the PUT be issued once prior to any output. Each additional execution of a PUT causes the record located at the previously supplied location to be written. The final record is written by the CLOSE macro. In the move mode, the control program moves the output record from the indicated work area to an output buffer. The address of the work area is returned in register 1. The mode of operation for the PUT is specified by the MACRF operand of the associated DCB.

13.1 Macro Instruction GET

symbol   GET   *dcb address, area address*
where *symbol* is an optional reference symbol, *dcb address* is a symbolic reference to the DCB associated with the data set under consideration, and *area address* is an optional symbolic reference to a work area.

Causes the next logical record of the data set associated with the indicated DCB to be obtained. The address of the record is returned in register 1. The logical-record-length field of the DCB is set to the length of the record. If the DCB specifies the locate mode, *area address* is omitted and the record remains in the input buffer. If the DCB specifies the move mode, the record is moved to the *area address* and C(R1) is set to the *area address*. See IBM Reference C28-6647 for the meaning under the substitute mode. In the event of reading beyond the end of the data set, the routine specified by the EODAD operand of the DCB is given control. In case of an error, the routine specified by the SYNAD operand of the DCB is given control.

13.2 Macro Instruction PUT

symbol   PUT   *dcb address, area address*
where *symbol* is an optional symbolic reference, *dcb address* is a symbolic reference to the DCB associated with the data set under consideration, and *area address* is an optional symbolic reference to a work area.

Causes the information provided to be written on the associated data set. The length of the record is specified by the LRECL field of the associated DCB. If the locate mode is specified by the DCB, the PUT macro returns, in register 1, the address of a buffer for the next output record. The record is not actually written until another PUT is issued, at which time another buffer address is supplied. *Area address* is omitted for the locate mode. If the move mode is specified, the information at *area address* is physically moved to an output buffer by the control program. For compatibility purposes, *area address* is returned in register 1. In case of an error, control is given to the routine specified by the SYNAD operand of the DCB.

The PUT macro is formally defined in Definition 13.2.

If an uncorrectable error is detected in either the GET or PUT macros, control is given to a routine whose address is specified by the SYNAD operand of the associated DCB. If an error routine is not supplied, abnormal termination of the program occurs. Upon entry to a supplied error routine, general-purpose register contents are as shown in Appendix 4. Certain status indicators are also made available for error analysis. The meaning of these indicators is presented in Appendix 5. For those readers who are interested, a special macro called SYNADAF is available for automatic analysis of I/O error conditions. For details of this macro refer to IBM Reference C28-6647.

If an end of data-set (EODAD) exit routine is not specified by the DCB associated with the data set, abnormal termination of the program occurs when an end of file is detected. Under normal operating conditions the programmer should specify such an exit, at which point a CLOSE macro is issued, logically disconnecting the data set from the processing program. It is quite proper to read data sets using QSAM techniques not knowing how many records the data set may contain. There will also be occasions when no further processing is required after exhausting all input records; thus the absence of an exit routine would be acceptable. During the resulting abnormal termination, the operating system, with high probability, will successfully close all presently open data sets.

A third processing macro, PUTX, allows an input record from a sequential data set, after desired update is complete, to be returned to the same position of the same data set. However, this operation cannot be performed on any device except a direct-access unit. For example, a data set residing on a tape unit cannot be updated in this fashion. In order to update a tape using QSAM, a second tape file must be written on a second tape unit. A second restriction on the use of PUTX requires that the updated record be the exact same size as the original input record. Because of these rather limiting restrictions, discussion of the PUTX macro is pursued no further here. Details can be found in IBM References C28-6646 and C28-6647.

13.2   LOCATE VERSUS MOVE MODE USING GETS AND PUTS

Several different processing strategies can be formulated using various combinations of the two modes of GET and PUT operation. This section discusses the different possibilities, showing the possible relationships among input buffers, work areas, and output buffers.

Input can be processed in an input buffer and then moved by the access routines to an output buffer. A second version provides that the access routines move the input record to an output buffer before processing occurs. A third approach is to have the system move the input record from the input buffer to a work area for processing and then move the output data to an output buffer. A fourth method involves the processing program in the movement of data from one buffer to another.

It might be mentioned in passing that the inclusion of the substitute mode, the PUTX macro, and exchange buffering, alluded to previously, would extend the processing variations even further. In fact, one sophisticated combination of techniques allows input from one data set, processing of that information, and final writing into a second data set all without any transfer of data from one buffer to another. Only the initial input and the final output transfer of data into and out of main storage is required. The discussion that follows is limited to the first four variations, involving only the locate and move modes using GET and PUT.

13.2.1   GET-locate, PUT-move Combination

This method of processing uses the GET macro to obtain the address of the next input record. Using this address, the problem program processes the record in the input buffer. After processing is complete, the resulting information is moved by the system to an output buffer by the execution of the PUT macro. Figure 13.1 illustrates this mode of operation.

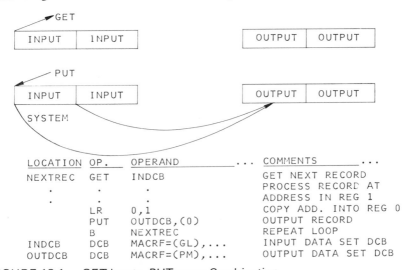

LOCATION	OP.	OPERAND	...	COMMENTS ...
NEXTREC	GET	INDCB		GET NEXT RECORD
.	.	.		PROCESS RECORD AT
.	.	.		ADDRESS IN REG 1
	LR	0,1		COPY ADD. INTO REG 0
	PUT	OUTDCB,(0)		OUTPUT RECORD
	B	NEXTREC		REPEAT LOOP
INDCB	DCB	MACRF=(GL),...		INPUT DATA SET DCB
OUTDCB	DCB	MACRF=(PM),...		OUTPUT DATA SET DCB

FIGURE 13.1   GET-locate, PUT-move Combination

13.2.2   GET-move, PUT-locate Combination

This method of processing QSAM records uses the GET macro to obtain the next input record. The system automatically moves the record into an area indicated in register 0 at the time the GET is issued. By first issuing a PUT in

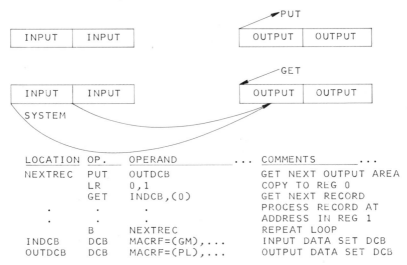

```
       LOCATION  OP.     OPERAND          ...  COMMENTS          ...
       NEXTREC   PUT     OUTDCB                GET NEXT OUTPUT AREA
                 LR      0,1                   COPY TO REG 0
                 GET     INDCB,(0)             GET NEXT RECORD
          .       .       .                    PROCESS RECORD AT
          .       .       .                    ADDRESS IN REG 1
                 B       NEXTREC               REPEAT LOOP
       INDCB     DCB     MACRF=(GM),...        INPUT DATA SET DCB
       OUTDCB    DCB     MACRF=(PL),...        OUTPUT DATA SET DCB
```

FIGURE 13.2   GET-move, PUT-locate Combination

locate mode, the address of a new output buffer is returned in register 1. The address is copied into register 0 before issuing the GET. The PUT does not cause the record currently being processed to be written until the next PUT is issued. Thus, the PUT macro is actually running one record behind the ones being processed. See Figure 13.2 for the program segment and diagram illustrating this process.

13.2.3   GET-move, PUT-move Combination

In this method of processing, the GET causes the system to move the next input record into a specified work area. After processing is complete, the PUT then is used to cause the system to move the output record from the work area specified to an output area. Figure 13.3 illustrates this technique.

13.2.4   GET-locate, PUT-locate Combination

The fourth method involves the locate mode for both the GET and the PUT macros. The PUT is issued first to obtain an address of the next output area. While saving this address, a GET is issued obtaining the address of the next input record. Either after or before processing occurs, the problem program must then move the record from the input area to the output area. The example shown in Figure 13.4 assumes that all records are of fixed length and that the length is exactly 50 bytes.

Because of its general interest, Figure 13.5 shows an example of a program that performs the same function as that shown in Figure 13.4, except that the program is written in such a way that records of variable length can be handled. By obtaining the length of the current record from the LRECL field within the

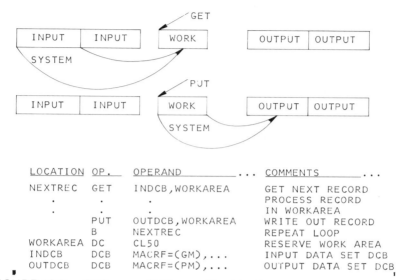

LOCATION	OP.	OPERAND	...	COMMENTS ...
NEXTREC	GET	INDCB,WORKAREA		GET NEXT RECORD
.	.	.		PROCESS RECORD
.	.	.		IN WORKAREA
	PUT	OUTDCB,WORKAREA		WRITE OUT RECORD
	B	NEXTREC		REPEAT LOOP
WORKAREA	DC	CL50		RESERVE WORK AREA
INDCB	DCB	MACRF=(GM),...		INPUT DATA SET DCB
OUTDCB	DCB	MACRF=(PM),...		OUTPUT DATA SET DCB

FIGURE 13.3   GET-move, PUT-move Combination

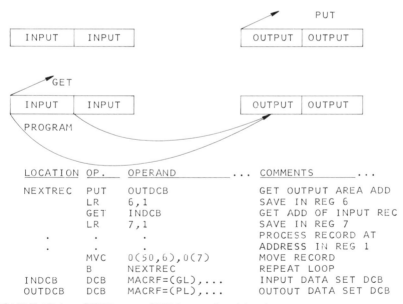

LOCATION	OP.	OPERAND	...	COMMENTS ...
NEXTREC	PUT	OUTDCB		GET OUTPUT AREA ADD
	LR	6,1		SAVE IN REG 6
	GET	INDCB		GET ADD OF INPUT REC
	LR	7,1		SAVE IN REG 7
.	.	.		PROCESS RECORD AT
.	.	.		ADDRESS IN REG 1
	MVC	0(50,6),0(7)		MOVE RECORD
	B	NEXTREC		REPEAT LOOP
INDCB	DCB	MACRF=(GL),...		INPUT DATA SET DCB
OUTDCB	DCB	MACRF=(PL),...		OUTOUT DATA SET DCB

FIGURE 13.4   GET-locate, PUT-locate Combination

DCB associated with the input data set, a move instruction can be indirectly
executed with the execute instruction, thereby changing the length specification
of the operand in an indirect manner. Obtaining the length is accomplished
through the use of a special DCBD macro that yields a dummy macro expansion

```
LOCATION OP.    OPERAND          ...  COMMENTS          ...
NEXTREC  PUT     OUTDCB               GET OUTPUT AREA ADD
         LR      6,1                  SAVE IN REG 6
         GET     INDCB                GET ADD OF INPUT REC
         LR      7,1                  SAVE IN REG 7
         USING   IHADCB,5             DEFINE SPECIAL BASE
         LA      5,INDCB              LOAD ADD OF INPUT DCB
         LH      4,DCBLRECL           LOAD RECORD LENGTH
         SH      4,=H'1'              SUBTRACT ONE
         EX      4,MOVEREC            MOVE RECORD
   .        .       .                 PROCESS RECORD AT
   .        .       .                 ADDRESS IN REG 1
         B       NEXTREC              REPEAT LOOP
MOVEREC  MVC     0(0,6),0(7)          MOVE INSTRUCTION
INDCB    DCB     MACRF=(GL),...       INPUT DATA SET DCB
OUTDCB   DCB     MACRF=(PL),...       OUTPUT DATA SET DCB
         DCBD    DSORG=(LR)           SYMBOLIC DCB EXPANSION
```

FIGURE 13.5   Program for Variable Record Lengths

of a DCB with symbolic references. By knowing that the location of the logical record length is found at symbolic location DCBLRECL, and by defining and loading a special base register that points to the beginning of the DCBD expansion, called IHADCB, one load instruction, using INDCB as the actual base address, is all that is required to retrieve the record length. Since object-code operand-length specifications must be one less than actual lengths, a one must be subtracted from the retrieved length before the execute instruction is performed.

13.3   DCB, OPEN, AND CLOSE REQUIREMENTS FOR QSAM

Special considerations are involved in correct specification of DCB, OPEN, and CLOSE macros for QSAM processing. The primary concern is for consistency in the coding of the various macro options that are to interact during access within a single data set. Central to all of the access methods and their associated processing routines is the data control block. All processing macros work out of or in conjunction with the DCB and its contents. In most cases, if an inconsistency does appear, one routine or another will detect it and cause an abnormal termination. A very comprehensive set of diagnostic messages, coded by completion codes, is available for reference. All System/360 computing installations have such a reference available for their users.

As noted in Chapter 12, two DCB operands are always required. They are the DSORG and MACRF operands. The first defines the organization of the associated data set. For QSAM, the code specification is either PS or PSU. Most problems can be handled by the PS option, as PSU is applicable only in those cases where the data set cannot be moved. Thus, the operand should usually be coded as DSORG=PS. The second mandatory operand is used to describe the macros that are going to be used to process the data set. QSAM choices are indicated by groups of certain letters coded within a pair of parentheses. The possible letters and their meanings are as follows:

Character	Definition
C	CNTRL macro to be used
G	GET macro to be used
L	Operation to be in locate mode
M	Operation to be in move mode
P	PUT or PUTX macro to be used
T	Operation to be in substitute mode

The CNTRL macro provides special functions, such as printer spacing, card-stacker selecting, and tape handling, which are all device dependent. Programs using the CNTRL macro are therefore device dependent and cannot be used for general processing. For details of the CNTRL macro consult IBM Reference C28-6647.

The six letters defined above can be coded in a variety of ways, as shown in the following list. The letter X represents either an M, L, or T. The letter C is optional in all cases.

Code	Meaning
(GXC)	GET in locate, move, or substitute mode.
(PXC)	PUT in locate, move, or substitute mode.
(GXC,PXC)	GET and PUT in locate, move, or substitute mode. Used for input and output of the same data set.

Thus, a typical choice for coding the MACRF operand for an input data set is MACRF=(GM). For an output data set, MACRF=(PM) would be a reasonable choice.

Most of the remaining DCB operands that are optional for QSAM can be omitted for most processing applications. For example, if buffer control is to be under automatic system control, as usually it is, BFALN, BFTEK, BUFCB, BUFL, and BUFNO can be omitted. The result is automatic simple buffering, two buffers being allocated. Note that even when the problem program controls all buffering, some of the buffer operands are still optional.

The DEVD operand should be omitted unless the data set is to reside on a particular device on a permanent basis. When omitted, direct access is chosen; thus the data set could reside on any device. It is especially useful, in a system employing spooling techniques, to specify a device that is as high in the independence ranking as possible. This allows data sets to be moved from one device to another, as they often are under spooling conditions. See Chapter 12 for further discussion of this operand.

The EROPT operand is used to specify what action is to be taken if an uncorrectable error is detected and no SYNAD exit routine is specified. The easiest and probably the most common choice of action is to terminate the job. This choice can be indicated by simply omitting the operand. See IBM Reference C28-6647 for other choices.

The EXLST operand is only useful to experienced programmers who need to perform special processing operations in connection with opening data sets, reading special user labels in input data sets, and creating special user labels in output data sets. This operand should therefore be omitted in most cases.

The OPTCD operand specifies that certain optional services are being requested of the control program. For QSAM, optional services include validity checking for write operations, chained scheduling, and special printer features. Again, except for the experienced programmer, this operand need not be coded.

The EODAD operand used to specify the end of data-set exit routine address, is a useful operand even for the beginner. If the programmer wishes to perform additional functions after exhausting input records, an EODAD exit address must be indicated. For example, the specification of EODAD=ENDUP would cause control to be given to that part of the user's program beginning with location ENDUP when the end of the associated data set was detected.

Unless special error analysis is to be performed, the SYNAD exit routine address operand should be omitted. If it is omitted and an error does occur, the program is terminated with an appropriate completion code, which may indicate the type of error upon reference to the diagnostic manual.

The remaining operands, BLKSIZE, DDNAME, LRECL, and RECFM, are usually coded. The DDNAME operand is used to coordinate the associated data control block with a data definition (DD) card to be included among the JCL cards accompanying the job. This DD card describes the physical location of the data set at the time the job is to be processed. For example, the specification DDNAME=CARDSIN might be used to associate the DCB in question with the data set being described by the following DD card:

//GO.CARDSIN DD *

This data set would normally be made up of the card records that follow this DD card in the job deck. Take note at this point that in a system involving spooling operations, the actual data set will most likely be residing on a direct-access device by the time the problem program attempts to process the data within the data set. By the same token, output data sets that are destined for the output printer or card punch will first be spooled to a direct-access device. To indicate such to the system, the associated DD card specifies a particular system (SYSOUT) class. Most System/360 systems reserve SYSOUT Class A for the printer and SYSOUT Class B for the punch. Thus, the operand DDNAME=LINESOUT and the associated DD card

//GO.LINESOUT DD SYSOUT=A

would cause the associated data set to eventually be printed on the system line printer.

The RECFM operand must be coded in the DCB or specified from another source to avoid defaulting to undefined-length records. For most simple applications, certainly those for beginners, the fixed-length blocked-records specification is a reasonable choice and is coded as RECFM=FB.

The LRECL operand should then specify the length of these fixed-length records. For records originating from cards, a length of 80 is appropriate. Records designed for the printer may have a length anywhere between 1 and 132, with values of 80, 100, 120, and 132 being the most common. When such records are finally printed, each record uses a line on the printer with single spacing in the absence of special control information or CNTRL macro operations.

Finally, the BLKSIZE operand should specify some multiple of the LRECL, such as 800 employing a blocking factor of 1 to 10. Again, under spooling conditions, existing input data sets may arrive at the processing stage with a predetermined blocking factor. However, the factor contained within the labels of the existing data set can be used to specify logical record length and block size by omitting the specifications from the DCB macro.

A typical DCB coding might appear as shown in Figure 13.6 along with its full expansion. This DCB is used for the input data set in the example in the next section.

Before a data set may be processed in any fashion, it must be opened using the OPEN macro. A QSAM data set may be opened for INPUT on any device if it is an existing data set residing on the device. Likewise, a data set may be opened for OUTPUT for any device that can receive a newly created data set. A magnetic-tape data set can also be opened for reading backwards (RDBACK). A direct-access data set can be opened for updating (UPDAT). Repositioning options for rereading (REREAD), no positioning (LEAVE), and DD card dispositions (DISP) can be specified for magnetic-tape and direct-access data sets only. The default option for the opening option is INPUT. The default option for positioning is DISP.

For most applications, particularly for beginning programmers, the OPEN options are INPUT for input data sets and OUTPUT for output data sets. The second option for repositioning should be omitted. Thus, for an input data set whose DCB is at symbolic location CARDS in a program, the OPEN macro operand field should contain (CARDS) or (CARDS,(INPUT)). For an output data set with DCB at location LINES, the OPEN macro operand field

```
LOC    OBJECT CODE         ADDR1 ADDP2  STMT  SOURCE STATEMENT

                                        4 CARDS   DCB   DSORG=PS,MACRF=GM,DDNAME=CARDSIN,EODAD=QUIT,
                                                        BLKSIZE=800,LRECL=80,RECFM=FB

                                                        DATA CONTROL BLOCK

000000                                  6+*
000000                                  7+*
000000                                  8+         ORG   *-0 TO ELIMINATE UNUSED SPACE
                                        9+CARDS    DS    OF ORIGIN ON WORD BOUNDRY
                                       10+         ORG   *+0 TO ORIGIN GENERATION

                                                        DIRECT ACCESS DEVICE INTERFACE

000000 0000000000000000               12+*
000000 00000000                       14+         DC    BL16'0' FDAD,DVTBL
000010 00000000                       15+         DC    A(0) KEYLE,DEVT,TRBAL

                                                        COMMON ACCESS METHOD INTERFACE

                                       17+*
000014 00                             19+         DC    AL1(0) BUFNO
000015 000001                         20+         DC    AL3(1) BUFCB
000018 0000                           21+         DC    AL2(0) BUFL
00001A 4000                           22+         DC    BL2'0100000000000000' DSORG
00001C 00000001                       23+         DC    A(1) IOBAD

                                                        FOUNDATION EXTENSION

                                       25+*
000020 00                             27+         DC    BL1'00000000' BFTEK,BFALN,HIARCHY
000021 000060                         28+         DC    AL3(QUIT) EODAD
000024 90                             29+         DC    BL1'10010000' RECFM
000025 000000                         30+         DC    AL3(0) EXLST
```

```
                                                          FOUNDATION BLOCK

                      32+*

000028 C3C1D9C4E2C9D540    34+         DC    CL8'CARDSIN' DDNAME
000030 02                  35+         DC    BL1'00000010' OFLGS
000031 00                  36+         DC    BL1'00000000' IFLG
000032 5000                37+         DC    BL2'0101000000000000' MACR

                      39+*                                 BSAM-BPAM-QSAM INTERFACE

000034 00                  41+         DC    BL1'00000000' RER1
000035 000001              42+         DC    AL3(1) CHECK, GERR, PERR
000038 00000001            43+         DC    A(1) SYNAD
00003C 0000                44+         DC    H'0' CIND1, CIND2
00003E 0320                45+         DC    AL2(800) BLKSIZE
000040 00000000            46+         DC    F'0' WCPO, WCPL, OFFSR, OFFSW
000044 00000001            47+         DC    A(1) IOBA
000048 00                  48+         DC    AL1(0) NCP
000049 000001              49+         DC    AL3(1) EOBR, EOBAD

                      51+*                                 QSAM INTERFACE

00004C 00000001            53+         DC    A(1) RECAD
000050 0000                54+         DC    H'0' QSWS
000052 0050                55+         DC    AL2(80) LRECL
000054 00                  56+         DC    BL1'00000000' EROPT
000055 000001              57+         DC    AL3(1) CNTRL
000058 00000000            58+         DC    F'0' PRECL
00005C 00000001            59+         DC    A(1) EOB
```

FIGURE 13.6   A Typical DCB Macro Expansion

235

should contain (LINES,(OUTPUT)). To open both data sets with one statement, the operand field should contain (CARDS,,LINES,(OUTPUT)) or (CARDS,(INPUT),LINES,(OUTPUT)).

In closing data sets, only positioning options of REREAD, LEAVE, and DISP are available for QSAM. Again, for beginners, the operand field of the CLOSE macro should specify only the DCB addresses of the data sets being closed, omitting the option. Thus, for the same two data sets discussed above, the proper operands for closing would be as follows. To close only one data set at a time, the operands are (CARDS) or (LINES). To close both in the same statement, the operand is coded as (CARDS,,LINES).

13.4   A COMPLETE EXAMPLE USING QSAM I/O

The example shown in Figure 13.7 is extremely basic in that all it does is print the contents of input data cards. In other words, it lists the data cards that follow the program. Thus, there is no processing between the application of the GETs and PUTs. Because of its straightforward simplicity, the GET-move and PUT-move strategy is used in this program. Only the source program is shown; therefore no macro expansions appear in Figure 13.7.

The first thing the program does after loading the base register is open the two data sets. The input data set, whose DCB is at location CARDS, is opened for input. The output data set, whose DCB is at location LINES, is opened for output. The program then enters a loop at location READ. Within the loop a GET is issued for the CARDS data set, specifying that the next record is to be moved by the system into the 80-byte field called WORKAREA. Notice that the size of the work area coincides with the logical record length given in the DCB. The contents of the work area are then moved by the system to an output buffer when the PUT is issued. The program then branches back to READ.

```
LOCATION  OP.    OPERAND             . . .    COMMENTS          . . .
LISTER    START  0                            SET LOCATION COUNTER
          BALR   12,0                          LOAD BASE REGISTER
          USING  ::,12                         DEFINE BASE REGISTER
          OPEN   (CARDS,,LINES,(OUTPUT))  OPEN DATA SETS
READ      GET    CARDS,WORKAREA                GET NEXT RECORD
          PUT    LINES,WORKAREA                PUT IT OUT
          B      READ                          REPEAT READ LOOP
QUIT      CLOSE  (CARDS,,LINES)                CLOSE DATA SETS
          ABEND  101                           TERMINATE
WORKAREA  DS     80C                           RESERVE 80 BYTES
CARDS     DCB    DSORG=PS,MACRF=(GM),DDNAME=CARDSIN,            X
                 EODAD=QUIT,BLKSIZE=800,LRECL=80,RECFM=FB
LINES     DCB    DSORG=PS,MACRF=(PM),DDNAME=LINESOUT,           X
                 BLKSIZE=800,LRECL=80,RECFM=FB
          END    LISTER
```

FIGURE 13.7   Example of QSAM I/O

```
JOB CARD
PASSWORD CARD
// EXEC ASMFCLG
//ASM.SYSIN DD ::
         .
    ASSEMBLY-LANGUAGE PROGRAM FROM FIGURE 13.7
         .
/::
//GO.SYSUDUMP DD SYSOUT=A
//GO.LINESOUT DD SYSOUT=A
//GO.CARDSIN DD ::
         .
    DATA CARDS
         .
/::
```

FIGURE 13.8   Card Layout for Program in Figure 13.7

If, during the process of reading input records, the end of the data set is reached, control is given to location QUIT. At this point a CLOSE macro is issued, closing both data sets. The program then terminates with a completion code of USER 101.

Figure 13.8 shows the card layout for running the program shown in Figure 13.7. Notice the DD cards with the same DDNAMEs as given in the DCB macros of the program.

PROGRAMMING EXERCISE

Reprogram the problem of either Chapter 7, 8, or 9, using QSAM techniques to eliminate the Fortran main program. In other words, the assembly-language program becomes the main program and does its own I/O. The proper card layout with JCL is shown in Figure 13.8. The //GO.SYSUDUMP DD SYSOUT=A card should be included in case an error occurs.

STUDY EXERCISES

1. What are the major advantages of the Queued Sequential-Access Method of performing I/O operations?
2. Discuss the GET and PUT macros, distinguishing between the locate and move modes of operation.
3. In the four variations of GET and PUT processing combinations, which ones involve data movement by the system and which ones by the problem programmer?
4. List the QSAM DCB macro operands in order of relative use from highly used to very seldom.

5. List the various possibilities for the MACRF operand.
6. What would be involved in making the program of Figure 13.7 punch card copies of the input data cards?
7. Reprogram the program in Figure 13.7, using the GET-locate and PUT-move combination technique.
8. Reprogram the program in Figure 13.7, using the GET-move and PUT-locate combination technique.

Chapter **fourteen**

Basic Direct-Access Method

The Basic Direct-Access Method (BDAM) of I/O is somewhat more difficult to learn than QSAM; however, it is very useful in allowing the reading and writing of data in a random or nonsequential manner. This technique is invaluable in environments where rapid access to data is desired and where the user is unable to predict beforehand which data block will be requested. To gain this direct-access advantage, automatic synchronization of I/O operations and the blocking and deblocking of logical records is sacrificed; therefore the problem programmer must perform these functions.

The BDAM approach to I/O, as other basic-access techniques, utilizes the READ and WRITE macros to read and write blocks of data from and to direct-access data sets. It might be mentioned in passing that direct-access data sets can be read or written sequentially using a sequential technique, such as QSAM. However, the data set must be residing on a direct-access device for access using BDAM. It is common practice, where possible, to create new data sets using QSAM or BSAM and then use BDAM to process the data sets at later dates.

Since control is normally returned to the problem program following a READ or WRITE macro before the associated I/O operation is completed, the programmer must verify that requested input is actually in core before processing the input, or that output is actually written before reusing the output buffer. A special macro, called CHECK, is provided for verifying the completion of I/O requests. The CHECK also determines if an I/O error has occurred and, if so, passes control to the SYNAD routine. If error processing is not to be automatic, the WAIT macro can be used instead of CHECK. In either case, the associated task (problem program) is placed in a wait state until the respective I/O request is complete. This is an explicit wait request, unlike QSAM where the GET and PUT macros carry an implied wait in their execution. The discussion of the CHECK and WAIT macros, as well as the READ and WRITE, involves another entity, the Data Event Control Block (DECB).

As with QSAM, there are many coding variations and considerations for BDAM operations that are beyond the scope of this text. Thus, only the most fundamental and, hopefully, the most useful concepts are presented. Where a major variation exists and is not discussed, an appropriate IBM reference is given. Section 14.1 discusses the concepts of the DECB and the READ, WRITE, CHECK, and WAIT macros. Section 14.2 describes typical DCB, OPEN, and CLOSE macro operands required for BDAM applications. Finally, Section 14.3 presents a few examples of the many ways that the various macros can be coded and used.

14.1   MACROS FOR BDAM OPERATIONS

Input from a direct-access data set is performed by the control program at the request of a READ macro. This macro causes a block (one physical record) of data to be retrieved from the data set and placed at a specified location in main storage. The problem program usually regains control following the READ prior to the completion of the input request. The CHECK (Definition 14.4) or WAIT (Definition 14.5) macro can be used to test for completion of the input operation. In order to overlap I/O with computation, the problem programmer should do as much data-independent computation as possible following the READ and before issuing the CHECK or WAIT.

The specific block of data being requested by the READ can be identified in one of several ways. An understanding of these block identification methods is somewhat device dependent and requires a short excursion into direct-access storage-device (DASD) characteristics. A typical DASD is physically composed of a set of disks, about the size of a large phonograph record, stacked vertically and mounted as a unit called a disk pack. This unit is placed in a disk drive, which spins the pack about its vertical center (see Figure 14.1). Access arms, carrying read/write heads, move in and out of the disk pack between the several disks. Data are stored on the magnetic coating of the disks in concentric circles called tracks. A typical DASD has ten recording surfaces, 200 tracks per surface,

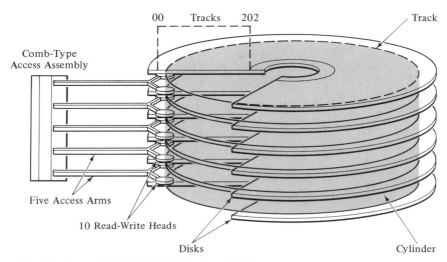

FIGURE 14.1   IBM 2311 Disk Pack and Drive

and the total capacity of approximately 7 million bytes. The ten tracks that are directly in a vertical line form what is called a cylinder. Thus there are 200 cylinders in our typical DASD.

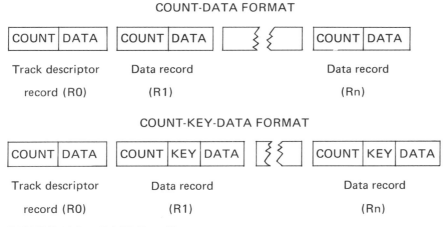

FIGURE 14.2   DASD Data Formats

Information stored on direct-access devices is always recorded in one of two standard formats, as shown in Figure 14.2. The first record on every track, called the track descriptor record, contains, in the case of BDAM, a count of the number of records recorded on the respective track. All additional records on each track are made up of either count and data fields or count, key, and data fields and, in either case, make up the data records of the data set. The two formats cannot be intermixed within the same data set. Within the count fields of both descriptor and data fields are found numbers not considered part of the data, which identify the record location in terms of cylinder, head, and relative block location in the track. Key and data lengths are also contained within the count fields. The key fields normally contain numbers supplied by the user and are ordered numerically from low to high. Keys can be used to represent account numbers, part numbers, serial numbers, or some other characteristic of the user's data to aid retrieval.

Each data record or block recorded on the DASD is identified by a unique address called the *actual block* address. Each address is composed of an eight-byte number of the form MBBCCHHR, where M is a one-byte binary number that specifies a relative location of an entry in a data-extent block (DEB), which is created when a data set is opened. The DEB contains entries that identify sets of contiguous tracks allocated to the data set. BBCCHH is a six-byte group of two-byte binary numbers that specify the bin (for IBM 2321 Data Cell, otherwise zero), cylinder, and head for the record in question. Finally, R is a one-byte binary number that specifies the relative block number with respect to record R0 on the track.

In addition to actual block-address references, BDAM allows records to be located by relative addresses of three different forms. One form, *relative block* addressing, is indicated by a three-byte binary number that identifies the desired record relative to the first data record of the data set. This is the easiest and probably the most popular method of block identification. A second form of relative addressing, *relative track* addressing, is of the form TTR, where TT is a two-byte binary number that specifies the track relative to the first track of the data set, and R is a one-byte binary number that identifies a record relative to the first data record of the selected track. A third form is the *relative track and actual key* address. Besides the three-byte binary number TTR, an actual key value is also provided. The system searches the indicated track for the record containing the specified key. Noncontiguous allocation of tracks does not affect any of the above relative addressing schemes.

Returning to the discussion of the READ macro, a 28-byte area is created within the macro expansion called the Data Event Control Block (DECB). This control block, whose symbolic name is supplied by the programmer in the READ statement, contains some of the information required to carry out the read operation. Table 14.1 describes the contents of the DECB.

The first word of the DECB contains an Event Control Block (ECB), which is used to signal completion of an event. The status of the ECB is tested by the CHECK or WAIT macro to determine the progress of the I/O operation. A fuller discussion of the ECB appears with the CHECK and WAIT macro presentation.

TABLE 14.1   DECB Contents for BDAM Operations

Byte	Contents
0	Event Control Block (ECB)
4	Type of search indicator
6	Length of data block
8	DCB address
12	Address of buffer area
16	Address of status indicators
20	Address of key
24	Address of block identification

The next two bytes of the DECB indicate the specific search and process-ing method to be used in the I/O operation. The various options are specified in the READ macro with one of the following letter codes:

DI: Data search to be performed using a block identification to be supplied by the READ macro

DK: Data search to be performed using a key to be supplied by the READ macro

DIF: Same as DI with the addition of *feedback* of the actual block address, which can be used by a subsequent WRITE macro

DIX: Same as DIF with *exclusive control,* a feature that prohibits any further access to the current block until a WRITE or RELEX macro is issued for the same block

DKF: Same as DK with feedback

DKX: Same as DKF with exclusive control

The next two bytes of the DECB contain the length of the data block being read. The third word of the DECB contains the address of the DCB associated with the direct-access data set. The fourth word contains or will contain the address of the buffer being used for data transfer. The fifth word points to status indicators that reflect conditions upon error detection. See Appendix 5 for the meaning of these indicators. The sixth and seventh words contain addresses pointing respectively to areas of core containing the search key and block identification. The various operands of the READ macro specify all of the information discussed above.

The READ is formally defined on p. 244.

Only one major specification remains unanswered for the READ macro operation. The type of block identification, whether it is to be an actual block address, relative block address, or relative track address, has not been specified by any of the READ operands. This decision is made when choosing the codes for the OPTCD operand of the DCB and is discussed in Section 14.2.

Features not discussed here are exclusive control, alluded to previously, considerations for variable- and undefined-length records, and the extended-

14.1 Macro Instruction READ (BDAM only)

symbol   READ   *decb,type,dcb,area,len,key,blk*
where *symbol* is an optional location reference, *decb* is a unique symbol, *type* is either DI, DK, DIF, DIX, DKF, or DKX, *dcb* is the DCB symbolic address, *area* is a buffer address, *len* is a block length, *key* is the key address, and *blk* is the block identification address. Operands *area* and *len* may be coded as 'S'. Operand *key* may be coded as 'S' if *area* is coded 'S'. Operand *key* may also be coded as zero.

Causes the *len* length block identified by either a key, pointed to by *key*, or an id, pointed to by *blk*, of the data set associated with the DCB at *dcb* to be read into the buffer at *area* using the technique indicated by *type*. If *area* is coded as 'S', a dynamic buffer is supplied by the system and its address is stored in *decb*+12. If *len* is coded as 'S', the length is taken from within the DCB. If *key* is coded as 'S' and a key search is not indicated by *type*, the recorded key is also read into *area* along with the data. If *key* is 0, no key is read. If F or X is coded in *type*, the actual block address may be returned in *blk*. (See Section 14.2.)

search option. The reader may consult IBM References C28-6646 and C28-6647 for discussions of these topics.

Two forms of the WRITE macro exist for BDAM. One form is used exclusively for creating a direct-access data set, while the other form is used exclusively for an existing direct-access data set. The latter is discussed first to show the similarity between it and the READ macro just presented. In most BDAM applications, an existing direct-access data set is involved in an update operation where a particular record is retrieved, updated, and rewritten at its original location. Thus, a READ/WRITE sequence is required within such a processing program; we shall now discuss this matching relationship.

The formal definition of the WRITE macro (Definition 14.2) appears very similar to that of the READ.

The additional two type codes of DA and DAF which may be coded in the WRITE macro are used to add blocks of data to an existing data set. This operation is predicated upon leaving the appropriate amount of unused space during the creation of the data set. The code DA causes the control program to write the data at the first available location randomly found in the track associated with the address supplied at the block-address operand of the READ

14.2 Macro Instruction WRITE (Existing BDAM only)

---

symbol   WRITE *decb,type,dcb,area,len,key,blk*
where the elements are syntactically identical to those for the READ
macro, Definition 14.1, except that *type* may be additionally coded as
DA or DAF. See the discussion following this definition.

Causes the *len* length data block at *area* to be written in the data set
associated with the DCB at *dcb* at the block address identified by either
a key pointed to by *key*, or an id, pointed to by *blk,* using the
technique indicated by *type*. If *area* is coded as 'S', the data must be
located in the dynamic buffer supplied by a READ. The address of the
buffer must be moved from the READ DECB to the WRITE DECB.
The dynamic buffer is released by the WRITE. *Key* may be coded as 'S'
only if *area* is coded as 'S', indicating that the key appears in the same
buffer area as the data. Zero may be used for *key* if no key is to be
written.

---

macro. The code DAF is the same as DA together with the feedback of the
actual block address of where the record is actually written.

One should notice several points about READ and WRITE macros. The
DECB for a WRITE macro is unique from the DECB of any other READ or
WRITE macro. One or more macros may refer to the same DCB associated with
one data set. The buffer areas specified are not required to be the same in a
read/write operation unless a dynamic buffer is involved. The key and block
addresses specified by one or more macros may or may not be identical, as the
programmer chooses. Various items of information, such as a buffer address,
may be transferred from one DECB to another.

A very important point to remember concerns dynamic buffering. If
dynamic buffering is requested by a READ macro, the supplied buffer must be
released either by a WRITE macro with *area* coded as 'S' or by issuing a
FREEDBUF macro. The latter would be required if records were being read but
not rewritten. The FREEDBUF macro is very simple and is coded for BDAM as
follows:

symbol   FREEDBUF   decb,D,dcb

The operands *decb* and *dcb* would be the same as the corresponding operands of
the READ that originally requested the dynamic buffer.

The create form of the WRITE macro *must* be used with a DCB with a

---

14.3 Macro Instruction WRITE (Create BDAM only)

---

symbol   WRITE *decb,type,dcb,area,len*
where *symbol* is optional, *decb* is a unique symbol, *type* is either SF, SD, or SZ, *dcb* is the DCB address, *area* is the address of the data, and *len* is the data length. Operand *len* may be coded as 'S'.

Causes either a data block with or without a key (SF) or a dummy data block with a key (SD) located at *area* to be written at the next available location in the data set associated with the DCB at *dcb*. The DSORG operand of the DCB must specify PS or PSU. The MACRF operand must specify WL. For a *type* code of SZ, the system writes a capacity record (used only for variable and undefined-length records, see IBM Reference C28-6647). If keys are used in SF, *area* must contain the key preceding the data. For SD, *area* need only be large enough for the key plus one byte. Length specification *len* is used only for undefined-length records. A *len* of 'S' causes the length to be taken from the DCB. A return code is returned in register 15 by this form of WRITE. See discussion below.

DSORG operand equal to PS or PSU; however, the DEVD operand *must* equal DA to specify a direct-access device. The MACRF operand *must* be WL, which actually is a BSAM (Basic Sequential) option. The associated DD card for this data set *must* specify direct access by the inclusion of DCB=(DSORG=DA or DAU) in the data definition.

The SF type operand is used for all records that are to contain actual data. If keys are to be included in the records, they must appear in the same area as and in front of the data. If space is to be left available for future record insertion, while writing fixed-length records with keys, the SD type operation is used. The system constructs a dummy key with the first byte set to all ones and adds the block number on the track in the byte following the key. This allows the system to detect dummy records during later processing using the WRITE macro with the DA option. For fixed-length records without keys, dummy records must be created by the programmer using the SF specification. Either the user must remember which records are dummy records or the records must be written containing codes that indicate to the user that the data blocks are dummy. The user must then use a READ macro to find these records during later processing.

The problem of variable- and undefined-length records and the use of the SZ operand is beyond the scope of this book. The system automatically writes capacity records when using SF and SD operands with fixed-length records.

A return code in register 15 is made available by the create form of the

WRITE macro immediately upon returning control to the processing program. The values and meanings of this return code are as follows:

Code	Meaning
00	Block will be written; more space is available on current track
04	Block will be written, followed by capacity record
08	Block will be written; next block will fill primary space allocation
0C	Block will not be written; issue a CHECK macro for the previous WRITE macro, then reissue

Different meanings are attributed to some of the above codes for variable and undefined records. See IBM Reference C28-6647.

Synchronization of I/O operations under BDAM and the problem program is accomplished with either a CHECK or WAIT macro instruction. The operation of these two macros is based on an Event Control Block (ECB). The ECB is a full word with the representation shown in Figure 14.3.

W	P	Completion codes

Bit   0   1   2   31

FIGURE 14.3   ECB Representation

When a concurrent operation is initiated that must later be synchronized with the problem program, an ECB is initialized by setting its wait (W) and post (P) bits to zero. The same ECB can be reused by resetting the W and P bits to zero for each new operation. When the problem program then reaches the point where synchronization is required, either a CHECK or WAIT macro is issued. This causes the supervisor to set the W bit of the associated ECB to one and places the problem program in a wait state until the associated concurrent operation is completed. Upon completion, the concurrent routine issues a POST macro that sets the P bit of the ECB to one. If the W bit is already one, the system returns control to the problem program following the CHECK or WAIT. Likewise, if when the CHECK or WAIT is issued the P bit is already one, control is immediately returned to the problem program. Based on this operating principle, I/O routines initiated by READ or WRITE macros always set the W and P bits of the ECB within the DECB associated with the READ or WRITE to zero. After initiating the requested I/O operation, control is returned to the problem program. When the I/O completion interrupt occurs, the READ and WRITE interrupt handling routines then issue a POST macro setting the P bit of the ECB to one. Thus, the programmer is required only to issue a CHECK or WAIT macro when synchronization is desired.

The definitions of the CHECK and WAIT macros follow.

14.4 Macro Instruction CHECK (BDAM, BPAM, and BSAM)

symbol   CHECK *decb*

where *symbol* is an optional reference symbol and *decb* is the symbolic reference to a DECB of an associated READ or WRITE macro instruction.

Causes the task in which the CHECK appears to be placed in the wait state and the W bit of the DECB to be set to one. When the associated I/O operation completes, a POST macro is issued by the interrupt handler setting the P bit to one. Control is then returned to the CHECK routine. The CHECK routine proceeds to check for errors and exceptional conditions resulting from the I/O operation. In case of errors, control is given to the SYNAD routine. If no SYNAD routine address is provided, the task is abnormally terminated. If the I/O operation completed successfully, control is returned to the problem program following the CHECK macro instruction. Additional functions are performed for BPAM and BSAM. See IBM Reference C28-6647.

If I/O operation error checking is not to be automatically performed, the CHECK macro must be replaced by the WAIT macro. Several forms of the WAIT macro exist within the Operating System; only the one applicable to a single I/O operation is defined here. Consult IBM Reference C28-6647 for the other forms.

14.5 Macro Instruction WAIT

symbol   WAIT ECB=*address*

where *symbol* is an optional reference symbol and *address* is a reference symbol to the associated ECB. (The I/O ECB is at the same address as the READ or WRITE DECB address.)

Causes the task in which the WAIT appears to be placed in the wait state and the W bit of the ECB to be set to one. Upon completion, the task being waited upon issues a POST macro, setting the P bit of the ECB to one. If the W bit is also on, control is returned to the program following the WAIT macro. No error checking is performed for I/O operations.

14.2   DCB, OPEN, AND CLOSE REQUIREMENTS FOR BDAM

We now consider the special considerations required in correct specification of DCB, OPEN, and CLOSE macros for BDAM processing. The primary concern is for consistency in coding of the various macro options that are to interact during access within a single data set. Central to all of the access methods and their associated processing routines is the data control block. All processing macros work out of or in conjunction with the DCB and its contents. In most cases, if an inconsistency does appear, one routine or another will detect it and cause an abnormal termination. However, a very comprehensive set of diagnostic messages, coded by completion codes, is available for reference. All System/360 computing installations have such a reference available for their users.

As noted in Chapter 12, two DCB operands are always required: the DSORG and the MACRF. The first defines the organization of the associated data set. For BDAM, the code specification for existing data sets is either DA or DAU. If actual block addresses are used in READ or WRITE macros, the user may be forced to specify that the data set is unmovable (DAU); otherwise the normal specification is DA. When creating a direct-access data set, the organization must be specified as PS or PSU. However, the associated DD card must specify DCB=(DSORG=DA).

The MACRF operand specifies the macros and facilities to be used in processing the data set. The following letters and meanings are used in coding this operand:

Letter	Meaning
A	Blocks are to be added to the data set
C	CHECK macro (absence denotes WAIT)
I	Search to be made by block identification
K	Search to be made by key
R	READ macro
S	Dynamic buffering is requested
W	WRITE macro
X	Exclusive control is requested

The following combinations are possible:

MACRF=(RDEC)	C and E are optional
MACRF=(WFC)	C is optional
MACRF=(RDEC,WFC)	C and E are optional

where   D can be either K, I, or KI,
        E can be either X, S, or XS,
        F can be either A, K, I, AK, AI, KI, or AKI.

A typical MACRF operand coding might be MACRF=(RISC), MACRF=(WIC), or MACRF=(RISC,WIC). The first denotes the READ and CHECK macros, a block identification search, and dynamic buffering. The second specifies the WRITE and CHECK macros with a block identification search. The third specifies a combination of the first two codings. For creating data sets, MACRF=(WL) must be used.

A great many of the remaining DCB operands can be omitted for BDAM processing—with notable exceptions. The BFALN operand is needed only if special data-alignment requirements will exist while processing data blocks within main storage. The BLKSIZE operand is required only when creating a new data set, since the size is automatically taken from the label of an existing data set. The BUFCB operand is required only if the problem program uses the BUILD macro to build a buffer pool. If dynamic buffering is used or if the user supplies work areas for buffers, no BUFCB entry is required.

The BUFL operand is required if dynamic buffering is specified in the MACRF operand. If required, BUFL can be set equal to the block size specified by the BLKSIZE operand or the value known to be contained within the data set label. If 'S' is specified for the key-address operand of the READ or WRITE macro instruction, the buffer length must include the key length.

The BUFNO operand is required only if the BUILD macro is used to build a buffer pool. If dynamic buffering is used, the number of buffers is optional. Two are provided if the operand is omitted. If the user provides work areas for buffer use, this operand is omitted.

The DEVD operand is required only when creating a direct-access data set and should be coded as DEVD=DA.

A DDNAME is usually supplied to associate the DCB with a DD card and data set at execution time.

The EXLST operand is required only if special label or DCB processing is required while opening or closing a data set.

The KEYLEN operand may be omitted if an existing data set is being used. If keys are to be written while creating a new data set, this operand must be supplied.

The OPTCD operand under BDAM is entirely different than under QSAM. The type of relative or actual block addressing to be used for reading and writing in direct-access data sets is specified by this operand. Letters and meanings used in coding the OPTCD operand are on p. 251.

If neither R nor A is coded, relative track addresses are assumed to be presented by the READ and WRITE macro instructions. A typical coding for this operand would be OPTCD=R.

The LIMCT operand is useful only if the extended-search option is requested in the OPTCD operand. Refer to IBM References C28-6646 and C28-6647.

The RECFM operand for BDAM specifies that records are of either fixed

Letter	Meaning
W	Requests that a validity check be made for each write operation. A validity check is made automatically if the device is the IBM 2321 Data Cell Drive.
E	Requests that an extended search be made for the requested record. This option is not discussed in this text. Refer to IBM Reference C28-6646 and C28-6647.
F	Specifies that if feedback is requested in a READ or WRITE macro, then the address returned is to be of the same form as that presented to the system by the user. If F is omitted, any requested feedback is of the form MBBCCHHR and is the actual block address.
R	Specifies that relative block addresses are to be presented by the READ and WRITE macro instructions.
A	Specifies that actual device addresses are to be presented by the READ and WRITE macros. Any request for extended search is ignored.

(F), variable (V), or undefined (U) lengths. For fixed-length records, the user can also specify that records may be written onto overflow tracks by coding FT. The FT option is required if compatibility is desired with a direct-access data set written with the Fortran IV direct-access facility. If relative block addressing is used, no special consideration must be made for overflow records. Coding FT does require less DASD storage space under most conditions. The simplest coding for RECFM would be RECFM=F or FT.

The remaining DCB operand SYNAD should be specified if an error-analysis routine is to be provided by the user. Otherwise the program is abnormally terminated if an error is detected.

The OPEN macro operand choices are fewer for BDAM than for QSAM. No operand two choices are allowed at all; thus it automatically defaults to the DISP specifications of the associated DD card. Only three choices for operand one are possible: INPUT, OUTPUT, and UPDAT. Under BDAM, OUTPUT is equivalent to UPDAT.

The CLOSE macro usually is coded showing only the DCB address. Positioning is indicated by the associated DD card.

14.3   SOME METHODS OF BDAM PROCESSING

Techniques of processing BDAM data sets depend strongly on the original organization of the data set in terms of data contents, data structure, key relationship, data length, and so forth. Organizations can range from a very simple one involving fixed-length records without keys through fixed-length records with keys to variable- and undefined-length records. Data sets containing fixed-length records with or without keys can be organized in such a way that records can be located directly without any search. This can be done even with relative block numbers, since the system can compute the actual address of a record knowing the beginning of the data set, the device characteristics (track capacity), block length, and the relative block address. This direct address computation can also be accomplished with fixed-length records containing keys. The key approach is useful in data collections where data for some key values may be missing. When the data set is created, dummy records are written for those key values not having associated data. This allows new records to be inserted at a later date with relative ease. The WRITE macro, used in the add mode (DA), searches for an available dummy record and inserts the new record at that location. An example of this operation is shown later in this section.

Data sets can be organized in which no vacant space is left at creation time; however, direct computation of block addresses is not possible if data items are missing in the key sequence. A much more complicated approach of using and maintaining a cross-reference table is required to relate a key with its address. Other, more sophisticated techniques are more commonly used, which eliminate the cross-reference table but are more complicated to describe. These techniques, sometimes referred to as indirect addressing, involve the manipulation of key values into addresses where searches for the desired block can be initiated. These methods are also sometimes known as hash codings or randomizing techniques.

```
LOCATION OP.    OPERAND          ...      COMMENTS          ...
DIRECT   START
  .         .
         L      9,=F'1000'                LOAD CONTROL
         OPEN   (DALOAD,(OUTPUT),TAPEDCB)
         LA     10,COMPARE
NEXTREC  GET    TAPEDCB
COMPARE  C      9,0(1)                    COMPARE KEY WITH
         BNE    DUMMY                     CONTROL VALUE
         LR     2,1
         WRITE  DECB1,SF,DALOAD,(2)       WRITE RECORD
         CHECK  DECB1
         AH     9,=H'1'                   BUMP CONTROL
         B      NEXTREC                   BRANCH TO GET
DUMMY    C      9,=F'8999'                HAVE 8000 RECORDS
         BH     ENDJOB                    BEEN WRITTEN?
         WRITE  DECB2,SD,DALOAD,DUMAREA   WRITE DUMMY
         CHECK  DECB2
         AH     9,=H'1'                   BUMP CONTROL
         BR     10                        BRANCH TO REG(10)
INPUTEND LA     10,DUMMY                  CHANGE BRANCH
         BR     10                        POINT IF END
ENDJOB   CLOSE  (TAPEDCB,DALOAD)
  .         .
DUMAREA  DS     CL5
DALOAD   DCB    DSORG=PS,MACRF=(WL),DDNAME=DAOUTPUT,DEVD=DA
TAPEDCB  DCB    EODAD=INPUTEND,...
```

FIGURE 14.4   Creating a BDAM Data Set

Methods of handling variable- and undefined-length records are just as complicated as those discussed immediately above, since again the direct computation of a block address is not possible. Thus the discussion and examples that follow involve only fixed-length records.

The first example, shown in Figure 14.4, involves the creation of a direct-access data set using as input a magnetic tape containing a sequence of records arranged in key sequence. QSAM is used to read the tape, while the create form of the WRITE macro is used to create the data set desired. The tape contains 204 character records, the first four bytes of which contain keys ranging from 1000 to 8999 in binary. Space is therefore required for 8000 records in the BDAM data set. Notice that dummy records are written for all key values that are not represented by records on the input tape. Also note that a key value need not be provided for dummy records, since the system creates a special key entry for these records. See the discussion of the create form of the WRITE macro with the SD option. The associated DD cards might appear as follows:

```
//DAOUTPUT  DD  DSNAME=SLATE.INDEX.WORDS,DCB=(DSORG=DA,
//                  BLKSIZE=200,KEYLEN=4,RECFM=F),SPACE=(204,8000)
//TAPINPUT  DD   – – –
```

The example shown in Figure 14.5 illustrates how additional records, contained within a tape file in key sequence, can be added to the data set created by the previous example. It is assumed that all of the new records represent data for keys that did not exist at the time the data set was created. When available space in a given track is exhausted (that is, all dummy records are replaced), a nonzero code is stored in the second and third bytes of the DECB. Since the CHECK macro would cause termination in the absence of a SYNAD routine for this condition, a WAIT macro should be used instead. The two-byte DECB code can then be tested to see if a successful record insertion occurred. If

```
LOCATION OP.   OPERAND            ...         COMMENTS        ...
DIRECTAD START
      .         .
              OPEN  (DIRECT,(OUTPUT),TAPEIN)
NEXTREC GET    TAPEIN,KEY
        L      4,KEY                           COMPUTE RELATIVE
        SH     4,=H'1000'                      BLOCK ADDRESS
        ST     4,REF                           STORE AT REF
        WRITE  DECB,DA,DIRECT,DATA,'S',KEY,REF+1
        WAIT   ECB=DECB
        CLC    DECB+1(2),=X'0000'              TEST FOR ERRORS
        BE     NEXTREC
      .                                        ERROR ACTION ROUTINE
DIRECT  DCB    DDNAME=DIRADD,DSORG=DA,RECFM=F,KEYLEN=4,
               BLKSIZE=200,MACRF=(WA),OPTCD=R
TAPEIN  DCB    – – –
KEY     DS     F
DATA    DS     CL200
REF     DS     F
```

FIGURE 14.5   Adding to a BDAM Data Set

not, special recovery action is necessary. See IBM Reference C28-6646. Again, a correct and successful write is indicated by all zeros in the second and third bytes of the DECB. Notice that the relative-block-address method of block identification is used, and that this is computed from the key by subtracting 1000. Also notice that the location of the block address is referred to by REF+1, since the relative block address must be a three-byte binary number, and a four-byte value is stored at REF. The associated DD cards might appear as follows:

//DIRADD　DD　DSNAME=SLATE.INDEX.WORDS,– – –
//TAPEDD　DD　– – –

The next and final example involves the updating of records within a direct-access data set, using records obtained from an input tape. The existing data set contains space for 25,000 records composed of five-byte zoned decimal keys and 30-byte data fields. The key values range from 00001 to 25000. It is assumed that corresponding data records exist in the DASD data set for every record on the input tape. Since relative block addressing is desired, the relative address is computed by subtracting one from the key. Since the input key is in zoned decimal, a pack and convert to binary is required. The update operation consists of a simple replacement of the existing data field with the 30 bytes of data read from the tape. Notice that dynamic buffering is being used; thus the buffer address must be obtained from within the DECB and used in the

```
LOCATION  OP.    OPERAND              ...  COMMENTS          ...
DIRUPDAT  START
    .          .
           OPEN  (DIRECT,(UPDAT),TAPEDCB)
NEXTREC    GET   TAPEDCB,KEY
           PACK  KEY,KEY
           CVB   3,KEYFIELD
           SH    3,=H'1'
           ST    3,REF
           READ  DECBRD,DI,DIRECT,'S','S',0,REF+1
           CHECK DECBRD
           L     3,DECBRD+12
           MVC   0(30,3),DATA
           ST    3,DECBWR+12
           WRITE DECBWR,DI,DIRECT,'S','S',0,REF+1
           CHECK DECBWR
           B     NEXTREC
    .          .
KEYFIELD   DS    0D
           DC    XL3'0'
KEY        DS    CL5
DATA       DS    CL30
REF        DS    F
DIRECT     DCB   DSORG=DA,DDNAME=DIRECTDD,MACRF=(RISC,WIC),  X
                 OPTCD=R,BUFL=35
TAPEDCB    DCB   ---
```

FIGURE 14.6　Updating an Existing BDAM Data Set

move-characters operation for replacement of the record. The buffer address is then placed in the output DECB for use by the WRITE macro. The dynamic buffer is therefore released after the write operation is complete. The program is shown in Figure 14.6. The associated DD cards might appear as follows:

```
//DIRECTDD  DD  DSNAME=SLATE.INDEX.WORDS,– – –
//TAPINPUT  DD  – – –
```

PROGRAMMING EXERCISE

An existing direct-access data set will be identified by the instructor as to its name and location. The data set will be composed of 100-byte fixed-length records written without keys. Each student will be given a unique number corresponding to the relative block address of a particular record within the data set. The format of these pilot records is as follows:

Byte	Contents
1–4	Relative block address in zoned decimal
5–6	A value N in zoned decimal
7–($4N$+6)	N fields of four columns each containing relative block addresses in zoned decimal

The object is for the student to insert into the N records, identified by the pilot record, his name, social security number, date, and time along with a sequence number that identifies each record in the same order as listed in the pilot record. The format for the updated records should be as follows:

Byte	Contents
* 1–4	Relative block address in zoned decimal
5–6	Sequence number in zoned decimal
7–36	Name
37–45	Social security number in zoned decimal
46–50	Year and day in zoned decimal
51–56	HHMMSS-time in zoned decimal
* 57–100	Prerecorded information

Information identified by * is to be left unchanged. The student should verify that the relative block address recorded in the first four bytes is actually equal to the value being specified in the READ macro before modifying the record. Use QSAM to print the pilot and updated data records in the order specified in the pilot record. Note that in order to update a record, the entire record must be read, updated, and then completely rewritten.

STUDY EXERCISES

1. What are the major differences between the basic- and queued-access techniques?
2. Describe a Direct-Access Storage Device.
3. Show the two basic DASD data formats.
4. How are records identified?
5. What is a Data Event Control Block?
6. Describe the behavior of the READ and WRITE macros.
7. What is dynamic buffering?
8. What is address feedback?
9. How are BDAM I/O operations synchronized with the problem program?
10. Discuss the various DCB operands used under BDAM.
11. How is it possible to directly address a record in BDAM?
12. Describe a data organization that allows direct addressing of data.
13. Describe a data organization that does not allow direct addressing of data.
14. What is a dummy record and what is its purpose?

Chapter **fifteen**

User-Defined Macros

Chapters 11 through 14 were concerned mainly with the concepts and uses of predefined system macro instructions, which should by now be fairly familiar to the reader. This chapter focuses on the facilities within the assembler, as under OS/360 and most other modern computing systems, that allow the user to define new and additional macro instructions within a problem program. Often a programmer is forced to use a sequence of operations several times throughout a program with few, if any, variations within the sequence. The macro programming approach saves considerable time and reduces the chance of error under such conditions.

The concepts embodied in macro programming can be applied at many levels and to many degrees. A programmer can define one or more macros to be used only within his own program. The same macros could be placed within a private direct-access library for use by a limited number of people. The same macros could be added to the existing system library, usually called SYS1.MACLIB, for use by anyone with access to the computing system. Occasionally, a macro has such universal application that it finds its way into the system distributed by a manufacturer and is applicable to all users of the system. Some unique programming systems, such as SNOBOL IV, originating from Bell Laboratories, are implemented entirely in terms of basic macro instructions. This allows such a system to be easily reimplemented for a different computing system by simply redefining the basic macro definitions and reassembling the system on the new computer.

Complementary, but not exclusive, to macro programming is the concept of conditional assembly. Within macro definitions, conditional-assembly instructions can be used to generate different macro expansions, depending on operands specified in the macro instruction application. An excellent example of variation in macro expansions is found in Chapter 11 in connection with the ABEND system macro. These same conditional-assembly instructions can be used outside of macro definitions to conditionally control the ordinary assembly of a program. This is a particularly useful concept on large-system generation, where variations are desired in tailoring a general system to a particular installation. A notable example of such a system is the WATFOR compiler, a Fortran system originating at the University of Waterloo. The system programmer changes a few parameters at the beginning of the source program and then, by reassembling the program, generates an object program that is tailored to the needs of his compiler users.

The sections that follow present the components, statements, and concepts of macro and conditional-assembly programming.

15.1   MACRO DEFINITION COMPONENTS

Basic to user-defined macros, as in conditional-assembly operations, are assembly variables. Just as in Fortran and assembly language there are symbolic variables that represent quantities that change during the course of computation in the execution phase, symbolic assembly variables are provided to represent program elements that can change during the course of assembly in the assembly phase. Two types of assembly variable are allowed in 360 assembly language; they are distinguished by the first character in the symbol. *Parameter symbols*, used primarily in macro programming, begin with an ampersand (&). *Sequence symbols*, used only in conjunction with conditional-assembly operations, begin with a decimal point (.). In either case, the first character is followed by one to seven letters or digits, the first of which must be a letter.

Parameter symbols are also known as *set symbols*. Which name applies to a given symbol depends on the context in which the symbol is used. Parameter symbols may appear only within macro definitions, while set symbols can be used both inside and outside of macro definitions.

Parameter symbols are used to transfer macro instruction application operands, such as the completion code in the ABEND macro, into the definition of the macro to find their way into the macro expansion during macro generation. Any parameter symbols found within the macro definition are set equal to associated operands found in the macro instruction application. At every point where these symbols appear within the macro definition, their corresponding values are substituted. Thus, the applied macro instruction operands appear within the macro expansion at those points after generation.

15.1 Parameter and Set Symbols

An ampersand followed by one to seven letters or digits, the first of which must be a letter.

Represents an assembly-language element that may change during the course of assembly.

15.2 Sequence Symbols

A decimal point followed by one to seven letters or digits, the first of which must be a letter.

Represents a transfer point for reference by a conditional-assembly operation for purposes of transfer during the course of assembly.

15.3 Assembler Instruction MACRO

blank   MACRO   blank
No name or operand field entries are allowed for this instruction. Must appear before any executable statements.

Causes the assembler to begin processing of a macro definition.

Set symbols are used for computational purposes during the process of assembly. Three types of set symbols exist: alphabetic, called SETA symbols; binary, called SETB symbols; and character, called SETC symbols. Each type of set symbol must be declared as such, using specific assembler instructions to be discussed in Section 15.2. Set symbols and parameter symbols may not be represented by the same symbol. However, parameter symbols may be used in arithmetic expressions whose result may be represented by a set symbol.

Sequence symbols are used to represent transfer points to be used by conditional-assembly instructions. This allows certain parts of a program to be either skipped or repeated on a conditional basis during the assembly process.

Macros are defined using special assembly operations in conjunction with ordinary machine and assembly operations already familiar to the reader. All macro definitions, if not obtained from a library, must appear at the beginning of a source program before any executable statements. Each macro definition

15.4 Assembler Instruction MEND

.symbol   MEND   blank
where *.symbol* is an optional sequence symbol. No operand field entry
is allowed. Must appear before any executable statements.

Causes the assembler to end the processing of a macro definition.

15.5 Macro Definition Prototype Statement

&symbol   symbol &symbol1,&symbol2, ...
where *&symbol, &symbol1, &symbol2, ...* are optional parameter
symbols and *symbol* is a unique mnemonic operation code. This statement must follow a MACRO operation statement.

Causes the assembler to recognize within the source program the new
mnemonic code *symbol* as meaning a new macro defined by the
statements following the prototype statement through the next MEND
statement. The symbols *&symbol, &symbol1, &symbol2, ...* are retained as parameter symbols to be used as assembly variables during
macro expansion.

must be delimited by a special start-macro-definition operation and an end-
macro-definition operation. These are called the MACRO and MEND operations.

The first statement following a start MACRO instruction is called the
macro instruction prototype. This statement describes in general how the macro
instruction will appear when it is written as an application in the body of the
source program. Through the use of the parameter symbols in the name and
operand fields of the prototype statement, variable information can be transmitted from the macro application into the expansion. The contents of the
operation field of the prototype specify the new mnemonic operation code for
the new macro instruction being defined. This mnemonic code obviously should
be unique from any existing machine, assembler, or system macro instruction.

The actual procedural definition, if any, of a macro occurs between the
prototype and MEND statements. Statements appearing in this context are
called *model statements*; they can, in general, be composed in a great many
ways.

The operation of concatenation, mentioned in Definition 15.6, allows a
single name, operation, or operand field entry to be specified by a combination

15.6 Macro Definition Model Statement

name   *code*   *x,y,z,...*
where *name, x, y, z,...* are optional name and operand field entries and *code* is an existing machine, assembler, or macro instruction mnemonic. The symbols *name, code, x, y, z, ...* can all be ordinary symbols, parameter symbols, or a concatenation of parameter symbols and/or characters. See the discussion following this definition. Parameter symbols used in a model statement must appear in the prototype statement. All model statements must follow a prototype statement and preceed a MEND statement.

Causes the assembly-language instruction represented by the model statement, with all parameter symbols replaced with their respective values specified by operands within the macro instruction application, to be generated into the macro expansion for assembly along with the rest of the source program.

of parameter symbols and/or other characters. For example, any single entry could be represented by two or more parameter symbols by writing them together without any intervening blanks. The resulting entry at generation time would be composed of the two or more variable values appearing as one entry written side by side in the same order as the symbols being replaced. If a fixed letter, digit, left parenthesis, or period is to be concatenated to the end of the value of a parameter symbol, a period must appear between the parameter symbol and the character. A period is optional for all other special characters being concatenated to a parameter.

As an illustration of how a macro is defined and used, the example in Figure 7.3 is coded as a macro. The complete macro definition is shown in Figure 15.1.

```
LOCATION OP.   OPERAND           . . .       COMMENTS          . . .
         MACRO                                MACRO HEADER
&NAME    FILL  &FIELD,&LEN,&CHAR              PROTOTYPE
&NAME    MVI   &FIELD,C&CHAR
         MVC   &FIELD+1(&LEN),&FIELD
         MEND                                 MACRO TRAILER
```
FIGURE 15.1   An Example of a Macro Definition

The macro, named FILL, can now be used later within the program as shown in Figure 15.2. All statements following the FILL macro instruction are generated from the macro definition with appropriate replacement of all parameter symbols.

```
LOCATION OP.    OPERAND            ... COMMENTS          ...
   .         .
         FILL   AREA,79,' '
         MVI    AREA,C' '
         MVC    AREA+1(79),AREA
   .         .
```

FIGURE 15.2   An Application of the FILL Macro

Notice that the parameter symbols are replaced as follows. Symbol &NAME is replaced by the null string; thus the name field of the MVI instruction is generated as a blank. Symbol &FIELD is replaced by the string AREA in all three places where the symbol appears in the model statements. Symbol &LEN is replaced by the string 79 and appears within the proper operand of the MVC instruction. The final symbol &CHAR is replaced by a string containing one blank enclosed in apostrophes, which then appears in the MVI instruction. A second application example is shown in Figure 15.3.

```
LOCATION OP.     OPERAND           ... COMMENTS         ...
   .          .
HERE        FILL   TABLE,49,'$'
HERE        MVI    TABLE,C'$'
            MVC    TABLE+1(49),TABLE
   .          .
```

FIGURE 15.3   Another Application of the FILL Macro

```
LOCATION OP.     OPERAND              ... COMMENTS        ...
   .          .
            MACRO
&NAME       SUM    &DATA,&R1,&R2,&R3,&R4,&LIMIT
&NAME       LA     &R1,0
            LA     &R2,0
            LA     &R3,4
            LA     &R4,&LIMIT
            A      &R1,&DATA.(&R2)
            BXLE   &R2,&R3,*-4
            MEND
   .          .
            SUM    A,9,5,6,7,96
            LA     9,0
            LA     5,0
            LA     6,4
            LA     7,96
            A      9,A(5)
            BXLE   5,6,*-4
   .          .
```

FIGURE 15.4   A More Extensive Macro Illustration

As a more extensive illustration, which also demonstrates parameter concatenation, the example of Figure 6.5 is implemented as a macro. Figure 15.4 contains the macro definition followed by a typical application and expansion.

Two types of comment statements may be included within macro definitions. Those beginning with an asterisk will also appear within expansions involving the macro. Those beginning with a period followed by an asterisk are not included within the macro expansion.

Information in the comment fields of model statements is reproduced in the statements of the expansion. Parameter symbols found in comment fields are not replaced by their values at macro expansion time.

15.2   CONDITIONAL-ASSEMBLY CONCEPTS

Basic to most conditional-assembly operations are set symbols as defined in Section 15.1. To use set symbols within a macro definition, one or more of three instructions are required to indicate the name and type of set symbols desired. These instructions are LCLA, LCLB, and LCLC.

15.7 Assembler Instructions LCLA, LCLB, and LCLC

blank   LCL*x*   *&symbol1,&symbol2,...*
where *x* is A, B, or C and *&symboli* are assembler variables. The name field must be blank. This statement must appear within a macro definition.

Causes the indicated symbols to be considered as either A, B, or C set symbols.

15.8 Assembler Instructions SETA, SETB, and SETC

&symbol   SET*x*   *expression*
where *&symbol* is a set symbol, *x* is A, B, or C, and *expression* is an arithmetic, logical, or character expression. The type of the set symbol, *x*, and the expression must all be consistently of either A, B, or C type.

Causes the value of the indicated set symbol to be set equal to the value of the expression. See the discussion that follows for what constitutes an expression.

Computations involving set symbols within macro definitions are indicated by three instructions: SETA, SETB, and SETC.

Expressions in SETA statements may be composed of parameter symbols, other SETA, SETB, or SETC symbols, and constants. SETB operands have values only of 0 (false) or 1 (true). SETC operands to be used in SETA expressions must contain decimal-digit values. Other more specialized operands are also allowed in SETA expressions. See IBM Reference C28-6514. Allowable arithmetic operations in SETA expressions are addition (+), subtraction (−), multiplication (∗), and division (/). The result of an expression is a 32-bit binary integer. Parentheses may be used to group operations to change the normal hierarchy.

Expressions in SETB statements are logical expressions and must be enclosed in parentheses. The result is either 0 (false) or 1 (true). SETB expressions are composed of one or more logical terms connected by AND, OR, and NOT logical operators. A logical term is composed of either SETB symbols or arithmetic or character expressions connected by the relational operators EQ, NE, LT, LE, GT, or GE. Any valid SETA or SETC expression may appear with appropriate operators in a SETB expression. These logical and relational operators are identical to the Fortran operations, except that blanks must appear before and after each operator instead of periods as in Fortran.

Expressions in SETC statements involve character strings as operands. The only operator allowed is concatenation, specified by a period between the terms being joined. SETA symbols used as operands contribute decimal-digit strings with leading zeros deleted. A zero value yields one zero. SETB symbols used as operands contribute either a numeral zero or one.

Set symbols may be used in model statements in the same way as parameter symbols. Thus, elements of macro statements generated during macro

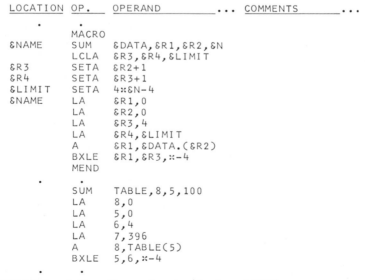

```
LOCATION   OP.    OPERAND         ...  COMMENTS        ...
      .      .
            MACRO
&NAME       SUM    &DATA,&R1,&R2,&N
            LCLA   &R3,&R4,&LIMIT
&R3         SETA   &R2+1
&R4         SETA   &R3+1
&LIMIT      SETA   4∗&N-4
&NAME       LA     &R1,0
            LA     &R2,0
            LA     &R3,4
            LA     &R4,&LIMIT
            A      &R1,&DATA.(&R2)
            BXLE   &R1,&R3,∗-4
            MEND
      .      .
            SUM    TABLE,8,5,100
            LA     8,0
            LA     5,0
            LA     6,4
            LA     7,396
            A      8,TABLE(5)
            BXLE   5,6,∗-4
      .      .
```

FIGURE 15.5   A More Comprehensive Version of SUM

expansion can be specified by results of arithmetic, logical, or character expressions. Figure 15.5 illustrates this technique through the use of a more comprehensive version of the macro in Figure 15.4.

SETB symbol values and/or logical expressions can also be involved in a conditional-assembly instruction, called AIF, which provides for conditional branching during the assembly process.

15.9 Assembler Instruction AIF

.symbol   AIF   *(expr).symbol1*
where *.symbol* is an optional sequence symbol, *expr* is a logical expression, and *.symbol1* is a sequence symbol. May appear anywhere in a program.

If the expression *expr* is true, the assembler next processes the statement whose name is *.symbol1*. If *expr* is false, the next sequential statement is processed next.

The following operations are also useful in conditional assembly or macro programming.

15.10 Assembler Instruction AGO

.symbol   AGO   *.symbol1*
where *.symbol* and *.symbol1* are sequence symbols and *.symbol* is optional. May appear anywhere in a program.

Causes the statement to be processed next by the assembler to be the one named *.symbol1*.

15.11 Assembler Instruction ANOP

.symbol   ANOP   blank
where *.symbol* is a sequence symbol. No operand is allowed. May be used anywhere in a program.

The next sequential statement following the ANOP is processed by the assembler.

15.12 Assembly Instruction MEXIT

.symbol   MEXIT   blank
where *.symbol* is an optional sequence symbol. No operand is allowed.
May appear only within a macro definition.

Causes the current macro expansion to terminate and assembly processing to continue with the next statement following the macro instruction invoking the current expansion.

15.13 Assembly Instruction MNOTE

.symbol   MNOTE   *n,message*
where *.symbol* is an optional sequence symbol, *n* is an optional severity
code < 255, and *message* is a character string in apostrophes. May
appear only in a macro definition. Parameter symbols may be used to
generate *n* or *message.*

Causes the *message*, usually indicating an error condition, to be printed
in the assembly program listing following the last statement generated.

The example of the FILL macro in Figure 15.1 is not very sophisticated.
Conditional-assembly and set-symbol statements can be used to increase its
sophistication. For one thing, the length of the field being filled had to be
specified as one less than the actual length. Second, no check was made for a
length greater than 256, the maximum number of characters that can be moved
by one MVC instruction. Figure 15.6 shows a better version of the FILL macro.

```
LOCATION  OP.    OPERAND           ... COMMENTS        ...
          MACRO
&NAME     FILL    &FIELD,&LEN,&CHAR
          LCLA    &N
&N        SETA    &LEN-1
          AIF     (&N GT 256).NOGOOD
&NAME     MVI     &FIELD,C&CHAR
          MVC     &FIELD+1(&N),&FIELD
          MEXIT
.NOGOOD   MNOTE   'ERROR...LENGTH TOO LONG'
          MEND
```

FIGURE 15.6   A Better Version of FILL

An ultimate version of FILL would allow a length greater than 256 by
generating a sufficient number of MVC instructions to fill the entire field. Figure
15.7 contains such a version.

```
LOCATION   OP.     OPERAND          ... COMMENTS          ...
           MACRO
&NAME      FILL    &FIELD,&LEN,&CHAR
           LCLA    &L,&M,&N,&CNT
&CNT       SETA    &LEN-1
           AIF     (&CNT LT 0).NOGOOD
&NAME      MVI     &FIELD,C&CHAR
           AIF     (&CNT GT 0).GO
           MEXIT
.GO        ANOP
&L         SETA    256
&M         SETA    1
&N         SETA    0
.LOOP      AIF     (&CNT GE 256).SKIP
&L         SETA    &CNT
.SKIP      ANOP
           MVC     &FIELD+&M.(&L),&FIELD+&N
&CNT       SETA    &CNT-256
           AIF     (&CNT LE 0).STOP
&M         SETA    &M+256
&N         SETA    &N+256
           AGO     .LOOP
.NOGOOD    MNOTE   'ERROR...LENGTH < ONE'
.STOP      MEND
```

FIGURE 15.7   The Ultimate FILL Macro

A step-by-step analysis of the macro definition in Figure 15.7 follows. As before, the prototype describes the FILL macro as having three operands: the data-field name, the field length, and the fill character. Four SETA symbols are required for computational purposes; they are defined as &L, &M, &N, and &CNT by the LCLA statement. The SETA statement then reduces the field length by 1 and sets &CNT equal to the result. Throughout the macro expansion process, &CNT indicates the remaining number of bytes to be filled. A test is then made for a valid positive length using the AIF instruction. Assuming the field length is at least one, the MVI instruction is then generated. A test is then made by another AIF instruction to determine if the original field length is greater than one. If not, the macro expansion terminates with the MEXIT instruction. Otherwise, transfer is made to the sequence symbol .GO. Notice that an ANOP instruction is required at this point, since transfer cannot be made to a statement with a label other than a sequence symbol.

Set symbols &L, &M, and &N are now initialized to 256, 1, and 0, respectively. A test is now performed with an AIF instruction to determine if &CNT is actually less than 256, in which case &L must be reset to &CNT. Otherwise, the AIF transfers to sequence symbol .SKIP. Again, an ANOP instruction is required to supply a valid statement in which to place the sequence symbol. A MVC instruction is then generated, using the current values of &L, &M, and &N. Set symbol &CNT is then reduced by 256. A test is made using an AIF to determine if sufficient MVC instructions have been generated. If so, transfer is made to MEND and the generation is terminated. If not, 256 is added to set symbols &M and &N. An unconditional transfer is then made back to sequence symbol .LOOP. The eight-instruction loop continues to repeat until enough MVC operations have been produced to completely fill the data field.

Note especially that the AIF, AGO, and ANOP instructions can be used anywhere within a program and are not restricted to macro applications. However, local set symbols defined by LCLA, LCLB, and LCLC instructions are restricted to macro definitions. Set symbols in one macro definition are independent of those in other macro definitions, even if their names are identical. Provisions for defining global set symbols are made with the GBLA, GBLB, and GBLC instructions. Additional features of the macro assembler allow macros to be defined with key-word operands or combinations of positional and key-word operands. Special system set symbols useful in more sophisticated programs are also available. Consult IBM Reference C28-6514 for a full discussion of these additional features and for further details of macro and conditional-assembly programming in general.

PROGRAMMING EXERCISE

Choose a problem and apply techniques of macro and/or conditional-assembly programming in its solution.

STUDY EXERCISES

1. What are the advantages of macro and conditional-assembly programming techniques?
2. What are the various parts, on a statement basis, of a macro, and in what order are they written?
3. What are parameter or set symbols?
4. What are sequence symbols?
5. Describe the difference between a macro definition, a macro application, and a macro expansion.
6. Write an application of, and show its expansion for, the macro defined in Figure 15.1.
7. Repeat Exercise 6 for Figure 15.4.
8. Repeat Exercise 6 for Figure 15.5.
9. How does the conditional-assembly AIF operation work?
10. Repeat Exercise 6 for Figure 15.6 for both valid- and invalid-length operands.
11. Repeat Exercise 6 for Figure 15.7 for length operand values of 1, 176, 257, 430, and 1000.
12. What are the purposes of the MNOTE and MEXIT operations?

Chapter **sixteen**

Differences Between System/360 and 370

During 1971, IBM initiated delivery of a new line of computing machines called System/370. These computers are based on the System/360 but contain several new design features and extensions. For the most part, programs written for use in System/360 computers are compatible with System/370. The primary differences exist within the area of privileged operations; thus the major changes in software occur in the supervisor or control programs. However, a few new instructions are available to the problem programmer in System/370 that are not available in System/360. Therefore, any program written for the System/370 incorporating one or more of these new operations would not be compatible on a 360 machine and, if executed on it, would cause an illegal-operation interrupt.

This final chapter will indicate the major differences between the two systems. Several extensions represent some interesting concepts of sophisticated control and supervisory functions beyond those found in 360 machines. Of particular interest are provisions for more comprehensive machine-failure detection and correction. These include storage-bit-level failure detection of single- and double-bit errors and single-bit error correction. Central-processor-unit retry capability is provided on some operations. Additional masking control is provided for more individual control of I/O and external interrupt sources. A time-of-day clock, designed for permanent operation, is included for easy access to the correct time without operator intervention. Section 16.1 describes the various features making up the major design variations beyond

System/360. Section 16.2 presents the thirteen new instruction codes found within the repertoire of System/370.

16.1   BASIC DESIGN EXTENSIONS OF SYSTEM/370

Fundamental to most of the additional features of System/370 over 360 is the inclusion of sixteen special control registers, each containing 32 bits. Various bit positions of these registers are allocated for controlling certain functions within the CPU and I/O channels. Table 16.1 gives the names and functions of those bit positions that are presently assigned specific duties. All sixteen control registers can be loaded or stored individually or in groups under program control (see Section 16.2) while the machine is in supervisor state.

As the table shows, the supervisor can choose to mask the three types of external interrupt on an independent basis. System/360 could only treat the external sources as one source with the single mask bit in the PSW. However, the PSW bit can still be used to mask all three types at once if desired. Thus, both the PSW bit as well as an extended mask bit must be one to accept the interrupt.

Since up to 32 I/O channels may someday be allowed on some System/370 models, channel masking on an individual channel basis is desired. Bits within control register 2 perform this masking service. Bits are assigned by associating bit position within register 2 with the I/O channel address number. Channels 0 through 5 are still under control of PSW System Mask bits 0 through

TABLE 16.1   Control Register Assignment

Register	Bits	Name	Function
0	0	Block-Multiplex Mode	Block-multiplexing control
0	24	Timer Mask	Extended external masking
0	25	Interrupt Key Mask	Extended external masking
0	26	External Signal Mask	Extended external masking
2	0–31	Channel Masks	Extended I/O masking
14	0	Hard Stop Mode	Machine-check handling
14	1	Synchronous MCEL Mask	Machine-check handling
14	2	I/O Extended Logout	Machine-check handling
14	4	Recovery Report Mask	Machine-check handling
14	5	Configuration Report Mask	Machine-check handling
14	6	External Damage Report	Machine-check handling
14	7	Warning Mask	Machine-check handling
14	8	Asynchronous MCEL Mask	Machine-check handling
14	9	Asynchronous Fixed Log	Machine-check handling
15	8–31	MCEL Pointer	Machine-check handling

Note: MCEL means Machine-Check Extended Logout

5. Control register 2 bits 0 through 5 do not participate in channel interrupt control. PSW System Mask bit 6 controls all channels above 5, with individual channel control performed by bits 6 through 31 in control register 2.

Machine-failure interrupt handling is a great deal more sophisticated in System/370. Instead of only one all-encompassing machine-check condition as in System/360, several subclasses of interrupt for equipment malfunction are possible in System/370. The single machine-check mask bit in the PSW of System/360 controls all machine-check conditions. If an interrupt is accepted in 360 machines, a single fixed-length *logout* of status indicators into a fixed area of storage is automatically performed. Within System/370 computers several types of logout are possible, depending on the type of machine-check condition occurring as well as on the model of 370. Mask bits within control register 14 are used to control the various types of logout and reports that can be generated by machine-check conditions.

Some equipment malfunctions can be automatically either corrected or circumvented. Recovery is made, if possible, through the correction of failing bits in storage or through the retrying of one or more failing instructions. Particularly in the case of instruction retry, the control of interrupts and interrupt logout is complicated considerably, since interrupt generation may not always occur at the same instant in relation to the timing of the failing instruction. Thus asynchronous, as well as synchronous, logouts are possible. In addition, some machine-check conditions can generate more logout information than the fixed-length logout mentioned above. This latter function is called a Machine-Check Extended Logout (MCEL). Following a MCEL, the starting address of the MCEL main storage area is found in control register 15.

By periodically saving information concerning machine status, called a hardware checkpoint, the machine may, upon detecting an error, return to the last checkpoint and retry the failing operations. If, during the retry, no further error is detected, a recovery condition is recognized and subsequently reported. If, after several attempts, the failure persists and processing cannot continue, a hard machine-check condition is said to exist. If any other equipment malfunction causes loss of information and subsequent loss of system integrity, a damage condition exists and is also classified as a hard machine-check condition.

Recovery conditions, as well as other alert or warning conditions, are called soft machine-check conditions. The sequence in which various interrupts, logouts, and condition reports are accepted is controlled by the various mask bits in control register 14.

In addition to all of the above machine-check condition information and control, a machine-check interruption code (MCIC) is also created and stored at location 232 at the conclusion of an interrupt. This MCIC contains some 24 bits, which indicate the validity of the other information stored for the interrupt along with damage reports, system recovery reports, warning information, time of interrupt (in terms of retry conditions), storage error types, and length of

MCEL information. A point of interest is that one type of warning report may indicate an impending power failure, so that recovery protection action might be initiated and carried out during the fraction of a second preceding final power failure. Additional permanently allocated main storage is set aside in System/370 for the various data discussed above. Table 16.2 contains the storage allocation beyond that of System/360.

TABLE 16.2   Permanently Allocated Storage Locations

Address	Purpose
232	Machine-check interruption code
240	Reserved for future use
248	Failing storage address
252	Region code
256	Fixed logout area
352	Floating-point register save area
384	General-purpose register save area
448	Control-register save area

Another interesting feature of System/370 is the provision for determining what model of machine is in use under program control. Two instructions are provided for storing CPU and channel ID information. This feature could allow generalized programs and operating systems to configurate or tailor themselves to match the requirements of the particular model. This ability could be particularly useful, it seems, in designing generalized diagnostic programs for machine-error detection and classification.

System/370 makes no provision for automatic recognition of the USASCII−8 code. Only the EBCDIC code characters are generated by code-sensitive instructions. If PSW bit 12 is ever set to one, a specification interrupt occurs.

System/370 contains a special time-of-day clock designed to operate for an indefinite period. The clock may be installed to operate even when power is turned off in the CPU. Presumably, the clock could be operated with batteries in the event of a power failure. The cycle time of the clock is approximately 143 years, represented by the left-most 52 bits within a 64-bit register. The clock is incremented every microsecond in the fifty-first bit position. Once the clock is set to the correct time, no further adjustment is anticipated unless the equipment malfunctions. The operating system then has access to the correct time, eliminating the need for operator intervention to supply the date and time of day at system start-up time. Two instructions are provided for initially setting and subsequently reading the clock. The set-clock instruction is effective only if a manually actuated security switch on the operator intervention panel is set to the proper position.

16.2   NEW INSTRUCTIONS IN SYSTEM/370

Thirteen new instructions are provided in System/370 computers. Their names, formats, and general characteristics are presented here, but no attempt is made to give all details concerning their operation. Table 16.3 contains the name, mnemonic code, format type, and whether the instruction is privileged.

TABLE 16.3   New System/370 Instructions

Name	Code	Type	Privileged
Compare Logical Characters under Mask	CLM	RS	No
Compare Logical Characters Long	CLCL	RR	No
Insert Characters under Mask	ICM	RS	No
Load Control Registers	LCTL	RS	Yes
Move Characters Long	MVCL	RR	No
Set Clock	SCK	SI	Yes
Shift and Round Decimal	SRP	SS	No
Start I/O Fast Release	SIOF	SI	Yes
Store Channel ID	STIDC	SI	Yes
Store Characters under Mask	STCM	RS	No
Store Clock	STCK	SI	No
Store CPU ID	STIDP	SI	Yes
Store Control Registers	STCTL	RS	Yes

The three operations, Compare Logical Characters under Mask (CLM), Insert Characters under Mask (ICM), and Store Characters under Mask (STCM), behave the same way (except for their comparing and moving functions) with respect to their first and second operands and the mask, specified by M3 in Figure 16.1. Bytes in the operand one register, specified by R1, corresponding in a one-to-one relationship with bits in the mask and selected by one bits in the mask, are compared with (for CLM), replaced by (for ICM), or replace (for STCM) consecutive bytes in main storage starting at the second operand address specified by B2 and D2. The length of the second operand is equal to the number of one bits in the mask. The condition code for CLM is set to zero if the selected bytes are equal, one if the selected bytes of the first operand are low, two if the selected bytes of the first operand are high, and three does not occur. The condition code for ICM is set to zero if the mask is zero or if all the inserted bits are zero, one if the first bit of the inserted field is one, two if the first bit of the inserted field is zero while the rest of the field is nonzero, and three does not occur. The STCM instruction does not change the condition code. All three operations may cause either operation, addressing, or protection interrupts. The operation interrupt would occur on a System/360.

The two RR type operations, Compare Logical Characters Long (CLCL),

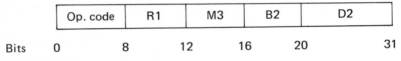

Op. code	R1	M3	B2	D2

Bits   0   8   12   16   20   31

FIGURE 16.1   Format of CLM, ICM, and STCM

and Move Characters Long (MVCL), are very simple on the surface, but are actually quite involved. Except that CLCL causes a compare and MVCL is a move operation, in basic organization the two operations are identical. Two even-odd pairs of general-purpose registers are specified by R1 and R2 of the instruction. The contents of bits 8 through 31 of registers R1 and R2 indicate the main storage addresses of the leftmost byte of the first and second operands, respectively. Bits 8 through 31 of registers R1+1 and R2+1 contain the length, in bytes, of the first and second operands, respectively. Bits 0 through 7 of register R2+1 contain a padding character. Bits 0 through 7 of registers R1, R1+1, and R2 are ignored.

For CLCL, the first and second operands are compared beginning with the leftmost byte. The compare is performed considering the operand data to be unsigned binary numbers. The operation ends as soon as an inequality is found or the end of the longest operand is reached. For unequal-length operands, the shorter operand is considered as extended with the padding character. Neither operand is changed by the operation. The condition code is set to zero if the operands are equal or if both fields have zero length, one if the first operand is low, two if the first operand is high, and three does not occur.

For MVCL, the second operand is moved into the first operand unless destructive overlap exists. Destructive overlap means that field overlap exists in such a way that part of the second operand would be changed by storing bytes into an area before that area had been fetched in the moving operation. The operation proceeds from left to right and terminates when the number of bytes specified by register R1+1 have been moved. If the second operand is shorter, the remaining first operand bytes are filled with the padding character. The condition code is set to zero if the operand counts are equal, one if the first operand count is low, two if the first operand count is high, and three if no movement occurs because of destructive overlap.

Both operations, CLCL and MVCL, may cause illegal-operation, protection, addressing, and specification interrupts. Either operation may be interrupted in the process of execution by a higher-priority task. In the event of such an interrupt, registers R1 and R2 are incremented, and R1+1 and R2+1 are decremented in such a way that the operation may be continued at a later time. Operands in either instruction may involve storage addresses, which wrap around from the highest address of 16,777,215 back to zero.

The only new SS type instruction is Shift and Round Decimal (SRP); this

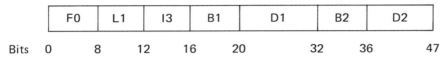

F0	L1	I3	B1	D1	B2	D2

Bits   0   8   12   16   20   32   36   47

FIGURE 16.2   SRP Format

is an added operation in the special decimal operation subset available on System/360 computers. The SRP instruction causes the first operand, specified by B1 and D1 (see Figure 16.2), to be shifted in the direction and number of decimal digit positions indicated by the second operand address, specified by B2 and D2. While shifting right, the first operand is rounded by the rounding factor I3.

Bits 26 through 31 of the computed second operand address are used as a shift count, expressed as a signed integer in two's-complement notation. If bit 26 is zero, the shift is to the left with the number of places expressed as a true number. If bit 26 is one, the shift is to the right with the number of places expressed as a two's-complement value.

The first operand is considered as a packed decimal number; thus digits and sign are checked for valid decimal data. The sign portion of the number does not participate in the shift. If a significant digit is shifted out of the left end of the field, a decimal overflow condition is recognized. During a right shift, the rounding factor, I3, is added to the digit being shifted out, and any carry resulting is propagated into the field. The sign of the first operand is ignored for the purpose of rounding. The condition code is set to zero if the result is zero, one if the result is less than zero, two if the result is greater than zero, and three if the result overflows. Operation, protection, addressing, data, and decimal-overflow interrupts can occur.

The two remaining RS instructions, Load Control (LCTL) and Store Control (STCTL), allow control registers to be loaded and stored in the exact same manner as LM and STM allow the loading and storing of general-purpose registers. The condition code remains unchanged. Illegal and privileged operation, protection, addressing, and specification interrupts may occur.

The Start I/O Fast Release (SIOF) instruction is used in conjunction with the block multiplexing mode of I/O operation—subjects which are beyond the scope of this book.

Two SI instructions, Set Clock (SCK) and Store Clock (STCK), are used to set and read the time-of-day clock. The SCK instruction is privileged, while anyone may use the STCK operation. In both operations, the first sixteen bits of the instruction are used as the operation code. The remaining sixteen bits, representing B1 and D1, specify the address of a double word. For SCK, the contents of the double word are used to set the clock, provided the clock security switch is in the set position. The condition code is set to zero if the clock is set, one if the clock is secure, two does not occur, and three if the clock is not operational. For STCK, the contents of the double word are either set to the clock value, zero, or are unpredictable depending on the state of the clock. If the condition code is set to zero, the clock value is stored and presumably represents the correct time. If the condition code is one, the clock value is stored and represents the time since the clock was turned on. This clock state can be used to measure elapsed time, but does not necessarily represent the correct time of day. If the condition code is two, the clock is in an error state and the stored value is unpredictable. If the condition code is three, the clock is not operational and the stored value is zero. Operation, protection, addressing, and specification interrupts may occur for both instructions. A privileged-operation interrupt may additionally occur for SCK.

The remaining two SI instructions, Store Channel ID (STIDC) and Store CPU ID (STIDP), are privileged operations, which can be used to determine the exact model, including certain variable information concerning the model, of CPU or channel within which the program is running. The STIDC instruction causes a full word of ID information concerning the addressed channel to be stored at location 168. The STIDP instruction causes a double word of ID information concerning the CPU to be stored at the address specified by the operand address. For STIDC, the condition code is set to zero if the ID is stored properly, one if the CSW is stored, two if the channel is busy, and three if the channel is not operational. The condition code is unchanged by STIDP. Illegal- and privileged-operation interrupts can occur for STIDC. Illegal- and privileged-operation, protection, addressing, and specification interrupts may occur for STIDP. Figure 16.3 shows the information stored by STIDC and STIDP.

Channel ID

Type	Channel model number	Max. IOEL length

Bits   0   4   16   31

CPU ID

Reserved	CPU serial number

Bits   0   8   31

CPU model number	Max. MCEL length

Bits   32   48   63

FIGURE 16.3   ID Information Stored by STIDC and STIDP

STUDY EXERCISES

1. What are control registers and how are they used?
2. What are the three subclasses of external interrupt?
3. How are additional channels, beyond the six allowed on System/360, controlled for interrupt?
4. What are some subclasses of the machine-check condition?
5. What are machine-check logouts, and warning, recovery, and damage reports?
6. What is a MCEL, and what is its relation to control register 15?
7. Does System/370 handle the USASCII-8 code?
8. What is the time-of-day clock and how does it work?
9. Discuss the CLM, ICM, and STCM operations.
10. Discuss the CLCL and MVCL operations.
11. Discuss the SRP operation.
12. Discuss the LCTL and STCTL operations.
13. Discuss the SCK and STCK operations.
14. Discuss the STIDC and STIDP operations.

Appendix **one**
System/360
Instruction Summary

Name	Mnemonic	Type	Code	Operand
Add	AR	RR	1A	R1,R2
Add	A	RX	5A	R1,D2(X2,B2)
Add Halfword	AH	RX	4A	R1,D2(X2,B2)
Add Logical	ALR	RR	1E	R1,R2
Add Logical	AL	RX	5E	R1,D2(X2,B2)
AND	NR	RR	14	R1,R2
AND	N	RX	54	R1,D2(X2,B2)
AND	NI	SI	94	D1(B1),I2
AND	NC	SS	D4	D1(L,B1),D2(B2)
Branch and Link	BALR	RR	05	R1,R2
Branch and Link	BAL	RX	45	R1,D2(X2,B2)
Branch on Condition	BCR	RR	07	M1,R2
Branch on Condition	BC	RX	47	M1,D2(X2,B2)
Branch on Count	BCTR	RR	06	R1,R2
Branch on Count	BCT	RX	46	R1,D2(X2,B2)
Branch on Index High	BXH	RS	86	R1,R3,D2(B2)
Branch on Index Low or Equal	BXLE	RS	87	R1,R3,D2(B2)
Compare	CR	RR	19	R1,R2
Compare	C	RX	59	R1,D2(X2,B2)
Compare Halfword	CH	RX	49	R1,D2(X2,B2)
Compare Logical	CLR	RR	15	R1,R2
Compare Logical	CL	RX	55	R1,D2(X2,B2)
Compare Logical	CLC	SS	D5	D1(L,B1),D2(B2)
Compare Logical	CLI	SI	95	D1(B1),I2
Convert to Binary	CVB	RX	4F	R1,D2(X2,B2)
Convert to Decimal	CVD	RX	4E	R1,D2(X2,B2)
Diagnose		SI	83	

Name	Mnemonic	Type	Code	Operand
Divide	DR	RR	1D	R1,R2
Divide	D	RX	5D	R1,D2(X2,B2)
Exclusive OR	XR	RR	17	R1,R2
Exclusive OR	X	RX	57	R1,D2(X2,B2)
Exclusive OR	XI	SI	97	D1(B1),I2
Exclusive OR	XC	SS	D7	D1(L,B1),D2(B2)
Execute	EX	RX	44	R1,D2(X2,B2)
Halt I/O	HIO	SI	9E	D1(B1)
Insert Character	IC	RX	43	R1,D2(X2,B2)
Load	LR	RR	18	R1,R2
Load	L	RX	58	R1,D2(X2,B2)
Load Address	LA	RX	41	R1,D2(X2,B2)
Load and Test	LTR	RR	12	R1,R2
Load Complement	LCR	RR	13	R1,R2
Load Halfword	LH	RX	48	R1,D2(X2,B2)
Load Multiple	LM	RS	98	R1,R3,D2(B2)
Load Negative	LNR	RR	11	R1,R2
Load Positive	LPR	RR	10	R1,R2
Load PSW	LPSW	SI	82	D1(B1)
Move	MVI	SI	92	D1(B1),I2
Move	MVC	SS	D2	D1(L,B1),D2(B2)
Move Numerics	MVN	SS	D1	D1(L,B1),D2(B2)
Move with Offset	MVO	SS	F1	D1(L1,B1),D2(L2,B2)
Move Zones	MVZ	SS	D3	D1(L,B1),D2(B2)
Multiply	MR	RR	1C	R1,R2
Multiply	M	RX	5C	R1,D2(X2,B2)
Multiply Halfword	MH	RX	4C	R1,D2(X2,B2)
OR	OR	RR	16	R1,R2
OR	O	RX	56	R1,D2(X2,B2)
OR	OI	SI	96	D1(B1),I2
OR	OC	SS	D6	D1(L,B1),D2(B2)
Pack	PACK	SS	F2	D1(L1,B1),D2(L2,B2)
Set Program Mask	SPM	RR	04	R1
Set System Mask	SSM	SI	80	D1(B1)
Shift Left Double	SLDA	RS	8F	R1,D2(B2)
Shift Left Single	SLA	RS	8B	R1,D2(B2)
Shift Left Double Logical	SLDL	RS	8D	R1,D2(B2)
Shift Left Single Logical	SLL	RS	89	R1,D2(B2)
Shift Right Double	SRDA	RS	8E	R1,D2(B2)
Shift Right Single	SRA	RS	8A	R1,D2(B2)
Shift Right Double Logical	SRDL	RS	8C	R1,D2(B2)

Name	Mnemonic	Type	Code	Operand
Shift Right Single Logical	SRL	RS	88	R1,D2(B2)
Start I/O	SIO	SI	9C	D1(B1)
Store	ST	RX	50	R1,D2(X2,B2)
Store Character	STC	RX	42	R1,D2(X2,B2)
Store Halfword	STH	RX	40	R1,D2(X2,B2)
Store Multiple	STM	RS	90	R1,R3,D2(B2)
Subtract	SR	RR	1B	R1,R2
Subtract	S	RX	5B	R1,D2(X2,B2)
Subtract Halfword	SH	RX	4B	R1,D2(X2,B2)
Subtract Logical	SLR	RR	1F	R1,R2
Subtract Logical	SL	RX	5F	R1,D2(X2,B2)
Supervisor Call	SVC	RR	0A	I
Test and Set	TS	SI	93	D1(B1)
Test Channel	TCH	SI	9F	D1(B1)
Test I/O	TIO	SI	9D	D1(B1)
Test under Mask	TM	SI	91	D1(B1),I2
Translate	TR	SS	DC	D1(L,B1),D2(B2)
Translate and Test	TRT	SS	DD	D1(L,B1),D2(B2)
Unpack	UNPK	SS	F3	D1(L1,B1),D2(L2,B2)

FLOATING-POINT FEATURE INSTRUCTIONS

Name	Mnemonic	Type	Code	Operand
Add Normalized (Long)	ADR	RR	2A	R1,R2
Add Normalized (Long)	AD	RX	6A	R1,D2(X2,B2)
Add Normalized (Short)	AER	RR	3A	R1,R2
Add Normalized (Short)	AE	RX	7A	R1,D2(X2,B2)
Add Unnormalized (Long)	AWR	RR	2E	R1,R2
Add Unnormalized (Long)	AW	RX	6E	R1,D2(X2,B2)
Add Unnormalized (Short)	AUR	RR	3E	R1,R2
Add Unnormalized (Short)	AU	RX	7E	R1,D2(X2,B2)
Add Normalized (Extended)	AXR	RR	36	R1,R2
Compare (Long)	CDR	RR	29	R1,R2
Compare (Long)	CD	RX	69	R1,D2(X2,B2)
Compare (Short)	CER	RR	39	R1,R2
Compare (Short)	CE	RX	79	R1,D2(X2,B2)
Divide (Long)	DDR	RR	2D	R1,R2
Divide (Long)	DD	RX	6D	R1,D2(X2,B2)
Divide (Short)	DER	RR	3D	R1,R2
Divide (Short)	DE	RX	7D	R1,D2(X2,B2)
Halve (Long)	HDR	RR	24	R1,R2
Halve (Short)	HER	RR	34	R1,R2
Load and Test (Long)	LTDR	RR	22	R1,R2
Load and Test (Short)	LTER	RR	32	R1,R2
Load Complement (Long)	LCDR	RR	23	R1,R2
Load Complement (Short)	LCER	RR	33	R1,R2

Name	Mnemonic	Type	Code	Operand
Load (Long)	LDR	RR	28	R1,R2
Load (Long)	LD	RX	68	R1,D2(X2,B2)
Load Negative (Long)	LNDR	RR	21	R1,R2
Load Negative (Short)	LNER	RR	31	R1,R2
Load Positive (Long)	LPDR	RR	20	R1,R2
Load Positive (Short)	LPER	RR	30	R1,R2
Load (Short)	LER	RR	38	R1,R2
Load (Short)	LE	RX	78	R1,D2(X2,B2)
Load Rounded (Extended to Long)	LRDR	RR	25	R1,R2
Load Rounded (Long to Short)	LRER	RR	35	R1,R2
Multiply (Long)	MDR	RR	2C	R1,R2
Multiply (Long)	MD	RX	6C	R1,D2(X2,B2)
Multiply (Short)	MER	RR	3C	R1,R2
Multiply (Short)	ME	RX	7C	R1,D2(X2,B2)
Multiply (Extended)	MXR	RR	26	R1,R2
Multiply (Long/ Extended)	MXDR	RR	27	R1,R2
Multiply (Long/ Extended)	MXD	RX	67	R1,D2(X2,B2)
Store (Long)	STD	RX	60	R1,D2(X2,B2)
Store (Short)	STE	RX	70	R1,D2(X2,B2)
Subtract Normalized (Long)	SDR	RR	2B	R1,R2
Subtract Normalized (Long)	SD	RX	6B	R1,D2(X2,B2)
Subtract Normalized (Short)	SER	RR	3B	R1,R2
Subtract Normalized (Short)	SE	RX	7B	R1,D2(X2,B2)
Subtract Unnormalized (Long)	SWR	RR	2F	R1,R2
Subtract Unnormalized (Long)	SW	RX	6F	R1,D2(X2,B2)
Subtract Unnormalized (Short)	SUR	RR	3F	R1,R2
Subtract Unnormalized (Short)	SU	RX	7F	R1,D2(X2,B2)
Subtract Normalized (Extended)	SXR	RR	37	R1,R2

DECIMAL FEATURE INSTRUCTIONS

Name	Mnemonic	Type	Code	Operand
Add Decimal	AP	SS	FA	D1(L1,B1),D2(L2,B2)
Compare Decimal	CP	SS	F9	D1(L1,B1),D2(L2,B2)
Divide Decimal	DP	SS	FD	D1(L1,B1),D2(L2,B2)

Name	Mnemonic	Type	Code	Operand
Edit	ED	SS	DE	D1(L,B1),D2(B2)
Edit and Mark	EDMK	SS	DF	D1(L,B1),D2(B2)
Multiply Decimal	MP	SS	FC	D1(L1,B1),D2(L2,B2)
Subtract Decimal	SP	SS	FB	D1(L1,B1),D2(L2,B2)
Zero and Add	ZAP	SS	F8	D1(L1,B1),D2(L2,B2)

DIRECT CONTROL FEATURE INSTRUCTIONS

Read Direct	RDD	SI	85	D1(B1),I2
Write Direct	WRD	SI	84	D1(B1),I2

PROTECTION FEATURE INSTRUCTIONS

Insert Storage Key	ISK	RR	09	R1,R2
Set Storage Key	SSK	RR	08	R1,R2

Appendix **two**
EBCDIC Codes

RR FORMAT INSTRUCTIONS

Decimal	Hex	Mnemonic	BCDIC	EBCDIC	7-Track Tape	Card Code
0	00			NUL		12-0-1-8-9
1	01			SOH		12-1-9
2	02			STX		12-2-9
3	03			ETX		12-3-9
4	04	SPM		PF		12-4-9
5	05	BALR		HT		12-5-9
6	06	BCTR		LC		12-6-9
7	07	BCR		DEL		12-7-9
8	08	SSK				12-8-9
9	09	ISK				12-1-8-9
10	0A	SVC		SMM		12-2-8-9
11	0B			VT		12-3-8-9
12	0C	EBCDIC +		FF		12-4-8-9
13	0D	EBCDIC −		CR		12-5-8-9
14	0E			SO		12-6-8-9
15	0F			SI		12-7-8-9
16	10	LPR		DLE		12-11-1-8-9
17	11	LNR		DC1		11-1-9
18	12	LTR		DC2		11-2-9
19	13	LCR		TM		11-3-9
20	14	NR		RES		11-4-9
21	15	CLR		NL		11-5-9
22	16	OR		BS		11-6-9
23	17	XR		IL		11-7-9
24	18	LR		CAN		11-8-9
25	19	CR		EM		11-1-8-9
26	1A	AR		CC		11-2-8-9
27	1B	SR		CU1		11-3-8-9
28	1C	MR		IFS		11-4-8-9
29	1D	DR		IGS		11-5-8-9
30	1E	ALR		IRS		11-6-8-9
31	1F	SLR		IUS		11-7-8-9

Decimal	Hex	Mnemonic	BCDIC	EBCDIC	7-Track Tape	Card Code
32	20	LPDR		DS		11-0-1-8-9
33	21	LNDR		SOS		0-1-9
34	22	LTDR		FS		0-2-9
35	23	LCDR				0-3-9
36	24	HDR		BYP		0-4-9
37	25	LRDR		LF		0-5-9
38	26	MXR		ETB		0-6-9
39	27	MXDR		ESC		0-7-9
40	28	LDR				0-8-9
41	29	CDR				0-1-8-9
42	2A	ADR		SM		0-2-8-9
43	2B	SDR		CU2		0-3-8-9
44	2C	MDR				0-4-8-9
45	2D	DDR		ENQ		0-5-8-9
46	2E	AWR		ACK		0-6-8-9
47	2F	SWR		BEL		0-7-8-9
48	30	LPER				12-11-0-1-8-9
49	31	LNER				1-9
50	32	LTER		SYN		2-9
51	33	LCER				3-9
52	34	HER		PN		4-9
53	35	LRER		RS		5-9
54	36	AXR		UC		6-9
55	37	SXR		EOT		7-9
56	38	LER				8-9
57	39	CER				1-8-9
58	3A	AER				2-8-9
59	3B	SER		CU3		3-8-9
60	3C	MER		DC4		4-8-9
61	3D	DER		NAK		5-8-9
62	3E	AUR				6-8-9
63	3F	SUR		SUB		7-8-9

RX FORMAT INSTRUCTIONS

Decimal	Hex	Mnemonic	BCDIC	EBCDIC	7-Track Tape	Card Code
64	40	STH		SP		No punches
65	41	LA				12-0-1-9
66	42	STC				12-0-2-9
67	43	IC				12-0-3-9
68	44	EX				12-0-4-9
69	45	BAL				12-0-5-9
70	46	BCT				12-0-6-9
71	47	BC				12-0-7-9
72	48	LH				12-0-8-9

Decimal	Hex	Mnemonic	BCDIC	EBCDIC	7-Track Tape	Card Code
73	49	CH				12-1-8
74	4A	AH		¢		12-2-8
75	4B	SH	.	.	BA8 21	12-3-8
76	4C	MH	¤)	<	BA84	12-4-8
77	4D		[	(	BA84 1	12-5-8
78	4E	CVD	<	+	BA842	12-6-8
79	4F	CVB	‡	|	BA8421	12-7-8
80	50	ST	&+	&	BA	12
81	51					12-11-1-9
82	52					12-11-2-9
83	53					12-11-3-9
84	54	N				12-11-4-9
85	55	CL				12-11-5-9
86	56	O				12-11-6-9
87	57	X				12-11-7-9
88	58	L				12-11-8-9
89	59	C				11-1-8
90	5A	A		!		11-2-8
91	5B	S	$	$	B 8 21	11-3-8
92	5C	M	*	*	B 84	11-4-8
93	5D	D	]	)	B 84 1	11-5-8
94	5E	AL	;	;	B 842	11-6-8
95	5F	SL	△	→	B 8421	11-7-8
96	60	STD	−	−	B	11
97	61		/	/	A 1	0-1
98	62					11-0-2-9
99	63					11-0-3-9
100	64					11-0-4-9
101	65					11-0-5-9
102	66					11-0-6-9
103	67	MXD				11-0-7-9
104	68	LD				11-0-8-9
105	69	CD				0-1-8
106	6A	AD				12-11
107	6B	SD	,	,	A8 21	0-3-8
108	6C	MD	%(	%	A84	0-4-8
109	6D	DD	⋎	−	A84 1	0-5-8
110	6E	AW	\	>	A842	0-6-8
111	6F	SW	+++	?	A8421	0-7-8
112	70	STE				12-11-0
113	71					12-11-0-1-9
114	72					12-11-0-2-9
115	73					12-11-0-3-9
116	74					12-11-0-4-9
117	75					12-11-0-5-9

Decimal	Hex	Mnemonic	BCDIC	EBCDIC	7-Track Tape	Card Code
118	76					12-11-0-6-9
119	77					12-11-0-7-9
120	78	LE				12-11-0-8-9
121	79	CE				1-8
122	7A	AE	Ƀ	:	A	2-8
123	7B	SE	#=	#	8 21	3-8
124	7C	ME	@'	@	84	4-8
125	7D	DE	:	'	84 1	5-8
126	7E	AU	>	=	842	6-8
127	7F	SU	√	"	8421	7-8

RS, SI FORMAT INSTRUCTIONS

Decimal	Hex	Mnemonic	EBCDIC	Card Code
128	80	SSM		12-0-1-8
129	81		a	12-0-1
130	82	LPSW	b	12-0-2
131	83	(Diagnose)	c	12-0-3
132	84	WRD	d	12-0-4
133	85	RDD	e	12-0-5
134	86	BXH	f	12-0-6
135	87	BXLE	g	12-0-7
136	88	SRL	h	12-0-8
137	89	SLL	i	12-0-9
138	8A	SRA		12-0-2-8
139	8B	SLA		12-0-3-8
140	8C	SRDL		12-0-4-8
141	8D	SLDL		12-0-5-8
142	8E	SRDA		12-0-6-8
143	8F	SLDA		12-0-7-8
144	90	STM		12-11-1-8
145	91	TM	j	12-11-1
146	92	MVI	k	12-11-2
147	93	TS	l	12-11-3
148	94	NI	m	12-11-4
149	95	CLI	n	12-11-5
150	96	OI	o	12-11-6
151	97	XI	p	12-11-7
152	98	LM	q	12-11-8
153	99		r	12-11-9
154	9A			12-11-2-8
155	9B			12-11-3-8
156	9C	SIO		12-11-4-8
157	9D	TIO		12-11-5-8
158	9E	HIO		12-11-6-8

Decimal	Hex	Mnemonic	BCDIC	EBCDIC	7-Track Tape	Card Code
159	9F	TCH				12-11-7-8
160	A0					11-0-1-8
161	A1					11-0-1
162	A2			s		11-0-2
163	A3			t		11-0-3
164	A4			u		11-0-4
165	A5			v		11-0-5
166	A6			w		11-0-6
167	A7			x		11-0-7
168	A8			y		11-0-8
169	A9			z		11-0-9
170	AA					11-0-2-8
171	AB					11-0-3-8
172	AC					11-0-4-8
173	AD					11-0-5-8
174	AE					11-0-6-8
175	AF					11-0-7-8
176	B0					12-11-0-1-8
177	B1					12-11-0-1
178	B2					12-11-0-2
179	B3					12-11-0-3
180	B4					12-11-0-4
181	B5					12-11-0-5
182	B6					12-11-0-6
183	B7					12-11-0-7
184	B8					12-11-0-8
185	B9					12-11-0-9
186	BA					12-11-0-2-8
187	BB					12-11-0-3-8
188	BC					12-11-0-4-8
189	BD					12-11-0-5-8
190	BE					12-11-0-6-8
191	BF					12-11-0-7-8

SS FORMAT INSTRUCTIONS

192	C0		?		BA8 2	12-0
193	C1		A	A	BA 1	12-1
194	C2		B	B	BA 2	12-2
195	C3		C	C	BA 21	12-3
196	C4		D	D	BA 4	12-4
197	C5		E	E	BA 4 1	12-5
198	C6		F	F	BA 42	12-6

Decimal	Hex	Mnemonic	BCDIC	EBCDIC	7-Track Tape	Card Code
199	C7		G	G	BA 421	12-7
200	C8		H	H	BA8	12-8
201	C9		I	I	BA8 1	12-9
202	CA					12-0-2-8-9
203	CB					12-0-3-8-9
204	CC					12-0-4-8-9
205	CD					12-0-5-8-9
206	CE					12-0-6-8-9
207	CF					12-0-7-8-9
208	D0		!		B 8 2	11-0
209	D1	MVN	J	J	B 1	11-1
210	D2	MVC	K	K	B 2	11-2
211	D3	MVZ	L	L	B 21	11-3
212	D4	NC	M	M	B 4	11-4
213	D5	CLC	N	N	B 4 1	11-5
214	D6	OC	O	O	B 42	11-6
215	D7	XC	P	P	B 421	11-7
216	D8		Q	Q	B 8	11-8
217	D9		R	R	B 8 1	11-9
218	DA					12-11-2-8-9
219	DB					12-11-3-8-9
220	DC	TR				12-11-4-8-9
221	DD	TRT				12-11-5-8-9
222	DE	ED				12-11-6-8-9
223	DF	EDMK				12-11-7-8-9
224	E0		‡		A8 2	0-2-8
225	E1					11-0-1-9
226	E2		S	S	A 2	0-2
227	E3		T	T	A 21	0-3
228	E4		U	U	A 4	0-4
229	E5		V	V	A 4 1	0-5
230	E6		W	W	A 42	0-6
231	E7		X	X	A 421	0-7
232	E8		Y	Y	A8	0-8
233	E9		Z	Z	A8 1	0-9
234	EA					11-0-2-8-9
235	EB					11-0-3-8-9
236	EC					11-0-4-8-9
237	ED					11-0-5-8-9
238	EE					11-0-6-8-9
239	EF					11-0-7-8-9
240	F0		0	0	8 2	0

Decimal	Hex	Mnemonic	BCDIC	EBCDIC	7-Track Tape	Card Code
241	F1	MVO	1	1	1	1
242	F2	PACK	2	2	2	2
243	F3	UNPK	3	3	21	3
244	F4		4	4	4	4
245	F5		5	5	4 1	5
246	F6		6	6	42	6
247	F7		7	7	421	7
248	F8	ZAP	8	8	8	8
249	F9	CP	9	9	8 1	9
250	FA	AP				12-11-0-2-8-9
251	FB	SP				12-11-0-3-8-9
252	FC	MP				12-11-0-4-8-9
253	FD	DP				12-11-0-5-8-9
254	FE					12-11-0-6-8-9
255	FF					12-11-0-7-8-9

Appendix **three**
USASCII Codes

		00				01				10				11				←3
		00	01	10	11	00	01	10	11	00	01	10	11	00	01	10	11	←4
		0	1	2	3	4	5	6	7	8	9	A	B	C	D	E	F	←5
0000	0	NUL	DLE			SP	0					@	P			`	p	
0001	1	SOH	DC1			!	1					A	Q			a	q	
0010	2	STX	DC2			"	2					B	R			b	r	
0011	3	ETX	DC3			#	3					C	S			c	s	
0100	4	EOT	DC4			$	4					D	T			d	t	
0101	5	ENQ	NAK			%	5					E	U			e	u	
0110	6	ACK	SYN			&	6					F	V			f	v	
0111	7	BEL	ETB			'	7					G	W			g	w	
1000	8	BS	CAN			(	8					H	X			h	x	
1001	9	HT	EM			)	9					I	Y			i	y	
1010	A	LF	SUB			*	:					J	Z			j	z	
1011	B	VT	ESC			+	;					K	[			k	{	
1100	C	FF	FS			,	<					L	\			l	¦	
1101	D	CR	GS			−	=					M	]			m	}	
1110	E	SO	RS			.	>					N	Λ			n	~	
1111	F	SI	US			/	?					O	_			o	DEL	

1 — Bit positions 4, 3, 2, 1
2 — Second hexadecimal digit
3 — Bit positions 8, 7
4 — Bit positions 6, 5
5 — First hexadecimal digit

Appendix **four**
Register Contents
on Entry to SYNAD Routine

Register	Bits	Meaning
0	0–7	Value to be added to bits 8–31 to yield address of first CCW (QSAM only.)
	8–31	Address of the associated data event control block (DECB) for BDAM, BPAM, and BSAM; address of the status indicators shown in Appendix 5 for QSAM.
1	0	Bit is on for error caused by input operation.
	1	Bit is on for error caused by output operation.
	2	Bit is on for error caused by BSP, CNTRL, or POINT macros (BPAM and BSAM only).
	3	Bit is on if error occurred during update of existing record or if error did not prevent reading record. Bit is off if error occurred during creation of a new record or if error prevented reading of the record.
	4	Bit is on if request was invalid. The status indicators pointed to by DECB will not be present (BDAM, BPAM, and BSAM only).
	5	Bit is on if invalid character was found in paper-tape conversion (BSAM and QSAM only).
	6	Bit is on for hardware error (BDAM only).
	7	Bit is on if no space for the record (BDAM only).
	8–31	Address of the associated DCB.
2–13		Contents that existed before the macro was issued.
14		Return address.
15		Address of the error-analysis routine.

Appendix **five**
Status Indicators
for the SYNAD Routine

Byte	Bit	Meaning	Name
2	0	Command reject	Sense byte 1
	1	Intervention required	
	2	Bus out check	
	3	Equipment check	
	4	Data check	
	5	Overrun	
	6,7 ⎱	⎰ Device dependent;	
3	0–7 ⎰	⎱ refer to device manual	Sense byte 2
8	0–7	Begin channel status word	
9	—	Command address	
12	0	Attention	Status byte 1
	1	Status modifier	
	2	Control unit end	
	3	Busy	
	4	Channel end	
	5	Device end	
	6	Unit check—must be on for sense bytes to be meaningful	
	7	Unit exception	
13	0	Program-control interrupt	Status byte 2
	1	Incorrect length	
	2	Program check	
	3	Protection check	
	4	Channel data check	
	5	Channel control check	
	6	Interface control check	
	7	Chaining check	
14	—	Count field	

Appendix **six**
Hexadecimal and Decimal Conversion Chart

Hex Digits

	1		2		3		4		5		6
Hex	Dec	Hex	Dec	Hex	Dec	Hex	Dec	Hex	Dec	Hex	Dec
0	0	0	0	0	0	0	0	0	0	0	0
1	1048576	1	65536	1	4096	1	256	1	16	1	1
2	2097152	2	131072	2	8192	2	512	2	32	2	2
3	3145728	3	196608	3	12288	3	768	3	48	3	3
4	4194304	4	262144	4	16384	4	1024	4	64	4	4
5	5242880	5	327680	5	20480	5	1280	5	80	5	5
6	6291456	6	393216	6	24576	6	1536	6	96	6	6
7	7340032	7	458752	7	28672	7	1792	7	112	7	7
8	8388608	8	524288	8	32768	8	2048	8	128	8	8
9	9437184	9	589824	9	36864	9	2304	9	144	9	9
A	10485760	A	655360	A	40960	A	2560	A	160	A	10
B	11534336	B	720896	B	45056	B	2816	B	176	B	11
C	12582912	C	786432	C	49152	C	3072	C	192	C	12
D	13631488	D	851968	D	53248	D	3328	D	208	D	13
E	14680064	E	917504	E	57344	E	3584	E	224	E	14
F	15728640	F	983040	F	61440	F	3840	F	240	F	15

Appendix **seven**
JCL Listing
of FGALPCXS Procedure*

```
//FORT      EXEC PGM=IEYFORT
//SYSPRINT  DD SYSOUT=A
//SYSLIN    DD DSNAME=&&WRK1,DISP=(,PASS),SPACE=(CYL,(3,1)),UNIT=SYSDA,  X
//              DCB=(BLKSIZE=3200,LRECL=80,RECFM=FBS)
//ASM       EXEC PGM=IEUASM,PARM=(LOAD,NODECK),COND=(5,LT,FORT)
//SYSPRINT  DD SYSOUT=A
//SYSLIB    DD DSNAME=SYS1.MACLIB,DISP=SHR,UNIT=2314,VOLUME=SER=SYSLIB
//SYSUT1    DD DSNAME=&&WRK2,DISP=(,PASS),UNIT=SYSDA,SPACE=(CYL,(2,1))
//SYSUT2    DD UNIT=SYSDA,SPACE=(CYL,(2,1))
//SYSUT3    DD UNIT=SYSDA,SPACE=(CYL,(2,1))
//SYSGO     DD DSNAME=&&WRK1,DISP=(MOD,PASS)
//LKED      EXEC PGM=IEWLF880,PARM=(LIST,MAP),COND=((5,LT,FORT),         X
//              (5,LT,ASM))
//SYSPRINT  DD SYSOUT=A
//SYSLIB    DD DSNAME=SYS1.FORTLIB,DISP=SHR,UNIT=2314,VOLUME=SER=SYSLIB
//SYSLMOD   DD DSNAME=&&MOD(M),DISP=(,PASS),UNIT=SYSDA,                  X
//              SPACE=(CYL,(2,1,1))
//SYSUT1    DD DSNAME=&&WRK2,DISP=(OLD,DELETE)
//SYSLIN    DD DSNAME=&&WRK1,DISP=(OLD,DELETE)
//          DD DDNAME=SYSIN
//GO        EXEC PGM=*.LKED.SYSLMOD,COND=((5,LT,FORT),(5,LT,ASM),        X
//              (5,LT,LKED))
//FT05F001  DD DDNAME=SYSIN
//FT06F001  DD SYSOUT=A
//FT07F001  DD SYSOUT=B
```

*The symbols that are underlined may vary at different installations.

Index